E-Business:
The Strategic
Impact on Supply
Chain and Logistics

ISBN 0-9658653-5-5

Council of Logistics Management
2805 Butterfield Road
Suite 200
Oak Brook, Illinois 60523-1170
www.clm1.org

Printed in the United States of America.

E-BUSINESS:
The Strategic Impact on Supply Chain and Logistics

Michael J. Bauer
Charles C. Poirier
Computer Sciences Corporation

Lawrence Lapide, Ph.D.
John Bermudez
AMR Research

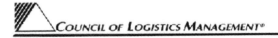

COUNCIL OF LOGISTICS MANAGEMENT®

TABLE OF CONTENTS

ACKNOWLEDGMENTS

An effort to create this kind of book requires the assistance of many external resources. Both of our organizations contributed much support and encouragement to create the materials and messages contained within the manuscript. But without the help of many willing and dedicated people and the cooperation of firms determined to build a logistics advantage in the new digital economy, the effort would have been fruitless.

Our special thanks go to individuals who took the time for interviews, so we could gather current information on details of what constitutes leading thinking and practices in the areas of supply chain, logistics, and e-business. These individuals include Richard D. Armstrong, Armstrong & Associates; Tricia Bratton, Federal Express Services; John Clark, Bayer; Mark Columbo, Federal Express Services; Douglas Christensen, USF Logistics; Ralph Drayer, Procter & Gamble; James Eccleston, Department of Defense; Steve Goble and Gregg Greve, e-Chemicals; Roger Kallock, Department of Defense; Terry Leahy, Modus Media International; Kevin Lynch, Nistevo; David Roussain, Federal Express Services; Tom Schmitt, Federal Express Services; Gary Scalzitti, W. W. Grainger; Kevin Schoen, General Mills; Mike Sprague, Tibbett & Britten Group; Kevin Wenta, CheMatch.com.; and Curtis Songer, General Motors.

More thanks go to the people who assisted us in finding the right contacts and providing valuable advice on how to proceed with our research. These friends include Chuck Davis, David Durtsche, Rene Bush, and Mike Gaffney of CSC and Mike Burkett, Tom Cook, Leif Eriksen, Roddy Martin, Chris Newton, and Kevin Prouty of AMR Research.

Special thanks goes to the Richmond Events, Inc., for allowing us to conduct and publish research for the book gathered during The Logistics Forum event in May 2000. We are grateful also to Bob Ferrari of AMR Research who planned, conducted, and analyzed the research.

Very special thanks go to members of the University of Maryland's Robert H. Smith School of Business: Dr Tom Corsi, Dr. Sandor Boysen, and Yulaing Yao.

Thanks and acknowledgement to the CLM Research Committee: Development of a Supply Chain Strategy Which Leverages the Use of E-Business Capabilities. Their patience and understanding is very much appreciated.

VIRGINIA E. CARMON, CHAIRPERSON
Principal Integration Services
IBM Corporation

CHRISTOPHER B. LOFGREN
Chief Operating Officer
Schneider National, Inc.

JOHN J. LING
Vice President Distribution and Logistics
Crate & Barrel

DR. ROBERT A. NOVACK
Associate Professor Business Logistics
Pennsylvania State University

MIKE SPRAGUE
President
Tibbett & Britten Group
North America, Inc.

Very Special Thanks to

DR. ELAINE M. WINTER
Director of Communication and Research
Council of Logistics Management

EXECUTIVE SUMMARY

Much has been written lately about the subjects of logistics, supply chain, and e-business. While there is considerable evidence that these subjects are at the forefront of concern for business executives, our research indicated the matter of practical application differs greatly—from desire to take advantage of these business practices and achieving results. Although some firms have made notable progress, others still lack the understanding or the determination to take advantage of what has become one of the most dramatic and dynamic changes to business commerce in the last hundred years.

The authors think that over the coming years, companies will gain the determination and motivation to accelerate efforts around e-business. They will do some because the long-term competitive and financial impacts will be apparent. Executives should understand that the current stock market (April 2001), beset by tumbling share prices and uncertainties is in no way an indicator of the business benefits and competitive positioning companies have begun to achieve. These accelerated plans will have the greatest impact on three key areas: supply chain's transitioning to value chains; logistics systems becoming a key competitive advantage; and the transformation of operating models.

Businesses would not be pursuing these supply chain activities without good reasons. A recent study by AMR Research provides some insight into why companies are still actively pursuing business-to-business (B2B) e-commerce activities. The potential financial benefits range up to $465 billion annually (see Figure 1). CSC Consulting predicts that the North American automobile industry alone could reap an annual benefit of up to $80 billion, if they master collaborative product development and transform supply chains into value chains— on average $5,000 per vehicle! (see Figure 4.1, "Auto Supply Chain Old and New"). The changes will come slowly and incrementally. Mopar, the DaimlerChrysler in-house supplier, recently reported savings of $7.5 million in the second half of 2000 (eCompany Now, April 2001). Using advanced supply chain management tools, Mopar was able to determine whether its warehouses and dealers had the right inventory on hand. While some individual benefits may seem small, cumulatively they have the potential of globally adding up to greater than $1 trillion annually.

B2B Technology Value Creation

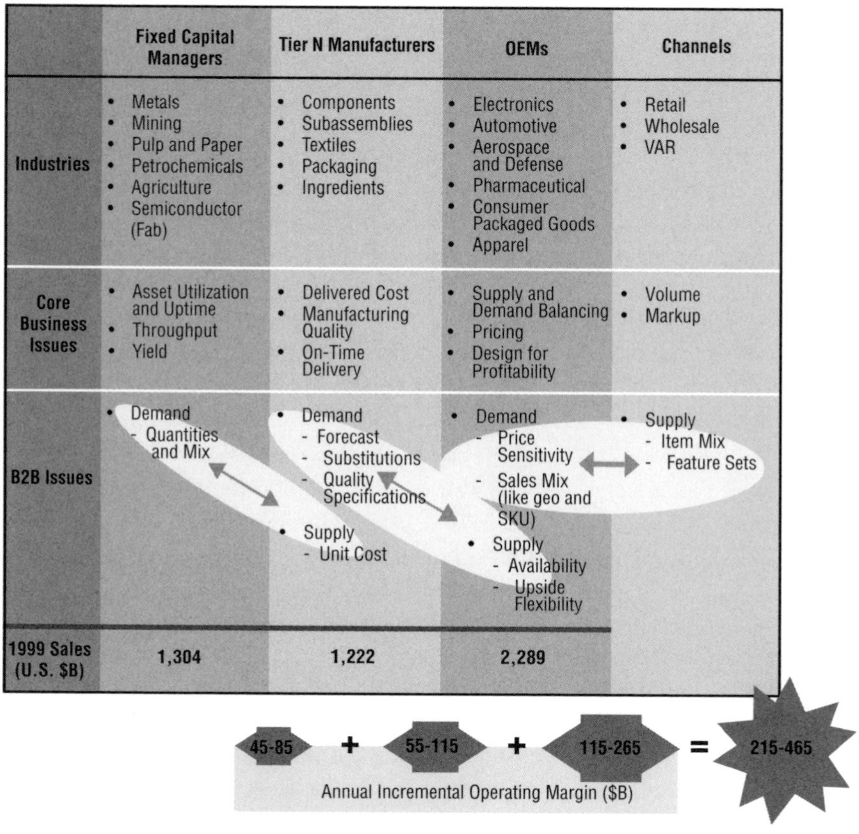

	Fixed Capital Managers	Tier N Manufacturers	OEMs	Channels
Industries	• Metals • Mining • Pulp and Paper • Petrochemicals • Agriculture • Semiconductor (Fab)	• Components • Subassemblies • Textiles • Packaging • Ingredients	• Electronics • Automotive • Aerospace and Defense • Pharmaceutical • Consumer Packaged Goods • Apparel	• Retail • Wholesale • VAR
Core Business Issues	• Asset Utilization and Uptime • Throughput • Yield	• Delivered Cost • Manufacturing Quality • On-Time Delivery	• Supply and Demand Balancing • Pricing • Design for Profitability	• Volume • Markup
B2B Issues	• Demand - Quantities and Mix	• Demand - Forecast - Substitutions - Quality Specifications • Supply - Unit Cost	• Demand - Price Sensitivity - Sales Mix (like geo and SKU) • Supply - Availability - Upside Flexibility	• Supply - Item Mix - Feature Sets
1999 Sales (U.S. $B)	1,304	1,222	2,289	

45-85 **+** 55-115 **+** 115-265 **=** 215-465

Annual Incremental Operating Margin ($B)

Source: AMR Research, 2000

figure 1

The benefits of e-business will cover more than supply chain and logistics. The benefits are across the board, from customer self-service to complicated B2B networks. Bristol-Meyers Squibb estimates its savings in procurement will be $100 million in 2000 (AMR Research, The Report on Supply Chain Management, October 2000). Janus, the mutual fund giant, was able to reduce its call center staff by 465 people, largely due to its customers accessing account information via the Janus Web site (NewYorkTimes, February 28, 2001). Figure 2 show some of the potential areas of benefit and the impact on both savings and revenue. Chapters 6 and 7 discuss methods of assessing a company's current position and developing a strategy to use advanced supply chain planning tools and achieve some of these benefits.

Overall Benefits of E-Business

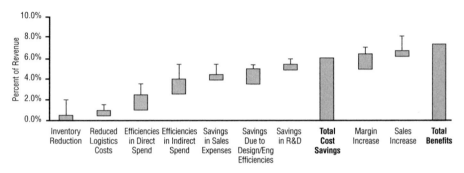

Source: CSC Consulting

figure 2

While some companies are moving ahead, we found a distinct difference in the gap between those showing significant progress and serious interest based on their industry segment or their geography. While the transportation, high-technology, aerospace and defense, utilities, and chemicals industries have grabbed hold of the advanced concepts and made serious gains, some players within those industries are still trying to figure out the right combination of ingredients to catch the leaders. At the same time, we found entire industries, such as construction and paperboard, trying to get a handle on how best to apply the right techniques. It is clear to the authors that business executives will only accelerate their activities in regard to e-business and the major areas impacted will be supply chain and logistics.

As we searched around the globe, we found very large companies a year or more behind the leaders. As we looked, however, at the rapid innovations being introduced with e-commerce techniques by the entertainment, books, travel, and high-technology industries in Europe, we found small gaps compared with U.S. rivals. The application field in general is littered with a potpourri of desires and results. Most important, we found there is still time to forge a commanding lead by applying the right techniques to find the right solutions for a particular market or industry.

The rate of technological innovation has never been greater and is expected to continue to accelerate. Those organizations that adopt the right technologies and lead the changes are setting a pace that is difficult to match. In no other area is the need to keep pace more crucial or the opportunity to catch up and take the lead greater than that of supply chain management and its sister discipline, logistics management. Using the enhancements made possible through applications conducted over the Internet, leaders are introducing new business models that take advantage of the most dramatic of all new technological innovations—the World Wide Web.

We have termed the new wave of thinking that permeates the leading practices "segmented logistic management systems." It represents the leveraging of modern technology, particularly the use of the Internet, with the best features of advanced supply chain management techniques. It is a business approach designed to develop compelling and differentiating values for the critical element of fulfilling the orders secured and the optimized processes behind the supply chain's connecting suppliers, manufacturers, and consumers.

OPPORTUNITIES AND PITFALLS ABOUND

If our research found one alarm, it was that the results of the best e-commerce applications could be interrupted, stalled, or destroyed by logistics problems. We can offer no better example than the near debacle that occurred during the 1999 holiday season, when various new e-tailers struggled to get the consumer orders they had secured via cyberspace to the intended destinations. Orders going to businesses were no less protected from inadequate logistics infrastructure, as computer parts, auto parts, and retail goods were hung up in distribution channels waiting for the right party to package the goods properly and get them to the point of need. Did Internet retailers learn any lessons from the 1999 holiday season?

> **Holiday Season 2000: Half Full or Half Empty?**
>
> The focus on unfulfilled orders, delivery nightmares, and question about the viability of direct consumer sales via Internet retailing after the holiday season in 1999 put a lot of focus on the holiday sales in 2000. In between 1999 and the holidays of 2000, several things happened.
>
> The Internet bubble collapsed as shareholders realized that new economy or not, companies need profits for long-term success. The 2000 presidential campaign captured the attention of the country, and large brick-and-mortar companies moved to shore up their online businesses.

The skeptics and/or cynics (half empty) would say that Internet retailing isn't working; the business isn't there. The optimists or visionaries (half full) are saying just wait—it will still happen. Without understanding the individual reader's view, our surveys, interviews, and statistics have given us a viewpoint and allowed us to draw some conclusions.

During the peak sales week of December 17, 2000, sales reached $1.6 billion; in 1999 the figure was $878 million.[1] For the 2000 holiday season, the sales figures topped $10 billion,[1] doubling the 1999 figures.

2000 Holiday Sales	1999 Holiday Sales[2]
$10.7 billion	$5.2 billion

Also, fewer of the problems reported in 1999 occurred. There were fewer nondeliveries, fewer out-of-stock situations, and more realistic delivery times. Also, early indicators are that customer satisfaction levels were higher. Whether this can be attributed to the steps Internet retailers took to rectify 1999 problems or a smarter buying community is currently unknown. The authors' insight is that it was a combination of the two.

Can any conclusions be drawn from the data?

- Online Internet retailing is a force to be reckoned with, and it will provide new requirements and opportunities for supply chain and logistics systems.

- Supply chain and logistics performance improved but needs more refinement.

- Traditional retailers have significantly increased their online presence and sales, so their supply chains and suppliers will continue to be impacted by Internet retailing.

[1] PC Data and Goldman Sachs reported in Information Week, January 1, 2001.
[2] PC Data (www.pcdata.com—www.pcdataonline.com/press/pcdo010901.asp).

A whole new fulfillment landscape is emerging, bringing new dimensions to the need for logistics response. As orders are received more quickly and cycle times shortened to gain competitive advantage, the demands on supply chains and their logistics heart has never been greater. The new business models clearly contain end-to-end perspectives that feature customer satisfaction but require online visibility of all material flows, ability to divert shipments in transit, and tracing and tracking systems that cover the globe. The leaders are pooling their distribution needs so utilization of trucks and planes reaches to 95% or higher on inbound and outbound shipments. The new requirement to handle the rapid appearance of return goods is also being handled efficiently by the leaders.

The Internet-enhanced supply chain systems have brought new requirements and meaning, opportunities and problems, to the traditional interactions that take place from initial supply of raw materials and services to final consumption and return and recycling of delivered products. Cycle times, customer satisfaction, elimination of errors, on-time deliveries, and out-of-stocks are the new measures of performance, and the leaders are establishing new high standards. In a previous book published by the Council of Logistics Management, Keeping Score, a whole new series of metrics was introduced for the logistics professional to measure whether his or her organization is keeping pace with the accelerated changes taking place. The leaders are embracing those metrics and drawing new high standards of performance.

At the same time, the rapidly evolving expectations of constituents to a typical supply chain are moving ever higher. Meeting these expectations—which include greater forecast accuracy, error-free order management, less purchasing time spent on tactical matters, no out-of-stock conditions, collaborative planning and scheduling, lower safety stock inventory, and minimal transportation and logistics costs—is placing new demands on systems already not up to the challenge. While new and established companies struggle with the pace of change and the need to meet the rising demands, one lesson is clear: Those who delay their participation are falling behind the leaders, and the gap can be measured in years, not months. Those who seize the opportunity to define new and better business models will excel. Those who fall prey to the problems and complications will be left in the wake of others.

The supply chains that do not meet the necessities of the new business models required in what has become a digital economy will have to be enhanced, or they will perish. Today, buyers want to deal with suppliers having the capability of flexible, short-cycle responses. They want sales representatives who supply solutions to their real needs. They want an online method of placing orders, being able to scan available global inventories and making the kind of changes that are present in any supply system with a click of a mouse. Manufacturing systems must be capable of responding to current online demand, as confirmed by cash register receipts. The financial and information technology communities are actively feeding the cost data and transaction systems to bring accuracy to where resources should be applied to improve supply chains and speed the transfer of money. And management is hard-pressed to keep pace with all the potential software, systems, and organizational changes that take advantage of the new possibilities.

Logistics Is at the Center of the New Requirements

At the core of these dynamic movements sits the logistics system, on which the burden of facilitating the new supply chain rests. It is now very clear that the e-businesses of the future will only be as good as the supporting logistics infrastructure. This need has two aspects. On the one hand, we fully expect that the majority of business for direct materials and branded finished goods will continue to move through traditional, physical supply chains with ongoing relationships between buyers and sellers and existing logistics partners. Some of the larger of these brick-and-mortar firms will most likely use their capital to acquire some of the better dot-com organizations that are showing how to best apply technology for business purposes.

On the other hand, when the excitement surrounding the use of the Internet settles down and reaches a sound business plateau, a significant percentage of business for most industries will be conducted over some form of cyber-based channel. No definitive data show just how much of a particular industry's orders will be cyber based. But the data available do show it grows by very large increments as the industry comes to embrace its version of Internet interaction. The grocery industry, for example, looks to be moving to an 85/15 ratio of physical to cyber-based shipments, while high technology could reach 60/40 or more. More important than the specific ratio is the fact that some portion of business in every industry will be supported by future Internet-based communication systems. Behind those systems has to be a solid supply chain and logistics infrastructure that assures the rapidity and accuracy of information flows will be supported by a delivery system that assures high quality and satisfaction.

From these aspects, we see that a firm cannot turn its back on the most dramatic changes ever encountered by business commerce. From a business-to-business perspective, the need for speed, accuracy, and availability of information has never been greater or more enhanced by use of a cyber channel of communication. Any company that overlooks the advantages to be gained in these basic business functions risks putting its future at risk to more capable competitors. At the same time, nothing turns off a Web-based business customer or consumer faster than a missed delivery, a late order, or mistakes in the shipment. The rise and fall of the new dot-com entrepreneurs has provided evidence that you can get the customer and consumer hooked on using an Internet-based system, but you better satisfy their demands effectively, or the switch to a new source is as near as another click of the mouse.

In this book, we will discuss how organizations can develop clear and consistent supply chain strategies for using electronic commerce features. More important, we will identify how organizations can develop meaningful solutions that will allow them to implement these strategies. A methodology is defined that will assist organizations in also creating and executing a tactical plan for achieving the desired results. Our presentation will be oriented around a future-state scenario. We believe business is moving to such a state, in which final consumption data, often referred to as point-of-sale (POS), from cash registers will be aggregated and shared by supply chain partners in specific industry networks. Use of this data will tend to augment the poor accuracy of typical sales forecasts and create a new and better dimension to what will become real demand information.

In the business-to-business sector, there will also be a linking of the demand data with supply data, so the need for as much inventory and warehouse space as exists today will be dramatically reduced. Access to information on availability and movement from the most basic raw materials to the final manufacture and delivery of products will be pervasive across the leading networks in particular industries. Meeting the visible demand will be accomplished through an e-fulfillment system in which needs are pooled in a collaborative manner across the supply chain network. Routing will be done based on real delivery time and use of total available assets in the network. Logistics systems will become leaner, while the use of assets—tractors, trailer, railroad cars, planes, warehouses, distribution systems, and so forth—move to near optimum conditions.

The new frontier of improvement in this scenario will be the taking of safety stocks and finished goods inventories to new low levels. All inventories, from beginning materials and supplies to finished products and any returned deliveries, will be fully visible through an online inventory tracking and tracing system. Diversion of product flow due to unforeseen conditions will be a click away in such a system, as the partners in a full supply chain will be coordinating activities in real-time, using the magic of the global Internet for communication.

The Internet provides a new platform and system of global communication that has dramatically shrunk the planet and all of the traditional cycle times required of business commerce. People are finding ways to free themselves from the onerous tasks required by a more labor-intensive era, to move from tactical issues to strategic capabilities. Buyers focus on how to enhance corporate profits, not spending days searching for sources. Sellers concentrate on key accounts, to bring novel and beneficial solutions to long-standing problems. Logistics managers find a new importance, as the enablers of facilitating the shorter cycles, smaller size orders, and more responsive supply chains. Manufacturers will use fewer inventories to produce and deliver smaller orders. Engineers and developers will collaborate across extranets to create the new products that match the current demands of consumers.

We document what has become the state of the art of electronic business communications, as we detail current practices employed by the leading performers. We point out the differences between global sectors of the world but will use case material to show that leaders exist in all of these sectors.

It is an era of opportunity. We intend to delve into those opportunities, particularly from the perspective of how an organization can leverage the new Internet connected world and take advantage of leading practices. The key will be determining how to synthesize the current applications into a business model and logistical plan. This will require communication of data across the full supply chain network that connects suppliers, manufacturers, distributors, business customers, and the ultimate consumers. It will require a rethinking of existing logistical systems and the harmonizing of an Internet-enhanced set of process steps that brings what the customer is demanding of modern supply chains—short-cycle, error-free, totally satisfying delivery of goods and services.

Our purpose is to supply an understanding of current e-business models and systems and to describe how a traditional business can take advantage of the new thinking to move their organizations to compete effectively with the e-commerce leaders. We will provide a road map for attaining such a capability, using the architecture that provides the best infrastructure, application development, and maintenance services needed to support an e-commerce-enhanced logistics system.

chapter 1

The Acceleration of
Supply Chain
and E-Business

S peed of reaction, order accuracy, supply chain visibility of product flow, low to just-in-time inventories, operational flexibility, sustained quality, and a reputation for no-hassle business processes are becoming the price of entry for doing business today. These characteristics and more have quickly become the basics for successful business in the last few years. The current emphasis is on optimizing process steps across the full supply chain, as the definitions of supply chain continue to be expanded, including capabilities to accomplish all of the new prices of entry.

At the center of this need is the requirement for electronic communications and a logistics infrastructure that backs up the improved processing, to continue to meet the new market expectations and keep the end consumer happy. As some firms succeed at this endeavor and some fail, a growing body of evidence shows how to leverage both the advances in supply chain and the accelerating application of Web technology. While companies are still getting used to these massive shifts, the next wave of transformation is already on the horizon, the change in business and operating models enabled by e-business. As this technology and new business concepts converge, almost faster than the mind can comprehend, understanding the implications can be the difference between future success and failure.

There is also a need for applying new tools, some of which are electronic and some simply better business practices that can be enhanced by electronics. These tools include advanced planning and scheduling (APS); Global Positioning Systems (GPSs); warehouse management systems (WMS); having visible inventories available-to-promise (ATP); collaborative planning, forecasting, and replenishment (CPFR); and vendor-managed inventories (VMIs). Without regard to the alphabet soup of acronyms, they focus on achieving measurable gains.

For example, using collaborative design and product development reduces cycle times. More effective use of total physical assets—from heavy machinery to tractors and trailers to warehouse space and material handling equipment—improves cash flow. The benefits continue with results from better managing inventory to get more use from invested capital, and end-to-end pooled logistics systems that operate with high accuracy and reliability. These systems must also contain the measurement and visibility capabilities the new business models dictate. As industry after industry attempts to reach new performance levels—with lower costs, shorter cycle times, better service, and new revenues—the message is clear: You aren't going to get there without the tools and techniques that e-business, advanced supply chain, logistics, and e-commerce practices can provide.

Let's consider the area of cycle times, where most industries and firms are trying to reach new and unprecedented performance levels. The aerospace industry is attempting to cut its cycle for delivering an airplane to an airline customer to 3 months. The automotive industry wants to deliver a car to a home in 25 days, from the time of a submission and acceptance of a customer order. The U.S. Department of Defense wants bombs on target in 72 hours, anywhere in the world. All of these objectives might have seemed impossible a few years ago. Now they are driving organizations to come together and find the keys to accomplishment. Companies that used to stand alone in all of their improvement efforts are finding the benefits of a nontraditional environment. With new allies, they are combining capital investments with sensible, innovative solutions to the supply, manufacturing, and delivery processes in their collective supply chains. And in a few years some players within the industries will achieve the targets mentioned.

In this chapter, we look at the results of some of our research and explain the concepts and applications that are setting the groundwork for these remarkable improvements. We'll consider the changes taking place as firms seek the next level of performance, when traditional cost-cutting efforts near the point of diminishing returns. We'll document what's been evolving as some companies become determined to apply the new tools and forge new paths to positions of leadership. We'll also explain why some companies don't seem to make the same progress. Moreover, we'll consider how you can take your company to a position of competitive advantage by applying the same techniques as those of the leaders.

E-Business Defined in Relation to Supply Chain

To begin our exposition, it would help to have some clear definitions on what we'll be considering. First, the larger context of e-business needs to be understood. It's the continuous optimization of an organization's value proposition and value-chain position, using the digitally connected marketplace and the use of the technologies of the Internet as the primary communications medium. It can include some or most of the business processes and commercial applications in a business system. These business processes will extend across full the supply chain. In most leading business models we studied, it did not include all processes, and the practitioners of e-business only have plans on the drawing board, not in daily use. The general rules of thumb are to apply e-commerce where the automation improves accuracy and flexibility and to make the transition to e-business as rapidly as your market and value chain permit, and where the improvement differentiates the company in the eyes of the business customer or end consumer. One caveat is in order: these improvements, based on e-commerce, will only differentiate a company for a short time.

Second, the supply chain represents the core business processes in an organization that create and deliver a product or service, from concept through development and manufacturing or conversion, and into a market for consumption. In a more appropriate context, it includes the interenterprise activities involved in the creation and efficient delivery of products and services. As we consider applications to supply chain, we'll be taking a broad end-to-end view, from primary supplies for a particular industry or company through the final consumption and return or recycling of the finished products through an end consumer group. As we describe the possible improvements, it will be apparent that we favor optimum use of both internal and external resources. This approach requires a scope that includes other companies as allies.

For your purposes, it may be more appropriate to take a smaller view if, for example, your company engages strictly in business-to-business transactions, and you see virtually no connection to end consumption. Our point is that you are not going to make significant and lasting improvement unless the scope of the effort is clearly understood in the beginning, which requires defining what you mean by "end to end." Many firms in the supply chain community espouse a limited view that considers one's supplier's suppliers and customer's customer. We prefer the broadest definition, as we see possibilities for improvement across the entire supply chain network. That type of effort leads to a competitive advantage for all constituent firms in the full supply chain system.

Third, supply chain management becomes the methods, systems, and leadership that continuously improve an organization's integrated processes for product and service design, purchasing, inventory management, planning and scheduling, logistics, distribution, and customer satisfaction. In a modern sense, most of these factors are being accomplished in a collaborative manner across a network of linked business partners. The more advanced supply chain management systems include extensive application of e-commerce features.

Fourth, as we refer to them, upstream processes are the actions that occur before manufacturing or production into a deliverable product or service—typically processes dedicated to getting raw materials from suppliers. Downstream processes are those actions that occur after manufacturing or production. They typically include steps dedicated to getting goods and services to business customers and end consumers.

Fifth, logistics, as defined by the Council of Logistics Management (CLM), is that part of the supply chain process that plans, implements, and controls the efficient, effective flow and storage and flow of goods, services, and related information from the point of origin to the point of consumption to meet customers' requirements. It includes forecasting, customer service, transportation, warehousing, and inventory management as inherent attributes.

Sixth, since we'll be considering the elements involved in e-commerce connectivity, three components must be described. The intranet is a private and privileged communications network, where a nucleus organization and its internal constituents are given digital access to private information to better add value to supply chain processing. This network is within the four walls of your organization. It's private and provides rapid data interchange. Through this type of system, cultural barriers to intraenterprise activities and cooperation break down and internal efficiency rises significantly by virtue of having quicker and more reliable access to vital information.

The Internet is the public forum, a relatively inexpensive communication network, where supply chain partners can share valuable data and marketplaces can be conducted. This network is outside of your four walls. It's public and information-rich. An extranet is a private communication network designed to use Internet technologies for access and data transfer, allowing selected supply chain and/or value chain constituents to share privileged information to address specific market conditions and situations. This capability is without physical boundaries and due to its nature easy to change and configure. You decide who participates and can make it secure by installing firewalls to protect private information. With such a system, solutions can be taken rapidly to the point of need, so customer and consumer satisfaction is enhanced. In short, an extranet is the physical network enabling your firm to become a networked organization.

Seventh, we define e-commerce as a critical component of supply chain management that includes the conduct of any business transaction using digital (electronic) rather than physical means (telephone, fax). In that sense, it covers the buying and selling of goods and services using a digitally connected marketplace or the transfer of vital information between supply chain constituents in a digital format. It can also be a vehicle to support networked business processes across the value chain—a critical component to success in the future.

Applying the concepts inherent in these definitions can bring distinct advantages to a firm in terms of cycle time, flexibility, accuracy, and efficiency. Creating an entirely new e-business model or introducing e-commerce features to a standard model can bring a contemporary look to the business offering. Conversely, those firms that overlook the possibilities offered by e-commerce applications risk being characterized as behind the times and not capable of collaborating with the leaders. In either case, there should be a clear purpose and set of objectives for making what will be a major transformation to the way a company conducts its business. Having a value proposition for your company's business that is enhanced with e-commerce features is the generally accepted initial driver.

The leaders are taking full advantage of the opportunities offered by an e-business orientation. Cisco Systems and Dell Computer have taken such applications to what is considered the most advanced level, as these firms are approaching or exceeding 80% Web-based business transactions. Consumer products firms such as Gillette, Procter & Gamble, and Kraft Foods are creating new markets and revenues by applying e-commerce in a new venture sense. Wal-Mart, Tesco, and Carrefour are leaders in the retail arena, using lower distribution costs to advantage over competitors. Hewlett-Packard, Intel, and Sun Microsystems are setting a torrid pace in the rapid development of high-technology products. The automotive industry is trying to rapidly deploy e-business features in an attempt to integrate suppliers, lower the delivered cost of the automobile, and to better react to the new buying patterns of their end consumers. At the same time, firms throughout the world are struggling with defining just what they want to accomplish by riding this wave of e-business change. As we move forward, we'll look at both camps as we pursue what's working and what isn't working.

A CULTURAL BARRIER AS THE FIRST OBSTACLE

Getting started is often the toughest part of any change process. In the case of logistics and supply chain, getting started was almost spontaneous. Unfortunately, the documented results show a littered background of success and failure. Every firm we studied or interviewed showed some degree of improvement, but the range of the results was much wider than expected. Getting started in the proper manner leads to a more fulfilling effort. In spite of the wide publicity given to leading logistics, supply chain, and e-commerce applications, some companies have not made the gains expected. A few have abandoned the effort. Our research shows that most often the complications and obstacles to greater progress are internally generated. Changing internal management processes and points of view is the critical enabler.

When AMR Research, with sponsorship from Richmond Events, had the opportunity to work with senior supply chain and logistics managers at its May 4–7, 2000, Logistics Forum event, some surprising results developed. The forum included seven focus groups with close to 100 attendees. Among the many issues discussed, these attendees gave their views on e-business and its impact on their supply chains. A significant consensus was that while e-business and trading exchanges generate high levels of interest, they have "not reached the status of allocating dedicated management time for value proposition development" (Ferrari 2000).

Inhibitors included no full understanding of the overall value proposition for e-business, as well as a lack of consensus and cross-organizational commitment. Marketing and sales were seen as leading advocates, using Internet activity to deliver customer content, followed by the rest of business functions working on applications. The attendees saw e-business as both an opportunity and as a threat—an opportunity to increase revenues and reduce supply chain costs and a threat to branded positions that could become a commodity. The conclusion was that there's additional management, leadership, consensus, and commitment work required in the leveraging of true benefits of e-business for the supply chain (Ferrari 2000).

A significant number of firms that attempted to apply supply chain and advanced logistics techniques remain mired in their traditional practices. They peruse leading-edge case studies, attend seminars devoted to extolling successes, and visit locations where exceptional progress has been made, but little changes are instituted in their own companies. As these firms continue their practices, they miss the opportunity to optimize their processes and will find themselves at a cost disadvantage vis-à-vis the industry leaders.

What's at the root of this problem? Many answers are possible, but we found two that dominate. The first is the lack of a clear articulation of the benefits for use of the Internet. The second appears to be the reluctance to adopt practices clearly proven to be successful because of a penchant to keep doing things in the usual manner. The latter problem starts with a lack of cooperation among internal constituents. In their recent book 21st Century Logistics, D. J. Bowersox and others (1999) state, "There is increasing evidence that failure to achieve internal integration is a leading cause of why strategic alliances do not work. A failure to operate on an integrated basis prevents making good on promises to supply chain partners".

Our research supports this contention. As firms move to the forefront of logistic and supply chain excellence, they do so by cleaning up weak practices within and between their internal business units, and with the help of a significant number of external resources and alliances with business partners, they extend the gains. As we interviewed those that did not make the same progress, we found a consistent pattern of an unwillingness to trust or to cooperate with internal constituents and an abhorrence of using external organizations. In extreme cases, some very prominent firms are losing ground in their industry because they have yet to learn how to integrate their internal business units to leading-edge practices. In these same companies, we found evidence that some business units were more able to collaborate with a few suppliers and key customers than with their fellow business units.

"There is no such thing as an old economy company or a new economy company," according to Brian Kelley, a Ford vice president and president of Ford Motor Company's CustomerConnect in the July 10, 2000, issue of *Automotive News*. Rather, "the winners in the global business environment will be the companies with new economy thinking."

One logistics manager told us he had more success in working with customers than with his own purchasing and manufacturing operations. Content to allow internal conflict and competition to exist, these firms consistently suboptimize their total efforts. Without the help of external alliances, they fail to capture the best practices being implemented by the leaders.

Another pitfall occurs mainly because of people's resistance to understanding and applying the new tools. Richard D. Armstrong, publisher of Who's Who in Logistics, calls it "kingdom surrender." He cites the phenomenon in logistics as a major inhibitor to progress, saying the laggards simply do not want to relinquish what they see as control of the transportation function to any external entity. In one supporting example, we found a company delivering food products on a regular basis with its own truck fleet. When shown that their cost per mile was 35% over comparable accomplishments by third-party logistics providers (3PLs), the CEO responded that it made no difference. He was not going to have any other company drive his trucks or give the transportation function to an outsider.

The cultural imperative that has to be overcome for real progress is the one stating only internal ideas are any good. With so much happening around the world in logistics, supply chain, and e-commerce, no one firm can have a lock on all of the best practices. Optimization requires a sharing of concepts and applications. The leaders we studied consistently cited examples of inter-enterprise collaboration and use of most competent partner as the secrets to breakthrough achievements. The element of trust was of crucial importance in developing these secrets.

CALIBRATING A POSITION IS NOT ALWAYS EASY

But how do you know where you are versus the industry or its leaders? Is there a gap between countries and geographic sectors? Do certain industries lead with new levels of performance? How much further can you go with improvements? These are typical questions we encounter as we study what is happening around the world. As we researched the answers, a pattern became clear. There is a difference in application and results between industries. Some are much further along the result curve than others. High technology, aerospace and defense, and motor vehicles appear to be leading industries, while heavy equipment and construction seem to be laggards in applying e-commerce and advanced supply chain techniques.

Table 1.1 is a synopsis of our research on the industries studied for this book and the differences we think exist in these industries on two dimensions—their assimilation of advanced supply chain techniques and the use of new e-business models. Using this chart as a guide, you have a chance to take a quick look at the differences within selected industries and the large opportunities still available to take a leadership position. Note that while some industries are definitely moving quickly forward on application of what have become better supply chain practices, the movement toward e-business models is much slower.

There is also a difference between countries and global sectors, but in some industries not as much as might be presumed. Europe appears to lag the United States in the leading supply chain applications by about a year. Asia is further behind. In some areas of the high-technology industry, however, we see virtually no lag between the United States and some parts of Asia. Japan leads in mobile telephony and its ability to impact business. In books, grocery, and entertainment, there is little difference between the United

States and Europe, except in warehouse management systems. Scandinavia has a clear lead in use and application of cellular technology. In chemicals and pharmaceuticals, it's a level playing field.

An Industry Comparison

Industry	Supply Chain Assimilation	Use of E-Business Models
Aerospace		
Automotive		
Chemicals		
Consumer Goods		
Department of Defense		
Fulfillment		
High Technology		

Little or no Capability   Complete Capability

table 1.1

In short, it's a mixed bag of results, and whether a firm can specifically calibrate itself with the leaders or not, the opportunity to develop a path to leadership is real. We find no leader so far in the forefront of any industry that the gap cannot be eliminated. Often it's regulatory as well as cultural barriers that inhibit progress. But our research certainly showed that there are good businesspeople everywhere in the world.

Let's elaborate on what we mean. Most firms anywhere in the world have been concentrating on logistics and supply chain improvement for some time, typically for 5 years or more. The better results have been a reduction in purchasing costs, greater internal cooperation, external alliances that lead to reduced transportation and warehousing costs, and some inventory reduction. In areas where labor costs for loading and handling are a large factor, some global sectors benefit by having a distinctly lower average labor cost. Eventually, however, most organizations approach a point of diminishing returns. There are just so many cost concessions a supplier can make. The cost of the drivers and trucks reaches optimum levels. Fuel becomes subject to market conditions. The cost of warehousing and distribution stabilize. Where do you go for the next improvements?

The difference seems to come in the application of e-commerce and use of the Internet. The next frontier includes real inventory reduction and collaborative development of new revenues, and it requires new e-business models. Ancillary benefits include reduced transaction costs, less selling and buying expense, lower errors and reconciliation, greater inventory visibility, safety stock reductions, less distribution costs, and further savings from pooled purchasing and aggregated transportation. More important, it includes better decision making by virtue of more accurate and timely information.

THE DIVERSE IMPACT OF E-COMMERCE

To appreciate the impact of e-commerce, we must understand that it has come to us in three waves. The first wave was full of hype and near hysteria to get into the act, reap unheard-of gains through stock offerings, and appear to be on the front edge of the newest business applications. The necessity to make a profit in the process seemed to get lost in that wave, but some very new entrepreneurs raised huge capitalization. With that capital, they introduced novel business models and changed a few industries in the process. Books, entertainment, bank loans, and travel stand out as affected industries.

In the second wave, a shakeout is taking place. Making a profit is becoming a necessity, and more rational business managers seem to be in control. The movement in this wave is certainly more focused on business-to-business (B2B) applications, in spite of the publicity given to the business-to-consumer (B2C) leaders. What we are witnessing is an evolution in terms of the business applications of what will be the most important new tool of the current century—use of the Internet or World Wide Web to enhance business and commercial processes. After the hype and near hysteria surrounding using the tool to make money has come a more disciplined approach to improving logistics and supply chains.

The second wave will define the real position of the new entrepreneurs and their business partners. Call them e-retailers, Internet retailers, I-marketers, or dot-coms, most of the successful ones, or those that endure, will be allied with very traditional business entities. Whether you are in the B2B or B2C scenario, using the new tools will enhance performance, perhaps more in terms of new revenues than in continued cost reduction. The e-commerce effect will force change in both areas, bringing shorter cycle times, more efficient order processing, and a host of better supply chain practices. With those changes will come the absolute necessity to improve your logistics and supply chain infrastructure or the benefits will be spurious. E-business models simply will not work if they are not supported by leading-edge practices in logistics and supply chain.

The most noted of the B2C examples affords us a chance to illustrate the differences between the two waves. Amazon.com has garnered more publicity than any other dot-com enterprise. In the first wave, this organization introduced a totally new book sales and distribution model. The result was the firm raised greater capitalization with its stock offerings than its two largest competitors had combined. With that capital, the owner and founder, Jeff Bezos, acquired a stable of other dot-com organizations. He also tried to create an infrastructure that included very large distribution centers to assure efficient delivery of the orders received over the Web. In the process, the firm lost money on a large scale. In the second wave, the pressure is clearly on Bezos to make a profit and to make better use of those megadistribution centers.

Of interest to us is the tactic of offering free or heavily discounted delivery charges during the first wave, as an inducement to secure the desired consumer base. Many dot-coms would overlook the actual costs in this area as a marketing ploy, only to find it was a significant drain on profitability. In the second wave, an opportunity arises for logistics and supply chain professionals to step in and show the entrepreneurs how to do the job right. These new entrepreneurs simply did not have the logistics or supply chain knowledge and infrastructures necessary to keep up with the demand created over the Internet. Many could not properly fill the orders they received. Several toy retailers were struck particularly hard by this aspect and have come under U.S. government scrutiny for making false promises. In the second wave the need for responsible, e-commerce-enhanced business models with a supporting infrastructure will be paramount.

The third wave will be full of mergers and acquisition, as our research shows a trend for the large brick-and-mortar companies to get in the act and acquire the better-constructed and -managed of the new dot-com organizations. Some well-funded Internet firms will acquire traditional firms, as AOL is attempting to do with Time-Warner. That means there will be a shakeout in the field as the weaker cyber players are eliminated and the stronger ones become candidates for takeover. In the logistics area, for example, we calculate that more than fifty marketplaces, trading sites, or other logistics-related Web sites are currently active. We see that number declining in the next few years to ten or fifteen at most. The strongest may remain independent, but we foresee the acquisition of the survivors by large transportation and manufacturing firms. In the chapter on the supply chain of the future, we'll discuss the fourth wave—where companies transform themselves into e-businesses.

In the interim, the tremendous hype associated with anything related to the Internet has fueled speculation around just how much growth will there be in the B2B segment of commerce and the role e-commerce will have in continued business expansion. People in a wide range of industries are wondering how much of their business will be cyber based by, say, 2004 or 2005. From our perspective, the actual percentage is not as important as the rate of adoption and what it indicates as a measurement of change in the way an industry conducts its business. No company wants to put even 5% or 10% of its business at risk.

PENETRATION OF THE WEB WILL VARY BY INDUSTRY

Our research indicates that virtually no industry will not be impacted by a growing and accelerated use of Web applications. We also find the amount of final impact will vary greatly by industry and possibly by country. In general terms, AMR Research projects that B2B e-commerce will reach $5.7 trillion by the end of 2004, or 29% of the dollar value of commercial transactions (see Figure 1.1). That amount does not include all of the information and Web-based applications that will support the 29/71 ratio of total transactions. Even the most physical of the 71% of transactions will be moved to the Internet in some form to take advantage of the speed and accuracy of future systems and to reduce errors and the inherent transaction costs. Moreover, the most important aspect of this projection is the indication that e-commerce has incredible momentum and will be adopted at a faster rate than most companies realize.

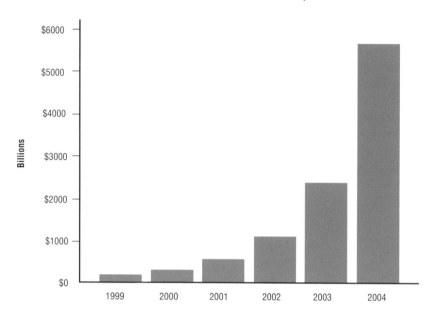

Growth of B2B Internet Commerce, 1999-2004

Source: AMR Research, 2000

figure 1.1

AMR also found a wide variation in the adoption rate of e-commerce between industries and leaders within the industry, as shown in Figure 1.2. These data show that service industries will progress to a 17% penetration. Transportation, trade and finance, which includes the communication, utilities, wholesale, and retail trade, will reach 34%. Manufacturing, which includes apparel, consumer goods, chemicals, pharmaceuticals, electronics, industrial equipment, and aerospace and defense, will hit 36%. Minerals and construction, including metal, coal, and oil and gas extraction, will settle at 15% penetration (Bermudez et al. 2000).

Within the broad industry classifications used in Figure 1.2, AMR expects the electronic industry Web usage to rise from 6.0% in 1999 to a leading 55% in 2004. Transportation should rise from 2.9% to 40% in the same time frame, while wholesale trade should go from a trace to 35% in that period. The most likely laggards will be the service and mineral and construction industries.

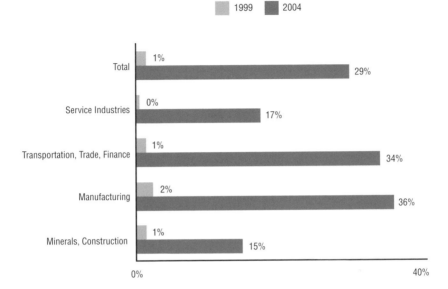

Internet Commerce Penetration Estimates
1999 vs. 2004

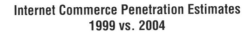
1999   2004

Total — 1% / 29%
Service Industries — 0% / 17%
Transportation, Trade, Finance — 1% / 34%
Manufacturing — 2% / 36%
Minerals, Construction — 1% / 15%

0%   40%

Source: AMR Research, 2000   figure 1.2

The data showed a wide gap between the projected adoption rate between industry leaders, such as Cisco Systems, Inc., Ingram Micro, Inc., General Electric, and General Motors, and those firms that expect a more gradual switch to Internet-based transactions. Evidence indicated that some industry leaders will use the Internet for the majority of their B2B transactions, some reaching as much as 80% by the end of 2001. As private trading hubs, independent trading exchanges (ITEs), and other cyber-based marketplaces enlarge the use of e-commerce throughout extended supply chains, the amount of Internet use by companies of all size can only be expected to increase. With more than 500 ITEs functioning across all vertical industries and the potential for thousands of private exchanges, B2B e-commerce is within the reach of any business with a computer and access to the Internet.

Whatever the actual equilibrium state percentages might be, the inference is clear. Some portion of every industry is going to move to Internet usage. That will require suppliers, distributors, and customers to keep pace with the technological innovations and the rapid transition to Web-based applications.

We encourage you to determine the ratio of cyber to physical transactions you expect will occur in your industry by 2004. With that projection and a reasonable implementation curve over the next 4 to 5 years, you can determine the impact the transition will have on your company. You can then determine the urgency with which you have to make the transition or accelerate current efforts to catch or beat the leaders.

POTENTIALLY MISLEADING GLOBAL ASPECTS

Regarding the global aspects of this expanded use of the Internet, we find another mixed bag of results. The fact is few companies are really global. Most become global through a set of alliances with other firms well established in areas of interest. So the game really becomes a competition between global business networks, centered on large nucleus companies wanting international positions for readily recognized brands or product lines. Such businesses in Europe are taking a hard look at the lessons being learned in the United States. While some industries consider themselves a year or more behind the United States, we found that estimate was moot.

If high technology in Europe lags that in the United States, the opportunity to make quick progress by adopting best practices is great. As markets in this arena continue on their global bent, the chance to make crucial alliances with leading supply chain and logistics partners affords the chance to make up ground rapidly. Furthermore, we saw evidence of very little gap between the United States and Europe in such industries as music, entertainment, travel, groceries, and books. As we viewed Asia, we found a similar scenario. Some industries and some companies lagged the U.S. progress, while some were very much at the same pace. American car manufacturers, for example, are still trying to catch the Toyota lead, while one of the leading e-commerce and supply chain stories still reside with Taiwan Semiconductor Manufacturing Corporation.

Our message is basic. The gap may be a point of indifference in the drive to gain a strategic or global advantage. So much is happening and so many new innovations have appeared that virtually every industry offers an opportunity to make up ground fast, if cultural barriers are subdued and the emphasis is placed on the right criteria. One concentration has to be on e-fulfillment, and we will cover that aspect in more detail in Chapter 5. Here the mistakes of the past have become apparent and the opportunities are large. It is not enough to secure a business customer or end consumer base that is disposed to using the

Internet for transactions. That accomplishment has to be backed with a fulfillment process that is nearly flawless, or the impact of the e-business model is wasted.

Another crucial concentration has to be on having the right supply chain partners so you can reach the most remote region of your sales territory, or the individual home addresses that may become part of your market. A further key element is compatibility of the communication infrastructure that is available. It does no good to choose a supplier partner if you can't move information accurately, quickly, and in a secure fashion. Understanding the communications capabilities of your partners will be as important as understanding their transportation resources.

We see a dichotomy of changes in this area. On the one hand, an emphasis will continue to be placed on creating full truckloads of goods going to large distribution centers or directly to stores. That situation is optimized by the physical transfer of goods from manufacturers to retail distribution centers and retail stores, through the expected Internet-enhanced systems of today and tomorrow.

On the other hand, as the B2C market grows and build to order from subassemblies increases, there will be another demand to take the loads down below pallet loads so a fulfillment center can deliver packages of one to a few items to a specific home address. This latter requirement has ushered in a new dimension to logistics and supply chain, creating a whole new market for some companies. We foresee a time in the near future when most logistics providers will have two parallel businesses in operation, either under their own direct control or with reliable channel partners.

IMPORTANCE TO LOGISTICS PRACTICES

We cannot stress too much the need for a supporting logistics and supply chain infrastructure in the business environment of the future. An e-business model will only be as good as that infrastructure. The holiday season of 1999 proved that fact, as several very large firms struggled once they received their electronic orders with fulfilling the promises made over the Web. As these firms committed to delivery to homes within hours after order receipt, they found their logistics infrastructure just wasn't prepared to fulfill on the commitment.

The future requirement is for a seamless, virtual network. Logistics can lead the way through the second wave, but there are weaknesses to overcome.

Companies must commit to membership in extended enterprise networks and then work out the details of having an Internet-enabled physical system of delivery as well as one that takes advantage of new orders received via the Web. This latter requirement must include some form of order segregation so packaging and delivery can be made in units down to one, to a large number of end destinations.

As you develop an e-business logistics/supply chain strategy, we cannot stress too much the importance of building in a full end-to-end capability to fulfill the commitments and promises that will be made over the new electronic communication system.

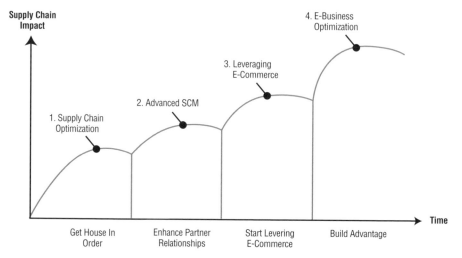

figure 1.3

PRACTICAL NEXT STEPS: A ROAD MAP

Figure 1.3 depicts how our research indicates progress is made. Consider the axes to represent the level of impact on your current business and the time the logistics and supply chain improvement effort takes to succeed. The level of impact is not meant to be absolute but relative in terms of the gains accomplished. The time frame can be 2 to 5 years.

Beginning in the first sector of the chart, we see that organizations pursuing supply chain and logistics excellence typically start by getting closer to the current leading practices, focused largely on internal operations. We call that area "get house in order." That means some form of supply chain and logistics effort is launched. Organizational changes are minimal, but someone is chosen to lead the effort. Internal inefficiencies are cleaned up through advanced planning and scheduling. Pressure is put on reducing costs and inventories. We find, in general, results in this sector lead to improved earnings of 2% to 4%, particularly from reduced inventories and lower distribution and transportation costs. The customer sees little impact in this area. It's a time of trying to develop a strategy and save some money by doing what leaders show can be done.

In the second sector, firms begin experimenting with advanced supply chain management processes aimed at enhancing partner relationships. Often under pressure from major customers, they look at vendor-managed inventory (VMI), begin some form of supplier synchronization, order promising improvements, and will even try collaborative planning, forecasting, and replenishment (CPFR) with major customers. This is a time of interacting with focus groups, listening to external counseling, and putting the business toe in the water. Pilot tests abound, and many people go off to see what is happening with the leaders. We find, in general, results in this sector lead to improved earnings of 3% to 4%, particularly from purchased materials, finished goods inventories, and plant utilization.

The third sector starts to leverage e-commerce and is a time when customers do become important and most companies try some form of Internet procurement. The more adventurous will dabble in online trading and consider one of the many logistics exchanges for partial or full outsourcing of their transportation needs. This is also the area where pushback from obliging suppliers starts to occur and the firm usually encounters diminishing returns from their trade-off of supply position for continued cost reduction.

Also in the third sector, the laggards try to catch the leaders that have continued to push forward. Now the requirement is to get very serious with e-commerce applications and to make important alliances with partners who can help you get to the top of the class. Web-based self-service is a feature added to call centers, so the service is matched appropriately with the need. Supply chain connectivity begins, as constituent firms link up their extranets to better serve designated business customers while leveraging their suppliers' capabilities, to a fuller extent. The savings in this area are typically another 4% to 5%, particularly from purchased materials, supplies and transportation, and new sales channels.

The final sector is open for participation as a company moves to build advantage through e-business optimization. There are no more than one or two companies per industry in this final phase we call "building an advantage." Here we see full global visibility of supply chain activities and virtual manufacturing and distribution systems are developed to provide speed and flexibility. Online tracking of everything from raw materials to finished product is possible. Collaborative planning and delivery is so pervasive, we term it supply chain kieretsu, after the Japanese concept of interlinked firms working together for a common purpose. Partners can see the systemic inventories, from beginning to end of the network. Demand data are linked directly from the point of consumption to the supply data at the various points of manufacture and delivery. In this sector, the savings come from real inventory reductions and working capital savings. Cycle times are slashed, and customer response ability goes up dramatically. New revenues, often from nontraditional sources, become a major factor.

Network transportation systems also show up in this fourth sector, as back hauls reach 90% or more by virtue of pooling logistics needs across many companies. The benefits here come from an absence of processing errors, lowest transaction costs, best constituent performance, more rapid and successful product introduction, and highest customer satisfaction ratings. The bottom-line impact of the fourth sector can be the final 5% to 7% available from a state-of-the-art, technically enhanced supply chain network.

OPPORTUNITIES, BENEFITS, AND CONSEQUENCES OF E-BUSINESS SUPPLY CHAINS

Ours is a simple thesis. We see a wide range of opportunity and results from the leveraging of logistics, supply chain, and e-commerce, resulting in a transformation to being an e-business. The opportunities come from developing new ways of doing old business. Getting a proper start is crucial, but when a clear vision is developed and articulated, and the total organization mobilizes to accomplish the vision, the results can be dramatic. Moving into the fourth sector of our road map can take 2 to 5 years, but once there a company wrings out just about the last dollar of savings from what becomes an optimized supply chain network. Firms do so by cleaning up the internal inefficiencies first and then moving externally in a trusting and collaborative manner to form alliances with other firms that can help them develop best practices across the end-to-end supply chain network, of which they are just one part.

The consequence of not participating in this new way of doing business is to be left out of important networks that dominate an industry. In the future, companies that are not participants will be invisible to many markets and suffer from a higher cost structure. Simply put, companies that do not participate will not be competitive.

This is very important alarm for small to midsize firms that never quite got through the electronic data interchange (EDI) stage. Avoiding what they saw as a costly system that had little benefits for themselves, these firms have no choice now but to be part of the next wave of electronic communication. Using the Internet is far less costly and can be quickly assimilated. Without that capability, the larger firms will simply avoid doing business with the technology-handicapped company.

E-business is still so new that the hype has to be separated from the positive benefits. It has to move from a game of making riches to sound business applications that support what becomes the new e-business model for conducting a company's commercial activities. Supporting that business model has to be a logistics and supply infrastructure that can conduct business on two bases—physical and cyber. The physical system of warehouses, distribution centers, and retail stores is not going to vanish. Indeed, it will continue to be the dominant mode of product and service delivery, for now and into the foreseeable future. A portion of every industry, however, will become cyber based. That means that orders will be taken, inventory and shipments tracked, payments made, and data transferred electronically.

Products will still be passed through some physical channel, but the size and destination for the deliveries could change dramatically. That will require logistics and supply chain professionals to plan on a dual channel of distribution, both of which should be electronically enhanced.

In Chapter 5, we'll present our future-state hypotheses. Our preview for now includes a state in which the dominant players in each industry are large nucleus firms surrounded by an alliance of partners helping them take products and services to designated markets, anywhere in the world, with the most efficient delivery system possible. No single firm will have all of the necessary elements.

The best will be sharing assets, ideas, and practices across an optimized supply chain system that extends from the most basic supplies to the final receipt and acceptance or rejection of the finished product. At the heart of such a network will be a cooperative logistics and supply chain system that has online access to all vital information, doing as many transactions and process steps in an automated manner as makes sense for added value for all constituents. Asset utilization will be a major consideration, as efficiency will be measured across an end-to-end fulfillment system.

FRAMEWORK FOR THE IMPLEMENTATION

As we proceed through the book, we'll build on the four-level evolution model described in Figure 1.3. To flesh out the position taken, we'll consider six industries and document leadership positions and practices. We'll fit the progression our research has found into the framework described in the four-phase evolution. The impact of the changes we're documenting will be shown on these industries. We'll then progress through the tools and methods important to making the gains shown by the leaders.

We'll take a look at the impact of the trading exchanges and new market-places appearing across the full business horizon, giving particular attention to what is working and what we expect will fail. A future-state hypothesis will be presented to synthesize our research and findings into a view of tomorrow. Early warning signals will be announced so you can decide on how to handle the many challenges you will face as you move along your journey. We'll tell you how to develop a supply chain and logistics strategy that leverages e-commerce and results in a distinguishing e-business model.

We'll conclude with the practical next steps that you can take to advance your current logistics and supply chain effort, by applying the best practices we found in our research. Finally, we'll issue our call for action, as we mentally step beyond the horizon and reflect on the vision synthesized from more than 100 discussions with senior managers and executive who are trying their best to decipher what is happening and what the future landscape will look like.

CONCLUSION

Every advantage is temporary. In today's rapidly changing business environment, firms have to reach out and grasp the best techniques and then continuously enhance the advantage they gain. The speed of e-business change is outrunning most organizations, so a special effort must be made to keep pace, let alone forge a commanding lead. The secret is not to panic. Consider e-business as both a threat and an opportunity and use it as a catalyst for positive change. It will be a struggle that starts inside the firm. It expands cautiously with the help of trusted partners intent on using the Internet collectively for market advantage.

If you don't understand what's really happening in your industry or fail to appreciate what the ultimate customer needs and expects, you'll probably design something that doesn't have any real value. The need is to define a new and compelling value proposition that is accepted by the most important of your customers and distinguished you from your competitors. This proposition becomes the new vision that is embraced by the organization and its partners and is easily articulated. As the process steps across the end-to-end value chain continue to be enhanced, the proper technologies are applied and fitted into the framework that gives the expected results—sustained profits and new revenue growth.

chapter 2

The Tools and Methods of
B2B E-Commerce

New tools and methods have become the creators of many of the terms and approaches outlined in this book. Prior to the e-business revolution, product price and quality defined success, and enterprise resource planning (ERP) systems that optimized operational productivity could create a competitive advantage. But then feature-rich, high-quality products became standard, making customer service mission-critical. Attracting and retaining customers—the underlying theme of customer relationship management (CRM) applications—differentiated suppliers. Now, rapidly advancing e-business processes create new ways of doing business, such as Internet auctions, trading exchanges, mobile communication, and Web-based self-service. Serving customers better requires not only mobilizing all of an organization's processes but collaborating in value chain communities as well. Collaboration will drive the next competitive advantage, time to market. In a collaborative market, B2B tools and methods become as much a core competency as the goods or services a company sells.

Participating in collaborative markets requires users to build successfully upon legacy systems and use new business processes, such as e-procurement, Web self-service, and automated channel partner support. Successful collaboration will mean extending these business processes across the value chain. It also means exploiting emerging services such as trading exchanges and business process outsourcing. CRM, ERP, and supply chain management (SCM) systems may wrestle for king-of-the-hill status, but they will not achieve it. These systems form the core of a company's back-office systems, to be embellished by analytic tools, such as data warehouse that yield actionable information, and supported by integration that intertwines the core applications and extends them out to participate in external markets. Leading software vendors in each of these markets are stretching toward a new systems blueprint; they are building functionality in unfamiliar components or binding their systems together with those of their partners. Nevertheless, no one vendor will ever provide all the applications needed to participate in collaborative markets.

From a more human perspective, business relationships were almost exclusively established through person-to-person interactions. While often spearheaded by the procurement and sales organizations, business relationships were established by many different organizations throughout a company. Many companies claim their greatest asset is their employees and this is often proved in the quality of the relationships employees establish. The companies with highly motivated employees often have the best relationships with their trading partners and help their companies dominate their market segment.

The tools and methods of B2B e-commerce give companies the potential to shift the balance of power from those corporations with good person-to-person relationship capabilities or internal systems to those with the best e-commerce strategies. Although back-office systems and person-to-person relationship building will always be important, a good e-commerce strategy can leverage a corporation's core competencies many times over to many new markets. For example, a good buyer might have two or three dependable suppliers he or she can go to with a rush order. A company participating in an industry trading exchange can post the same rush order and have it visible to hundreds of potential suppliers. Companies using exchanges for these types of orders have found that they not only can get what they want but may pay less for it because they found a supplier with excess capacity or inventory.

In this chapter we will introduce readers to the new tools of B2B e-commerce that are driving the recent interest in e-business concepts and that are largely predicated on use of the Internet to support a company's internal and external business processes. One type of these tools, trading exchanges, is of such paramount importance, that the next chapter, Chapter 3, is solely dedicated to describing them and their potential impact on business. They are expected to drastically alter the landscape of most value and supply chains—helping to create new ways of doing business and forever changing the nature in which companies interact.

THE NEW TOOLS OF B2B E-COMMERCE

The enormous potential of this leverage from B2B e-commerce has spawned a number of new concepts and processes. In turn, these concepts and processes are supported by a plethora of new software packages and Internet services (see Figure 2.1). The key concepts for B2B include

- buy-side e-commerce,
- sell-side e-commerce,
- content management,
- collaboration,
- XML and EDI, and
- trading exchanges.

Each of these is changing the way corporations need to look at their internal systems and external trading partner relationships. Each also plays a key role in developing an overall e-business strategy for the corporation. The relationship between the concepts listed is follows:

- Buy-side and sell-side software and processes enable buying, selling, and negotiation transactions in B2B commerce.

- Collaboration transforms these unidirectional transactions into a bidirectional information exchange to reduce the time required to adjust schedules, quantities, and terms.

- Content management provides the platform technology to manage and exchange vast amounts of product specifications, documentation, contracts, images, and Web pages in support of B2B commerce.

- Trading exchanges, or online hosted Web sites, provide the platforms that pull all of these concepts and technologies together to provide a Web site to host B2B commerce.

- XML and EDI provide the basis for a common communications protocol in a trading exchange.

E-Business Platform within the Collaborative Market Environment

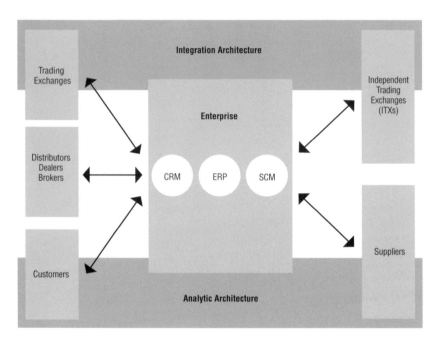

Source: AMR Research

figure 2.1

To summarize this, B2B tools and methods leverage the Internet in three broad areas:

- Internal processes supporting employee interaction

- External processes supporting customer and supplier interaction

- Value and supply chain processes supporting the intercompany interactions

Given these broad areas, the tools of B2B must be looked at from a different perspective than the business software applications and information technology (IT) investments of the last three decades. Foremost is that B2B tools are not simply an IT investment, but they must also be a commitment by the corporation to embrace e-business as we now know it. As you can see from the preceding list, the common ingredient of all B2B tools and methods is improved interaction, which leads us to the premise that commitment is more important than software. General Electric and Cisco Systems are B2B pioneers as a result of corporate commitment, not B2B software investments.

BUY-SIDE E-COMMERCE

As companies look for ways to take advantage of Internet technologies and demonstrate their ability to become e-businesses, many turn first to supplier-facing software applications. These applications, designed to help companies buy goods and services over the Internet, are commonly termed buy-side e-commerce. Buy-side e-commerce initiatives carry rapid payback and broad organizational impact, and they are less risky than customer-facing, sell-side e-commerce initiatives because they can be implemented with little disruption from corporate politics, such as sales channel conflict.

Buy-side e-commerce software applications fall into two broad categories:

- Indirect procurement—the acquisition of goods and services that do not become an inventory asset or go into a manufacturer's product

- Direct procurement—the acquisition of goods and services that become part of a product or that are resold.

Thus far, most of the activity and attention has been focused on the indirect procurement subset of buy-side e-commerce. Existing processes for indirect procurement are inefficient at most corporations, and loads of information need to be exchanged between buyers and sellers, often to complete even simple transactions. For example, consider the exorbitant amount of time that an employee might expend acquiring an additional piece of modular office furniture:

The employee might have to:

1. determine the original manufacturer,
2. seek out a catalog,
3. find the correct SKU for the right color and style,

4. fill out a requisition,

5. get it approved,

6. enter it into the requisition system, and

7. then send it the purchasing department, which then has to get a price, approve the quote, confirm the order, and acknowledge delivery.

All of this for a one-time purchase that was not likely leveraged with other purchases from the same manufacturer!

Indirect procurement systems are designed to leverage the Internet to streamline these processes to drastically save the buyer's time and money.

Although direct procurement has gotten much more IT investment over the last 30 years (e.g., using ERP systems and EDI), it too will be vastly improved by B2B tools and methods. Given that direct procurement often makes up to 80% of a manufacturer's or distributor's procurement spending, cost reductions and efficiency improvements have the great potential. Direct procurement processes and systems, however, are so intertwined with ERP, supply chain planning, EDI, and other systems that it is a much more complex task to introduce buy-side e-commerce. To date, some companies have leveraged the Internet to replace faxes and phone calls to introduce some rudimentary collaboration. Many of the indirect procurement software providers, such as Ariba and Commerce One, have begun to address direct procurement. In addition, ERP vendors, such as SAP, Oracle, JD Edwards, and PeopleSoft, as well as supply chain planning vendors, such as i2 Technologies, Manugistics, and Adexa, have begun to address direct procurement.

INDIRECT PROCUREMENT SOFTWARE APPLICATIONS

Indirect procurement software applications are designed to reduce the total cost of ownership of all commodities other than direct material and labor. ERP systems crafted to support direct material through traditional purchasing execution processes do not adequately support the highly variable nature of indirect commodities. This gap has created an opportunity for a slew of software vendors to enter the market, offering Internet-based procurement (IBP) applications, electronic catalogs, trading communities, application hosting services, integration tools, and system integration services. Leading indirect procurement vendors include Ariba, Commerce One, Oracle, PeopleSoft, i2 Technologies, Clarus, and PurchaseSoft.

Indirect Procurement Improvement—Evolutionary, Not Revolutionary

The idea of improving indirect procurement processes is not new. In the early to mid-1990s, some capital-intensive firms applied direct material improvement activities, such as supplier rationalization, commodity teams, private extranets, request for quotation (RFQ) processing, EDI, and supplier management, to indirect procurement, often with great success. Procurement cards, called p-cards, also emerged as a widely adopted self-service purchasing-control strategy intended to reduce purchase order (PO) volume and control maverick buying. The Internet's most recent impact on indirect procurement has been improved requisition-to-payment efficiencies and reduced maverick buying with electronic catalogs, sell-side system integration, Internet-based trading protocols, and self-service transactions for end-user buyers.

IBP Systems

To examine the benefits of IBP systems, it is important to understand the general procurement process (see Figure 2.2). It is also important to understand the similarities and differences between the direct and indirect procurement processes. The direct procurement process deals with the acquisition of products directly specified and required by the production plan. Meanwhile, the indirect procurement process involves the purchase of items not used as part of the product; hence, it is independent of the production plan and often

The Procurement Process

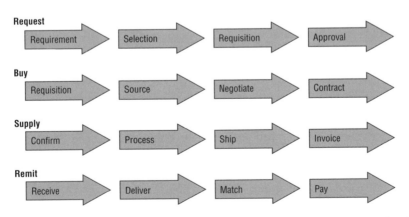

Source: AMR Research

figure 2.2

driven by budgetary plans. Generally, direct and indirect procurement follow the same basic processes, but the characteristics of process implementation are different (see Table 2.1).

Content Management Requirements for E-Commerce

Process	Direct	Indirect
Request	Requirements are normally generated in an automated fashion using traditional Materials Requirements Planning (MRP) algorithms. Formal requisitions and approvals are rarely required.	Requirements are usually generated on a reactive basis. If indirect inventories are involved, replenishment is frequently done on a reorder point model. Requisitions are completed and can require one or more approvals.
Buy	Sourcing and pricing are frequently predetermined. Orders are released to both blanket orders and individual purchase orders. This can vary based on the industry or the commodity being purchased.	There is some preestablished sourcing and pricing for common items. If there is no contract, buying can involve multiple quotes and extended negotiations, particularly for high-cost items.
Suppy	Formal order confirmation is rare. Carriers are usually predetermined based on consolidation strategies of the vendor or customer. Invoicing procedures can vary widely based on industry.	For more expensive items, order confirmations are common. Parcel/package shipment is frequently utilized. For contracted relationships, statement-based billing (instead of individual invoices)
Remit	Receipts are delivered to a stockroom or directly to the production line. Trust relationships can be fairly common in specific industries with little or no matching required for payment processing.	Bulk receipts often have to be burst into multiple deliveries within the organization. Trust relationships are less common for indirect procurement, resulting in considerable matching requirements.

Source: AMR Research

table 2.1

IBP Systems: Bringing Automation to the Procurement Process

Although the purchasing modules of ERP systems automate the ongoing process of direct materials and components, they have a number of prominent shortcomings:

- They do not provide much help in the vendor identification and selection process.

- They are cumbersome and expensive to use for infrequently and one-time purchases.

- They provide very little control over the cost of what is being purchased as it relates to budgets.

- They do not easily facilitate the aggregation of indirect purchase to leverage buying power.

IBP systems leverage the vast amount of information on the Internet to address these problems by providing the missing elements of typical ERP suites:

- Web-based, self-service requisitioning and receiving;

- workflow for the requisition approval process;

- aggregate purchases across departments and corporate divisions to leverage buying power;

- electronic catalog management to identify suppliers and products;

- integration to suppliers' order systems; and

- integration to back-office ERP systems to close the accounting loop.

IBP systems use combinations of external Web sites and in-house computing to accomplish these tasks. The typical system allows for the creation of custom catalogs that limit employee access to only authorized items. The catalogs may be resident on an in-house system, at the suppliers' Web site, or hosted on a Web site run by the IBP provider. The rapid evolution of Internet-based service models is causing most providers of IBP systems to transform their licensed-based software products into a hosted service provided on a transaction fee basis (see Figure 2.3).

High Return, Many Choices

Indirect procurement has become a popular application choice for initial B2B projects. The popularity results from the significant project return-on-investment (ROI) and the narrow implementation scope. ROI comes from three areas:

- Compliance: Maverick buying is eliminated by making the requisitioning process more convenient for employees.

- Improved negotiation: Having accurate aggregated information about spending improves a company's position when it negotiates with suppliers.

- Reduced process times: The inherent workflow automation substantially reduces the time and cost of processing.

The key components of an indirect procurement application can be evaluated along three dimensions:

- Content—involves how and where supplier product information is accessed. Most products offer the ability to use a hybrid approach-- catalogs that reside on the internal indirect procurement system and those that reside on an external Web site.

Market Landscape for Indirect Procurement Systems

Trading Communities:
Chemdex   Neoforma
Orderzone   PlasticsNet
MRO.com   mpresse
ec-Portal

Hosting Communities:
Connectq   Netscape/sun
OnDisplay   TRADE'ex
Vertical Net

ERP Buy-Side Vendor Products:
SAP *Business-to-Business Procurement*
Oracle *Strategic Procurement*
PeopleSoft E-Procurement (commerce One *BuySite*)
J.D. Edwards *OneWorld ORMS* (Ariba *ORMS*)
Baan *E-Procurement*

Buyer

Supplier

Back-Office System Data
Organization
Employee Master
Supplier Master
Approved Supplier List
Contacts/Pricing
Part Master
Purchase Requisition
Purchase Order
Accounts Payable
General Ledger

IBM Vendor Products:
Ariba *ORMS*
Commerce One *Buysite 5.0*
Clarus *E-Procurement*
Concur *CompanyStore*
RightWorks *RightWorks*
AGENTics *Supply Channel*
Hot Samba *net Procurement*
Intelysis *IEC-Enterprise*
Netscape/Sun *BuyerXpert*
ProcureNet *OneSource Procurement*
PSDI *mroBuyer*
PurchaseSoft *PurchaseSoft 5.1*
Remedy *Purchasing@Work*
SupplyWorks *SupplyWorks*
Trilogy *Buying Chain*

Content Aggregators:
Aspect Technology
Harbinger
Commerce One (MarketSite.Net)
PSDI
Requisite Technology
TPN Register
PartNET

Front-Office Sell-Side Systems

Back-Office System
Customer
Sales Order
Part Master
Inventory
A/R
Pricing

Self-Service Application Vendors
Capture Software
Clarus Corporation
Concur Technologies
Extensity
Necho Systems

EDI Vendors: GEIS, Harbinger, Sterling

Enterprise Application Integration (EAI) Vendors:
Crossworlds, Extricity, Viewlocity, Vitria, webMethods

Procurement Card Provider: American Express, Visa, Mastercard

System Integrators: Big Five, Anderson Consulting, CSC, Perot Systems, EDS/A.T. Kearney, IBM, Cap Gemini, Cambridge Technology Partners

Source: AMR Research, 1999

figure 2.3

- Workflow—directs the requisitions and encompasses the user interface (the requisition), approval automation, and integration with back-office systems

- Reporting—involves aggregating spending information across several dimensions, such as supplier, commodity, and cost center

How IBP Systems Work

IBP systems first help identify supplier rationalization opportunities by analyzing supplier spending within a commodity. Some systems assist with the RFQ and bidding process to select the preferred supplier or suppliers. To purchase some product or service, an end user starts by browsing a Web-based catalog that displays all the items the user can requisition. The catalog can be a locally hosted, hosted by the supplier, or hosted by a third party. The catalog is searched using either free-text searches or parametric searches of certain commodity attributes, often within a well-defined commodity hierarchy. The user-selected items, including company-specific pricing, are passed back to the IBP system shopping cart. When the cart is checked out, any needed approvals will be processed using Web-based workflows, e-mails, and extranet access. Approvals are based on user or cost-center limits, at the order level, or in aggregate. Upon approval, the shopping cart is usually turned into a purchase requisition, a purchase order, or both, usually in the back-office purchasing system. However, if the user is using a p-card, a purchase order is not needed because a consolidated invoice will be electronically downloaded from the purchase card's provider, with end users reviewing their charges on an exception basis. After purchase orders are batched and transmitted, users typically perform a desktop receipt, but the ERP system can also be used for centralized receiving. Vendors paid via terms usually receive an electronic funds transfer transaction at prespecified times.

DIRECT PROCUREMENT: ULTIMATELY THE DOMINANT FORCE IN B2B COMMERCE

While it might seem to be an easy transition from indirect procurement to direct, it is much more complicated than one might think. Indirect procurement relies on a requestor to initiate the buying process and define the requirement for the purchase. Many manufacturers purchase systems, rather than single components. Systems are inherently more complex than a single item. Often systems are highly engineered, complex components. In most manufacturing companies, direct procurement is initiated by the material planning system (usually part of the ERP system) based on the bill-of-material and production plan. The ERP system has its own purchasing function that is usually tightly integrated with the material planning function. Adding a Web-based procurement application requires a lot of complex integration to an ERP system in order to handle the continuous flow of part data, purchase orders, and release schedule updates to the suppliers. Further complicating this picture, many companies have begun to add advanced planning and scheduling (APS) systems to optimize the material planning function. This adds one more integration step to the implementation process.

While some of the other benefits of indirect procurement systems include finding suppliers for infrequently purchasing items (at one end of the spectrum) and aggregating buying power for similar items (at the other), these do not readily apply in direct procurement. For direct procurement, the purchasing department has generally already established contracts and negotiated favorable pricing from one or two suppliers. This leads to the obvious question: What benefits will Internet-based direct procurement yield?

Even with all the capabilities of ERP and APS systems, the direct procurement process can benefit from Web-based procurement systems in the following ways:

- Lower transaction costs

- Better communication with suppliers

- More visibility of suppliers' capacity and open-order status

- Collaborative planning

- Quicker response to changes

- Aggregated buying across divisions running on different ERP systems

Although most indirect procurement vendors are just beginning to tackle direct procurement, it is a forgone conclusion that Web-based indirect procurement systems will be adapted to the direct procurement process. Many of the leading indirect procurement providers including Ariba, Commerce One, and Oracle are already moving in this direction. For example, Commerce One is integrating its procurement application with SAP's ERP system, and PeopleSoft has embedded an early version of Commerce One to tackle direct procurement (see Figure 2.4 and Table 2.2).

SELL-SIDE E-COMMERCE

Every sale requires a buyer and a seller. Sell-side e-commerce spans a wide variety of applications, processes, and services designed to help sellers represent their products, brand, and companies in the digital marketplace. While sell-side e-commerce applications come in many shapes and sizes, they are generally aimed at giving Web sites the capability to conduct some part or all of the selling and customer relationship functions. Common sell-side software applications include:

- Web-based shopping carts,

- personalized response,

- channel management,

- self-service order management,

- configurators,

- product information delivery, and

- automated customer response.

E-Commerce Application Adoption in 2000-2001

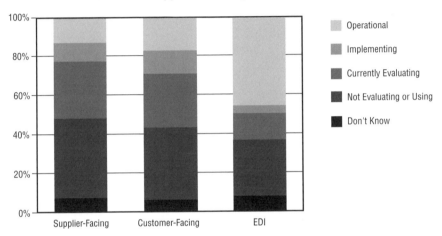

Source: AMR Research

figure 2.4

Buy-Side Vendors Ranked and Segmented by 2000 Total Revenue

1999 Revenue Rank	Company Name	Revenue, 2000 ($M)	Buy Side %	Other %	Buy Side $	Other $
1	Ariba	$391	46%	54%	$180	$211
2	Commerce One	$402	40%	60%	$159	$243
3	SAP	$5,744	2%	98%	$125	$5,619
4	Oracle	$2,865	3%	97%	$100	$2,765
5	RightWorks	$58	43%	57%	$25	$33
6	Clarus	$15	100%	0%	$15	$-
7	Peregrine	$584	7%	93%	$39	$545
8	Remedy	$317	9%	91%	$27	$290
9	Other	$112	100%	0%	$112	$-
Subtotal		**$10,488**	**7%**	**93%**	**$782**	**$9,706**

Source: AMR Research, 2000

table 2.2

A common thread behind sell-side e-commerce is creating a 24/7 (24 hours a day, 7 days per week) environment in which your customers can interact with your company via the Internet.

Sell-Side Commerce Has Broadened Its Meaning

This focus on serving the customer is quickly causing sell-side e-commerce application providers with an origin in building Web sites, such as Broadvision, to converge with CRM applications providers, such as Siebel Systems. (CRM systems are designed to help acquire, sell to, and maintain customer relationships.) This convergence has spawned another category of software, E-Business Relationship Management (ERM), that extends the CRM concept with capabilities that can only be achieved because the selling process occurs online. Examples of ERM include automated Web-based response from vendors such as Kana, personalized promotions and merchandising from such vendors as Blue Martini, and marketing automation from vendors such as e.Phiphany. As a result, sell-side e-commerce is now a broad label applied to CRM applications, Web site selling applications, ERM, and other specialty customer-facing applications.

Sell-Side Application Concepts

The applications that are available to support sell-side initiatives have been developed recently and rarely carry the complexity that usually comes with older legacy systems. These applications make full use of Web-centric computing techniques and are generally a collection of components that must be assembled by a systems integrator to create the finished application. Sell-side application components can be grouped into three basic categories:

- Presentation—displaying the right product, at the right time, to the right customer at the right price.

- Process automation—processing the order including entry, tracking, and settlement

- Administration—providing tools for non-IT personnel to maintain product information and the sales process

These three categories appear simple, but think about the vast number of employees in your company who are involved in making these steps happen in your selling and fulfillment processes. Now imagine a collection of software applications that will attempt to replicate the capabilities of all of these people, to allow your customers to do it via the Internet. Not so simple! Let's look at each of these concepts in a little more detail.

Product Presentation

Many of today's Web sites simply display crude product photos with limited information. Sell-side applications are designed to improve upon this by acting as an online sales representative. Generally, a sales rep discusses only the products that your company is interested in or may have bought in the past. The sell-side equivalent of sales rep knowledge of your company is called personalization. (See the sidebar "What Is Personalization?") In addition, a sales rep may help with custom configurations and special orders. This is handled by configuration applications. The sales rep may also make a call to the factory to determine the feasibility of a rush order. An available-to-promise (ATP) application would determine this feasibility. The presentation capabilities of sell-side applications are being designed to incorporate these capabilities so that a customer can do this unassisted. Enterprise application integration (EAI) software (i.e., software that is used to integrate and interface software systems in an enterprise) connects the online order process to the back-office ERP systems for further processing, which may include manufacturing, shipping, and billing.

What Is Personalization?

Personalization involves applying knowledge about customers (and their behavior) and products (and their characteristics) to present appropriate products, cross-selling opportunities, and up-selling opportunities. This functionality borrows heavily from artificial intelligence methodologies, particularly rules-processing and pattern recognition (a.k.a. case-based reasoning). Rules processing involves applying knowledge about the customer, such as demographics, customer type, or equipment installed, to generate the appropriate set of products. Rules about products are used to provide product configuration capability on a self-service basis. Pattern recognition is used to apply knowledge of past behavior (by either a specific customer or customers in a common group) to suggest products. Rules processing is common across all personalization implementations, while pattern recognition is most common in business-to-consumer (B2C) deployments.

Process Automation

Once the customer has selected a product, the process automation phase of sell-side e-commerce takes over. Here, the applications assist the customer in entering the order, confirming availability, and completing the order. Once an order is complete, enterprise application integration (EAI) software connects the online order process to the back-office ERP systems for further processing which may include manufacturing, shipping and billing.

Let's look at common Web-store sales scenario and the product presentation and process automation that might support it:

An industrial customer needs a rush order of 10,000 steel mounting brackets with an enlarged screw hole. To accomplish this, the customer comes to your Web site and is greeted by a Web page customized for this specific customer based on profile information from the ERM application. The page presents open-order status information driven out of the order management system and customized product specifications from a content management system. The customer enters the rush order request with the special modification. An ATP application from the advanced planning and scheduling (APS) system determine the availability of the raw materials and capacity to process the order by the date requested. The APS system determines that overtime will be needed and a premium price must be charged. The new price is determined by an online pricing engine. An automated call center application tied to the Web site provides human assistance to answer a question on the new price. An automated e-mail response system immediately sends a formal confirmation of the new price to the customer. At same time, an online product design collaboration application has accepted the modification and initiated the workflow to get the modification through engineering to the factory. A sales channel management system credits the distributor that normally services this customer with a new sale.

While no single software vendor's systems currently offer this complete a level of sell-side automation, all of the software to do this is currently available. E-Commerce pioneers such as Cisco and Dell are approaching this level of sophistication. Leading suppliers of sell-side applications are working with a number of other leading manufacturers to design similar systems.

Although buy-side e-commerce has received much of the early attention and spending, it is easy to see how sell-side applications can be much more valuable as they are visible to your customers (see Table 2.3). More important, sophisticated sell-side applications have been behind much of the success of early e-business leaders including Amazon and General Electric.

Administration

A key aspect of sell-side e-commerce is the capability to maintain the selling and customer services functions with a minimum amount of programming support from the IT department. The administration function provides the capability to reconfigure sell-side applications to accommodate price changes, new products, promotions, new channels, new catalogs, discounts, and so forth. For the most part, these changes must also be accomplished without disrupting the online selling environment. For example, Amazon cannot afford to shut its compact disk sales site while this week's new releases are added.

Common Sell-Side Application Functionality

Sell-Side Application Functionality	Description
Product catalogs	Organize product information for online presentation and searches
Personalization	Allows users some ability to customize the Web page to their individual needs. In advanced functions, some of this personalization may be done automatically.
Content management and product presentation	Creates and maintains the text and images that appear on the Web site.
Customer interaction	Supports an interactive dialogue with the customer, which may include invoking a personalized Web page.
Automated Web response	Automatically responds to a customer's request online, by e-mail, or may initiate a phone call.
Self-service order management systems	Order management systems designed for use online by the customer with zero prior training.
Configurators	Supports the order processing for complex products with customer-selectable options.
Payment processing	Supports the payment for good or service through a credit card, an invoice, or an electronic payment

Source: AMR Research   table 2.3

Administration tools support this type of hot maintenance. In addition, this maintenance function is designed such that customer service or marketing people can handle the changes through a utility application that does not require programming or IT support. Generally, an important attribute of B2B tools is that they are designed to be used and maintained by the department responsible for the content. As the Internet becomes more pervasive, each department will need to think about the how its contribution to the product life cycle must appear on the Web. In the near future, the process of creating a traditional paper version and then converting to the Web will be too slow and inefficient.

Channel Management

The Internet has given rise to a new category of sell-side applications called channel management applications. While the channel management concept is not new, the advent of online selling created a more pressing need to manage the conflict between the various ways your company's products are sold. Manufacturers that are committed to selling their products through sales representatives, retailers, and distributors cannot easily begin selling from their Web site without running into conflict with existing sales channels. Channel management applications help manufacturers manage these multiple channels online and, in some cases, compensate a sales partner that may have been impacted by an online sale. These applications often include rules engines so that complex relationships and associated compensation can be handled automatically.

CONTENT MANAGEMENT

As we move from a largely paper-based world to online e-business, all of the information about our products, services, contracts, advertising, and much more must also be moved online. Not only must it be moved online, but it must live online, which means that we need a whole new process for creating and maintaining it.

Content Management Software Applications

Content management software applications are designed to support the creation and maintenance of the vast amount of information, including text, images, audio, and video, found on today's Web sites. In addition to creating and maintaining the content, these applications must also support sharing this information across Web sites. For example, consider the vast number of items that appear on the Web site of an online office supplies retailer, such as Staples.com or OfficeMax.com. Ideally, the content describing each item has to be repurposed from the manufacturer's Web sites to the retailer's Web site using the collaboration capability of a content management application. In turn, the retailer may be asked by its customers to repurpose the content again for the in-house catalog of an e-procurement system.

At present, content management applications are in their infancy. Unique content management applications exist for both buy-side and sell-side e-commerce. Buyers want all commodity types supported, including high-volume maintenance, repair, and operations (MRO) goods, ad hoc spot buys, configurable goods, and complex strategic commodities. Buyers also want accurate, searchable multivendor content served up in context to their strategic sourcing and procure-to-pay processes, seamlessly integrated into their enterprise applications. Sellers want to provide timely, personalized content efficiently through all distribution channels to reach buyers. Yet, although content application vendors are offering improved commodity breadth, content quality, and implementation flexibility, the increasingly demanding e-business requirements to publish and subscribe content fluidly among buyers, sellers, and intermediaries has created a software functionality gap. For buyers, the single largest reason for delays in large e-procurement projects still continues to be catalog content management. Buyers, such as retailers, distributors, manufacturers, and trading exchanges, demand that sellers offer not just tailored sell-side functionality but also the ability to publish on-demand content in various formats—a challenge for even the most sophisticated suppliers.

Content management requirements for e-commerce differs from other forms of content management (see Table 2.4), such as document management, electronic publishing, or Web publishing, because of its emphasis on the following:

- Collaborative content generation: Content needs to suitable for buyers and sellers.

- Page layout management: Content on the Web is displayed one page at a time.

- User registration management: Unique content is often displayed to meet individual user needs.

- Customer feedback management: The content may generate customer questions that require response or further refinement of the content.

- Affiliate program management: The content will be repurposed by resellers or buyers.

- Merchandising, promotion management, personalization, and customization: Content display is dynamic and must be controllable by both customer and seller.

- Brand and product differentiation presentation: Brand image must be preserved.

- Limited or controlled support for comparison shopping and catalog presentation: Sellers want to control the impact of Web sites that use sophisticated programs called crawlers, spiders, or bots to search out the lowest price.

To accomplish these goals, the best content management applications include the following capabilities (also see Figure 2.5):

- Content collection and capture

- A metadata (metadata are data that describes other data) framework to define the different kinds of content required for and published on the buy-side or sell-side Web site

- A repository or storage for content and metadata

- Content publishing tools to extract component data from a content repository and to assemble components into final Web pages or portions of Web pages for presentation and publication

- Workflow management to control the process of creating, modifying, and producing the content

Content Management Requirements for E-Commerce

Content Types	Content Definitions
Raw Content	Unstructured, inconsistent, and inaccurate information from original sources
Clean Content	Raw content that has had inaccuracies and inconsistencies removed
Rationalized Content	Clean content that has been structured to reflect a specific environment or context
Normalized Content	Rationalized content that can be used for comparing alternatives, making decisions, and taking action
Syndicated Content	Normalized content available to those who need and can use it

table 2.4

Content Management Automation Is Required

Content generation, editorial review, and publication are extremely labor-intensive and iterative processes that require automation to scale well. Without automation, Web site growth is often constrained by the speed at which the organization can hire and train writers, editors, Web designers, creative directors, project managers, and Web site managers. These types of constraints to Web site growth can often be removed through the use of page templates and other authoring and version control tools. Effective content management applications allow specific users to operate on portions or components of

Content Management Architecture Simplified

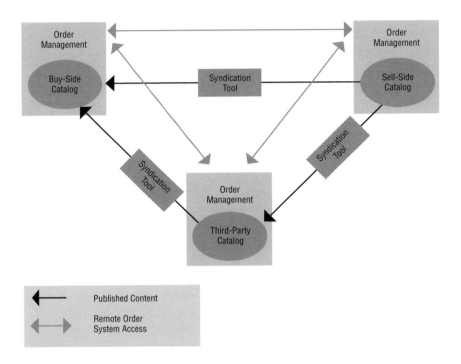

Source: AMR Research, 2000

figure 2.5

pages, not just entire pages. A high degree of granularity in what can be authored and edited is key to success.

The need for content management applications is dramatically growing as content that requires maintenance escalates and the competitive pressure for portals to be adaptive, rather than merely static, increases. For example, the Fishweb Web site holds between 75,000 and 100,000 pages and receives up to 1.5 million hits per month. Any user on the company's wide area network can access the documents, which translates into 12,000 employees world-wide. By adopting a content management strategy to support content pro-duction, Fishweb saw a 70% reduction in document publishing and manage-ment time, and document dispersal time was cut from up to 10 days to 1.

COLLABORATION

Collaboration is probably the most often cited and least understood of the potential benefits of B2B commerce. Broadly defined, collaboration is a two-way exchange of information between trading or design partners. This exchange of information ranges from a simple price negotiation between a buyer and a seller to a complex multiparty new product design session. The benefits cited for collaboration include shortened product development time, inventory reduction, and better customer responsiveness. In part, this originates from the belief that most supply chains carry excess inventory to cover for volatile demand and supply and that poor information flow hampers customer responsiveness. Conceptually, collaboration throughout the supply chain would smooth out much of the uncertainty of demand, thus reducing inventory while improving responsiveness.

The concept of collaboration is not new. Companies have found many ways over the years to share better demand information, including EDI, faxes, and phone calls. The Internet, however, has sparked a great deal of interest in collaboration because is offers a ready network that interconnects the value/supply chain. With such a network in place, many new software companies have sprung up offering applications and services that purport to handle collaboration. The inherent operating model of the World Wide Web allows for the entire supply chain to see changes in demand simultaneously. These new collaboration applications are attempting to transform the point-to-point collaboration (faxes, etc.) to many-to-many collaboration (see Figure 2.6). The belief that many-to-many collaboration is the key to dramatic reductions in supply chain costs has also led to the rapid growth of trading exchanges and marketplaces. Many of the new collaboration applications are being developed to leverage these marketplaces as the hub for many-to-many collaboration.

Connectivity Applications

Collaboration applications fall into two broad categories: connectivity and information sharing. Connectivity applications provide the conduit to get information from back-office systems, such as ERP, into a format that can be sent over the Internet. Many connectivity vendors got their start as EAI software vendors. These vendors provide adapters to connect their applications to the popular ERP, supply chain planning, and CRM systems. These adapters help get information such as purchase orders, release schedules, and planning data into the connectivity application that performs the transmission process. Generally, this process includes conversion of data into a more standard for-

Supply Chain Collaboration Model

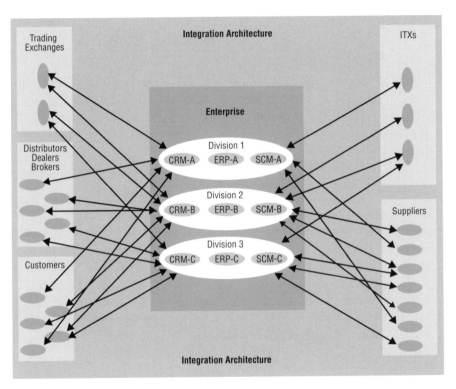

Source: AMR Research

figure 2.6

mat, usually Extensible Markup Language (XML). Widespread acceptance of XML is one the keys to making collaboration across an entire supply chain feasible. (XML is discussed in this chapter later.) Leading connectivity software vendors include Extricity, Vitria, WebMethods, Viewlocity, and Tibco.

Information-Sharing Applications

Information-sharing applications fall roughly into general categories: content (information) originators and collaboration coordinators. The content originators are applications such as supply chain planning, engineering design change applications, and ERM systems. Generally, these applications have another primary purpose, but they have been enhanced to share the information they create through collaboration. For example, supply chain planning applications from vendors, such as i2 Technologies, Adexa, and Manugistics, generate new plans and release schedules that can be sent to suppliers or customers. As supply chain planning applications provide much of the analysis that eventually initiates a change in the supply chain, they are natural applications to be a focal point for collaboration.

One of the elusive goals of supply chain planning is to get more accurate demand information from the ultimate consumer and pass it back through the supply chain without reinterpretation by each individual participant. Although this is a noble goal, collaboration has barely reached the stage where two companies can have a real-time, two-way dialogue about a single plan. Supply chain–wide collaboration is still 2 to 3 years from being viable and will require that marketplaces are successful.

A growing and certainly no less important subcategory of content originators are engineering design and change management systems, such as those from PTC, MatrixOne, Unigraphics, and Agile Software. These systems introduce one of the other major causes for change into a supply chain: new product designs and changes to existing designs. With time-to-market being a critical success factor for many companies, especially in the high-tech industry, vendors such as Alventive, Agile, and MatrixOne have pioneered applications to help designers and suppliers collaborate via the Internet to develop new products.

Collaboration coordinators fill the gap between the content origination systems and the connectivity applications. Some collaboration coordinators include some connectivity in their application. The coordination application may initiate a collaboration process, provide visibility across the supply chain, and act as a hub for multiple back-office systems that generate content for collaboration. Some collaboration coordination applications are also designed to handle person-to-person interactions over the Web. Many of these collaboration coordinators are also providing support for the development of private marketplaces (discussed in the next chapter). This category includes software providers such as Syncra, Atlas Commerce, Oracle, Eqos, Commerce One, and Ariba.

PORTALS

No discussion of B2B tools is complete without the inclusion of portals (see Figure 2.7). For many relationships within your business community, all you need to do is educate people with information. There's no transaction, no data collection—just plain old simple information sharing with the right people at the right time. Portals are a means of easily sharing content and information that can be fine-tuned to a particular role. One of the more critical tasks will be matching the content to a particular community. The intent is to prevent information overload, while still getting more essential information to a set of users or even an individual user. And just like the other elements in your e-business strategy, the portal will need to conform to a corporate level of security, leveraging existing security policies and products. You will also need to manage the portal as an exterior face to the world. In sum, portals can be defined as Web sites that aggregate content or information based on a defined role.

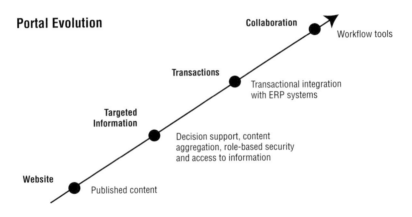

Portal Evolution

Collaboration — Workflow tools

Transactions — Transactional integration with ERP systems

Targeted Information — Decision support, content aggregation, role-based security and access to information

Website — Published content

Source: AMR Research

figure 2.7

A portal can be evaluated by several criteria: community definition, content, personalization, integration, and security and management. Portals merge all the traditional ways of communicating with a business community and supplement them with new communication styles. Companies are no longer relegated to just direct mail, e-mail, faxes, or phone communications, and the technology allows users to reach their business community with more than just a generic Web site. Portals can be looked at as the employees' window into B2B, as they can be designed to provide a consolidated and personalized view of buy-side and sell-side e-commerce.

XML: A KEY ELEMENT OF B2B

XML was originally designed to simplify Web publishing, but today its most anticipated use is simplifying the complex communication requirements of business community integration (BCI). (BCI is a term used to describe broad B2B collaboration across a value or supply chain.) XML can act as a facilitator for communicating with new partners, linking to a recently purchased e-commerce application, or sending information to and from a portal. At a base level, XML can replace proprietary message and metadata formats and create a canonical format for the data being exchanged. Within an integration framework, XML most directly simplifies the data transformation layer by using a standardized format for data that can more easily be mapped to another XML format, such as schema or document-type definition. XML documents can also help manage transactions by maintaining information about the state of the transaction within the XML document, overcoming the deficiency of Hypertext Transfer Protocol (HTTP) as a sessionless protocol. XML-based workflows can detail the path for the data. Although XML does not address every layer in the integration framework, it still makes BCI an easier goal to accomplish (see Table 2.5).

Products Available Today for XML

New products supporting XML are appearing every day, ranging from full-functioning systems for integration within a company and to the business community, all the way down to shareware parsers and limited-functionality XML servers available for download at no charge. Also on the market are countless packaged applications and application server and development tool vendors providing the ability to accept and send XML. For many vendors, adding support for XML is one step in a strategy to support mobile devices using Wireless Markup Language (WML). At this point, you will get what you pay for—the more expensive a system, the less manual coding you should have to do, and the more easily the system will support many schemas of XML.

Integration and connectivity vendors offer an array of products with a range of functionality. They include the ability to send and receive XML-formatted data and support XML to any data format exchange, XML parsing and mapping tools, and even prepackaged XML standards and the tools to extend and upgrade them in the future. The most sophisticated products will support XML queries, an XML metadata model, and the ability not only to receive XML documents at the gate but also to interpret business process directions.

XML Basics

XML Basics	Details
Document Type Definitions (DTDs)	Defines the elements (such as names and attributes) that can be used in a set of XML documents. The DTD specification was released by the W3C and is widely accepted.
XML Schema	More comprehensive than the DTD, this is an XML document that describes the structural rules,including the elements and their associated data types. As an XML document itself, it is easier to parse and edit. The W3C is preparing standard schema definitions.
XML Stylesheet Language (XSL)	Defines XSL Transformations (XSLT) to transform one XML document to another. SXLT can convert XML to HTML for display in a browser for machine-to-person interaction. XSL essentially adds rules to the documents for processing and parsing.

XML Sample (Source: W3C, 2000)	`<customer-details id-"AcPharm39156">`
	`        <name>Acme Pharmaceuticals Co.</name>`
	`        <address country-"US">`
	`        <street>7301 Smokey Boulevard</street>`
	`        <city>Smallville</city>`
	`        <state>Indiana</state>`
	`        <postal>94571</postal>`
	`    <</address>`
	`</customer-details>`

Metadata and Repositories	It's worth noting the increasing importance of metadata with XML documents and, therefore, the escalating requirements of a repository to act as a storage center for XML DTDs, schemas, transformation maps, and metadata. The W3C is also working on the Resource Description Framework (RDF) specification to allow document meta-data to be embedded directly into a document. The result could allow XML documents to be more process oriented, with process descriptions build directly into an XML document.

Source: *AMR Research*

table 2.5

Not a Replacement for EDI, but More Widely Adopted

Many companies have existing investments in EDI systems because of requirements from major partners, among other reasons. Those companies using EDI, required an initial investment in equipment and personnel to maintain the system. Furthermore, many EDI transactions are supplemented by phone calls or manual reentry into internal applications. EDI systems aren't perfect, but they have their benefits. While XML is gaining ground, it definitely won't supplant EDI overnight. Many EDI users will continue to use EDI for machine-to-machine automated exchange of information, following the wisdom of the old adage "If it ain't broke, don't fix it." Efforts are under way to make sure EDI and XML messages can be received and sent by the same integration systems.

Regard XML as part of a more accessible integration platform for a larger number of business partners than EDI ever was. In the long run, more companies will be able to use XML than EDI because of its cost structure and adaptability. Consider XML a widely accepted success when even existing EDI users turn off their EDI systems and transition to XML over the Internet. Before this final stage in XML's adoption, XML can still be useful by encouraging companies to consider XML formatted data as a viable alternative to traditional means of doing business, such as e-mail and fax. However, for XML to become a standard business practice, companies already valuing the process automation of EDI must demonstrate a willingness to accept XML. It will be a slow transition.

Start Planning Your XML Pilots

XML is here to stay, and companies are evaluating it now. Most XML pilots are very simple, with one supplier or customer involved in the network. Enough pilots are progressing onto implementations and enough vendor support exists to allow XML to continue to gain traction over the next few years. The XML standards effort is by no means complete, and the standards and how they are applied, as well as the products, will continue to evolve. The overwhelming impact of XML can be dramatic, partly because of the response from the technical and business community, and partly because of XML's wide span and generous scope for reuse. The application of XML within a business community can reach all the way from a purchasing agent's desktop to a supplier's warehouse. Fortune 500–level corporations have indicated that they are evaluating XML now to gain the expertise internally and win the opportunity to influence the vendor direction for tool selection and process definitions.

CONCLUSION

This chapter introduced readers to many new tools and methods of e-business and B2B e-commerce, with the possible exception of one very important type—trading exchanges. These are discussed in detail in Chapter 3, as they require a focused treatment because of the profound anticipated effects they will have on value and supply chains.

In this chapter we covered the sell-side, buy-side, content management, portal, collaborative, and other technologies that will also alter value and supply chains in the long run. This chapter also serves as a primer for readers on the new tools and techniques of e-business that companies are currently leveraging, as well as can be leveraged to enable value/supply chain strategies. However, before we move on to discussing these, let's consider trading exchange concepts, methods, and tools.

chapter 3

Trading Exchanges
The Hubs of
B2B Commerce

A trading exchange is an online Internet-based marketplace that facilitates
the transfer of goods, money, and information.

The basic concept of a digital marketplace, or trading exchange, is a Web site where buyers and sellers meet to carry out business transactions quickly and efficiently, without paperwork. The use of the Internet means that any browser device can be used to access the exchange unlike EDI, which requires special software at each end of the transaction. Also unlike EDI, it is inexpensive for buyers to take part and adds the promise of increased volumes to sellers. A key process of early marketplaces, auctions, and reverse auctions enable companies to buy and sell at the best possible price, with the exchange eventually acting as a vehicle for the whole supply chain. Trading exchanges also open up the possibility of electronic collaboration between partners and customers who can share information about products from sales trends to design information.

A Heavy Interest in Trading Exchanges

The number of online trading exchanges has exploded over the last two years, with more than 1,000 sites vying for business in virtually every industry. Many exchanges started as information and news sites with specific vertical industry content to create a community of users with similar interests. One of the early trading exchange pioneers, VerticalNet, created exchange communities for more than fifty different vertical industries. Each VerticalNet exchange caters to very narrow interest groups with sites such as SolidWaste.com and Nurse.com. Another trading exchange pioneer, Ventro Corporation, created it first site, Chemdex.com, to be a resource for chemists and scientists to find compounds and chemicals for specific applications. Most information sites have evolved from the community stage to facilitate the buying and selling of goods and services.

Trading exchanges will use the concept of community to go beyond the simple buying and selling of direct materials and services to offering a full range of other services that complement the commercial transactions. For example, MetalSite, a trading exchange for steel, not only provides a marketplace for steel products and services but offers logistics, banking, and credit services as well. This momentum will continue, leading to new business processes that combine multiple stages of the B2B supply chain in a sales transaction. For example, a buyer for molded parts might go to PlasticsNet.com to find a mold maker, a molding manufacturer, a specific plastic resin, and a logistics provider—to ship the mold and resin to the manufacturer and the finished parts to a public warehouse. In addition, a buyer might also use the exchange to confirm a revolving line of credit with a bank to pay for all of it. This buyer has just created a coordinated virtual supply chain using just an Internet browser. Far-fetched? Not at all. It is already possible, and trading exchanges are constantly establishing new relationships to extend their reach along supply chains.

Trading Exchanges: The Application Suites of the Future

The billions of dollars spent on ERP systems over the last decade were the final gasp in the old economy's attempt to create the perfect computing model. These systems promised standard applications integrated by the vendor that support activities in all areas of an enterprise, common data and process models, controlled revision processes, and a stable migration path validated by a large and prestigious installed base. What could be better than that? And the message played well in corporate boardrooms—one system to manage the entire company, with information at your fingertips. What a relief from the company's hodge-podge of systems, which accomplish little quickly or well and send the IT budget spiraling out of control.

Unfortunately, ERP software vendors never lived up to the expectations they set for the marketplace. Leaving aside the inevitable licensing issues pertaining to a captive installed base, ERP's Achilles' heel was in fact its strength—a broad array of tightly integrated applications that proved inflexible in the face of changing business models and technologies. Nowhere is this more apparent than in supply chain execution (SCE) applications, a development backwater for most ERP vendors. SCE applications control the processing of goods through the supply chain and include warehouse management, transportation management and planning, order management, and inventory replenishment systems. Now that the Internet enables the supply chain to extend beyond the enterprise, opportunities rise more quickly than any ERP vendor can capitalize on them. ERP systems and designs are characterized by rigidity: tightly defined and integrated processes and services. That degree of rigidity is nearly impossible to coordinate across today's complex supply chains. Trading exchanges offer collaboration within an entire trading community, unknown territory for ERP vendors.

Trading exchanges will become the center of community interaction, especially the private trading exchanges, and that means their value will extend far beyond the aggregation of demand and supply we associate them with today. Therefore, exchanges will become a catalyst for e-commerce adoption in B2B. AMR Research predicts they will represent as much as 52% of the revenue flowing through B2B processes in 2004 (see Figure 3.1).

To play such an integral role in the growth of B2B e-commerce, trading exchanges will act as the hub for business community integration by con-

Projected Growth of Trading Exchange Revenue Through 2004

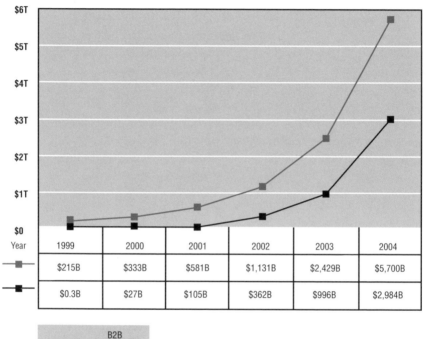

Year	1999	2000	2001	2002	2003	2004
■	$215B	$333B	$581B	$1,131B	$2,429B	$5,700B
■	$0.3B	$27B	$105B	$362B	$996B	$2,984B

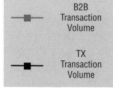

■ B2B Transaction Volume

■ TX Transaction Volume

Source: AMR Research, 2000

figure 3.1

necting partners, allowing collaboration through common ancillary process-es, and integrating with other exchanges for an even broader extension of the trading community (see Figure 3.2).

For most exchanges moving up the value chain, adding SCE functionality is one of the first steps in broadening community offerings. Unlike the four-wall enterprise model of the ERP vendors, the trading community is decentralized and requires a strong SCE foundation to function, both physically and sys-temically. A year ago, emerging vertical exchanges were handicapped by the lack of SCE functionality available to them on the Web. Now, SCE vendors are rushing to fill the gaps by building alliances with trading exchanges to pro-vide content and services that support commerce on a global basis.

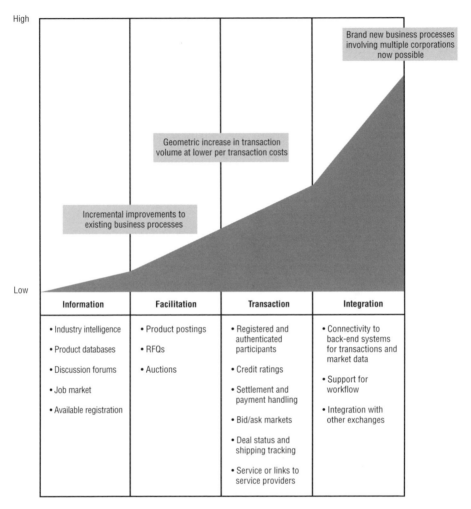

Value of Trading Exchanges to Participants

High

Brand new business processes involving multiple corporations now possible

Geometric increase in transaction volume at lower per transaction costs

Incremental improvements to existing business processes

Low

Information	Facilitation	Transaction	Integration
• Industry intelligence • Product databases • Discussion forums • Job market • Available registration	• Product postings • RFQs • Auctions	• Registered and authenticated participants • Credit ratings • Settlement and payment handling • Bid/ask markets • Deal status and shipping tracking • Service or links to service providers	• Connectivity to back-end systems for transactions and market data • Support for workflow • Integration with other exchanges

Source: AMR Research

figure 3.2

TRADING EXCHANGE MODELS

As Figure 3.3 shows, four types of trading exchanges are evolving, each displaying a different business model dependent on its ownership and goals: independent vertical exchanges, independent horizontal exchanges, private trading exchanges, and hybrid exchanges. Another type, logistics exchanges, are also discussed in this section. Let's consider each one in more detail.

Trading Exchange Landscape

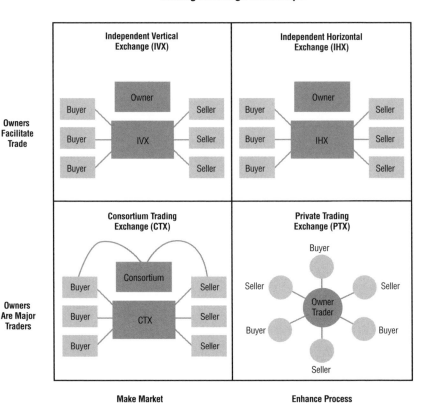

Source: AMR Research

figure 3.3

Independent Vertical Exchanges

An independent vertical exchange (IVX) is an independent intermediary that connects many buyers to many sellers within a vertical market segment. It operates as a profit-making enterprise, attracting liquidity by creating market and transaction efficiencies. A good example of an IVX is e-Chemicals, which enables manufacturers in the chemical industry to buy, sell, and negotiate transactions on specialty chemicals. In addition, the site contains value-added resources, such as news, market indices, and reports, to assist member businesses and encourage frequent visits. Other IVXs include the following:

- Agriflow—a community portal and marketplace for the agricultural industry

- ecFood—a marketplace focused on food manufacturers

- e-cement.com Ltd.—a marketplace for cement and heavy building materials

- eSteele—a marketplace for the steel industry

Independent Horizontal Exchanges

An independent horizontal exchange (IHX) is similar to an IVX, except that the focus of the exchange is not aimed at a single industry. For example, Ariba and Commerce One, in addition to selling procurement software applications, have exchanges that offer a wide selection of indirect materials pertinent across vertical industries. While the product complexity is low, users benefit from supplier rationalization and content aggregation. Other IHXs include the following:

- exchange.com—a marketplace for the procurement of high-tech goods

- mondus—a marketplace offering procurement services for small and midsize businesses

- GroupTrade.com—a marketplace for the procurement of office supplies, equipment, and services telecoms

- MRO.com—a marketplace offering maintenance, repair, and operations (MRO) goods

---

An IVX Profile: Altrade of Altra Energy Technologies, Inc.

Altra (Houston, TX) operates Altrade, an IVX for the natural gas, gas liquids, and electric power industries. The company also develops and markets risk management and enterprise applications for the utilities industry. It has consummated significant liquidity across its three segments, trading daily twelve billion cubic feet of natural gas, one million barrels of gas liquids (primarily butane and propane), and one million megawatts. The site has 1,800 buyers and sellers. Its annual revenue is in the $60 million range, although a large percentage can be attributed to software and services.

Altra has accepted limited equity stakes, but not majority stakes or board seats. It is also active with the Federal Energy Regulatory Commission. It benefits greatly from its legacy of installed applications, which decreases the pain associated with integrating into the

---

exchange. Altra was spun out from two pipeline companies, the Williams Company and Duke Energy Corporation, which bring excellent domain expertise to the table, as reflected in the senior management team down to the consulting services group.

In addition to information and facilitation functionality, Altrade offers strong transactional capability. Participants in the wholesale power market rank the credit risk of fellow participants, which is reflected in the trading. In the natural and liquid gas markets, a third-party insurance company rates participants, and Altra takes responsibility for title and settlement. The company offers process and supply chain integration across several dimensions. Altrade seamlessly integrates into Altra's risk management, scheduling and delivery, and reporting applications.

Consortium Trading Exchange (CTX)

A consortium trading exchange (CTX) is a consortium of major industry players, often representing a significant percentage of the commercial transactions in a specific industry. It operates primarily to reduce transaction and product costs to make the market more efficient for its users. Several major consortium exchanges are emerging, most notably the following:

- WWRE—which comprises 57 of the leading retail companies of the world (including Best Buy, Tesco, Marks & Spencer, and El Corte Inglés)

- Transora—a consumer product exchange, whose members collectively generate over 40% of the global revenue in that field. Global companies investing in Transora include Parmalat USA Corp., Cadbury-Schweppes plc, Campbell Soup Company, Danone Foods, Inc., Heineken International, McCain Foods Ltd., and Nestlé Holdings, Inc.

- CPGmarket.com—a European consumer products exchange headed by Nestlé, Danone of Switzerland, German food and chemical group Henkel, and SAP

Private Trading Exchanges

A private trading exchange (PTX) is owned and maintained by a single company to more effectively manage interactions with its trading partners. It is a one-to-many environment, with the owner a participant in each deal. The owner has the opportunity to improve process efficiency, optimize its assets, and provide collaboration within its community. A PTX tries to take market share by deflecting the attention of its trading partners away from competitors by providing additional services that make life easier for partners. Examples of PTX owners include the following:

- IBM

- Cisco Systems

- Sun Microsystems

- Wal-Mart

- General Motors

- Ford Motor Company

Hybrid Exchanges

Hybrids exist between the independent exchanges and exhibit the same characteristics, with the exception of focus. They focus either on a vertical sell-side market and promote to a wide horizontal buying audience, or the reverse. Many logistics-oriented exchanges are hybrids, such as FreightGate and National Transportation Exchange. Each operates exclusively with the sellers of transport capacity, but with multiple industries on the capacity buy-side. Another example of a hybrid is Utilyx, a procurement site for energy requirements like electricity. Utilyx deals with utility supply, but it is horizontally oriented on the buy side, encouraging large corporate customers to utilize their extensive value-added services as a forerunner to actual trading.

Another type of hybrid is a trading exchange created as an independent company to service groups with a certain affinity (see Figure 3.4). An example is HispanB2B, which provides horizontal services but for a vertical affinity group—Hispanics living in the United States. It provides a wide variety of services to Global 500 companies but promotes suppliers from the Hispanic business community. It also offers this community value-added services. HispanB2B is planning to provide similar functionality for African American–owned organizations in the near future. Another example of an affinity-based hybrid is MeetChina.com, which provides the same type of facilities to promote Chinese products and services.

Logistics Exchanges

Of special interest to CLM members reading this book is the logistics exchange (LX). An LX enables you to identify carriers and service providers, initiate a request for quotation (RFQ) process that will qualify partners based on your service and cost requirements, and establish a contract that will be monitored for

Independent Exchange Hybrids

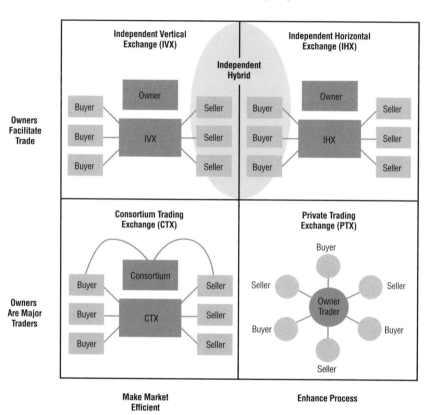

Source: AMR Research

figure 3.4

compliance throughout its entire life. You can also use the exchange to transmit replenishment orders to your supplier and schedule transportation arrangements for each shipment. The exchange may also provide the documentation required for international trade and give both buyer and seller full visibility to key events as products make their way from the supplier's dock to the buyer. With its combination of domain expertise, content, and technology, the LX becomes an extension of your company, allowing you to leverage its knowledge and network to set up supply chains anywhere in the world. The LX is about finding, cultivating, and sustaining relationships with your extended trading community, not shaving a percentage point off transportation spending (see Figure 3.5).

Relative Effectiveness of LX Service Types

	Market Efficiency	Transaction Efficiency	Asset Optimization	Coordination Execution
LX Freight Matching	◕	●	◕	◕
LX Auction	◑	◑	◑	◑
LX Portal	◕	●	◕	◔
LX Marketplace	●	●	●	●

No Effect   Very Effective

Source: AMR Research, 2000

figure 3.5

LX Profile: The National Transportation Exchange, Inc.

The National Transportation Exchange (NTE) caught a lot of attention in 1998 when it became the first mover in the LX marketplace. The company found itself in an endless cycle of evangelism, trying to sell a very sophisticated market-making approach in a period when the general concept of the B2B exchange was itself only beginning to gain acceptance.

NTE is not an auction of transportation services. It sets a market price for each shipment tendered to the exchange based on an algorithm that includes 150 market variables, including available capacity, seasonality, and time value of money—pretty esoteric stuff, but absolute accuracy of the market price isn't the key value here. NTE must keep rates high enough to attract carriers but low enough to deliver savings to its shippers.

Users can configure rules to designate which carriers are allowed to participate. A price ceiling can be set, usually the lowest contracted rate for the lane. If the market price exceeds the ceiling, or if the exchange cannot find carrier service, NTE will automatically tender the shipment to a default carrier designated by the shipper.

For a carrier, NTE's proposition holds more perceived risk. Granted, NTE allows a carrier to find freight to fill cargo space on already moving trucks, and the revenue for that incremental freight should translate into almost pure profit. But the fear of aggregation raises its head here, as carriers are sure to be concerned about creating a market dynamic over which they have no control.

Over time, we expect that each type of trading exchange will be used within supply chains to coordinate the B2B supply chain operations among a variety of trading partners. PTXs will be valuable in enabling and controlling B2B commerce, while many advanced supply chain concepts will be enhanced using them, altering supply chains as we know them today.

PRIVATE TRADING EXCHANGES AS B2B COMMAND CENTERS

In the future, PTXs will serve as command centers for B2B commerce. The best way to envision the PTX is to view it as the software application platform on which an individual company will build its trading interface to the outside world via the Internet. Even companies engaged with consortium exchanges will build their own PTX to provide a single integration point for B2B. A number of software vendors have begun to offer application platforms for PTXs (see Table 3.1). Although these trading exchange platforms are in still in the early release phase of maturity, it is clear that this has become a hot software market.

PTX Platform Providers

Private Trading Exchange Platform Providers	Headquarters
i2 Technologies	Dallas, TX
VerticalNet	Malvern, PA
Ariba	San Jose, CA
Oracle	Redwood Shores, CA
Atlas Commerce	Atlanta, GA
IBM	Armonk, NY
Commerce One	Pleasanton, CA

table 3.1

The leaders of hot software markets tend to drive de facto industry standards. This means that the various software applications it takes to create collaborative, B2B supply chains, will be designed to plug into the major exchange platforms. In this respect, trading exchange platforms will be to B2B commerce what major ERP systems were to internal business systems—a common conceptual business model and significant market presence to encourage other vendors to make their applications compatible with minimal integration effort.

In the next three years, most organizations will deploy a PTX as their interface between internal systems and the plethora of exchanges with which each company will interact. As result, PTX platform software will develop into one of the next great software application markets over the next several years.

ENHANCING ADVANCED SUPPLY CHAIN CONCEPTS

From their position as hubs in the supply chain, trading exchanges will support supply chain event management (SCEM), a new application software category composed of workflow rules, content, alert monitoring, and integration capabilities. SCEM applications provide visibility of the flow of raw materials and finished through supply chain and trigger alerts when problems arise. As supply chain management focus moves from the enterprise to the trading community, SCEM applications running on trading exchanges will be available as a service to coordinate and sequence activities as well as manage information distribution and processing. Already, VerticalNet has partnered with Yantra Corporation's PureEcommerce to act as the collaborative hub for SCE, and i2 Technologies is integrating Exceed eFS Fulfill Suite from EXE Technologies, Inc. into i2 Technologies' TradeMatrix. This represents a further shift of functionality from individual companies to the trading exchange, as well as a prime area of concentration for both investment and development.

Ultimately, the trading exchanges that survive will be those that go beyond the premise of being an industry marketplace to offer sophisticated software and services. In addition to offering SCE and SCEM applications, trading exchanges are also likely to offer supply chain planning and demand planning functions. Some trading exchanges including eskye.com (a liquor industry exchange) plan aggregate and analyze demand information for resale to marketplace participants. Some trading exchanges may go as far as hosting ERP applications for smaller suppliers.

CHANGING SUPPLY CHAIN FUNDAMENTALS

Although most trading exchanges have yet to turn a profit, they will change the way supply chains function. From the individual company perspective, the sophisticated software applications that will become available through trading exchanges will enable smaller (in terms of sales revenue and employees) participants in the supply chain to leverage more sophisticated software and services currently affordable by only the largest corporations. This will help smaller (and even some larger) companies become more responsive suppliers. Moving beyond company by company optimization, the largest impact will come from extended supply chain synchronization.

Of course, the obvious question is how will trading exchanges synchronize supply chains full of competing companies. In fact, the first of this synchronization is already happening in the preliminary transactions of some of the consortium and vertical industry exchanges. For example, one member company of the retail industry's Global Net Exchange (a consortium that includes Sears and Carrefour) needed to make a spot buy to fill a demand for greater than expected demand for a sale item. With their primary supplier at full capacity, they put the bid out on the exchange and got an immediate response from another supplier with excess inventory offering immediate delivery at a reduced price. Thus, this excess inventory came out of the supply chain for this item. Considering that, from a macroeconomic view, most retail items have relatively stable demand (a sale at one retailer usually means reduced demand at a competing retailer), this supply chain became more efficient. While this is a very trivia example, it demonstrates how trading exchanges and marketplaces can improve supply chains without cooperation among competitors.

Getting Electron Economy Off to a Good Start

The elevator conversation to describe the company had better take place in a very tall building, but SOFTBANK and Crosspoint Venture Partners have just invested $70 million in Electron Economy, Inc.'s, second round of financing. How do you make good on a significant investment in a concept that is only starting to emerge?

Electron Economy is a hub for business community integration, providing supply chain event management and workflow as well as data integration for a trading community. This is how you will run your extended supply chain in the future. While the company has several Internet retailers such as EggHead.com and Style365.com, along with

---

lead logistics providers including Copera, Inc., USF eLogistics and ODC Integrated Logistics, it still has a lot of evangelism to do to get payback on its backers' money. Over the longer term, Electron Economy wants to be a platform on which public and private trading exchanges can be built. Wall Street seems to think this will work!

AS FOR CTXS, WILL COMPETITORS COOPERATE?

Cynically, the original formation of many consortium trading exchanges was driven by the perceived dot-com peril of the independent exchanges. Initially, one wondered whether the competitors that were forming these CTXs could cooperate and make them successful. As many have had more than a year to contemplate their existence, there is growing acceptance of the idea that the benefits to the supply chain as a whole out weigh the competitive threats. In addition, many companies worry that not participating in a major consortium exchange will leave them perilously behind as B2B commerce shifts into high gear.

The evidence of this point is widespread. All major manufacturing industries now have one or more consortium exchanges. The companies forming these exchanges represent some of the biggest names in their respective industries, such as Hewlett Packard, IBM, Solectron, and Compaq in High Tech, and Sears, Marks & Spencer, Best Buy, and Kmart in retail. These companies have all made significant investments to join these exchanges. Investments range from several million dollars to more than $50 million. In most cases, these investments were made quickly without much input from the employees in the company that are closest to the supply chain. These rapid decisions will challenge logistics, sales, purchasing and IT personnel to adopt these exchanges into the organization's supply chain processes.

THE FUTURE VIABILITY OF TRADING EXCHANGES

With more than 1,000 independent trading exchanges, including numerous consortium exchanges, it is clear that most will not survive. The concept, however, is sound. Companies have been trying address supply chain inefficiencies for the last five years. The trading exchange brings together technology, concepts, and processes that can finally achieve significant improvements in overall supply chain efficiency. The innovative companies will make it work; the rest will follow.

Navigating through such a tumultuous environment will not be easy. Companies should take the following steps to minimize the impact of this turmoil:

- Develop a private trading exchange strategy. Consider that there will be options to building it in-house that include acquiring a failing industry vertical exchange or running a private, hosted version of a consortium exchange. An interim strategy could be to join or utilize a trading exchange. This provides a rapid mechanism for testing concepts and processes.

- Ask the following ten main questions before banking on a consortium to provide long-term trading exchange capabilities:

  1. What do we get for our founder's fee, and what is the ROI?
  2. What functionality will be delivered and when?
  3. What will the exchange cost over 5 years. and will we get everything promised without paying again?
  4. How will the exchange resolve contention among competing software vendors brought together to build the exchange?
  5. What's their plan to attract and retain suppliers?
  6. What's the business process model for collaboration, supply chain event management, logistics, and planning applications?
  7. How do members integrate exchange functionality with their back-office systems?
  8. How will the exchange handle exchange to exchange integration?
  9. Can we get there by adopting standards?
  10. What incentive will the exchange provide to encourage members to share best practices?

TRADING EXCHANGE EVALUATION METHODOLOGY

Is your company looking to join or start a trading exchange? Keep in mind that trading exchanges are still unproven business models. The evaluation methodology described here was developed by AMR Research to assess these new business models, especially the independent ones. You can also this methodology to assess what exchanges are most attractive to join or to evaluate how well your company's exchange stacks up against the competition.

Generally, exchanges should be rated across two dimensions: strength of business model and functionality.

Rating the Strength of Business Model

The following three components are integral to trading exchange's strategic position and viability: domain expertise, liquidity, and strategic position. Within each component, we assign a numeric value that assesses their progress. The exchanges with highest score are expected to be most viable.

Domain Expertise Component

How well does the exchange know the business with regard to process and nuance? Are other third-party affiliations within the industry recognizing the trading exchange? Another major consideration is expansion into verticals. As exchanges build liquidity through vertical expansion, do they bring domain expertise? If not, are they establishing the correct partnerships or acquiring the proper players? Maintaining domain expertise represents an interesting challenge for exchanges expanding their footprint. Also, does the exchange provide customer service staff familiar with the industry, or does it defer calls back to the supplier, in effect adding little value? Similar to wholesale distributors, exchanges need to do more than just move product.

Use the following point allocation scheme for rating an exchange for the domain expertise component:

0   Provides little more than a transaction platform, with no industry-specific added value

25 Delivers domain expertise primarily through content or spans multiple verticals, but does not differentiate business or customer service

50 Brings a strong senior management team from inside the industry, partners with industry organizations, and is a leader in the industry. Exchanges spanning multiple verticals demonstrate strong partnerships and acquisitions.

75 Supports industry-specific processes, offers strong customer service with domain expertise, and delivers strong industry knowledge

100 Is the definitive online source for industry and product information and innovation.

Liquidity Component

Liquidity measures the amount of business the exchanges are facilitating. Here, look for two early indicators: positive growth and transactional liquidity. Positive growth is measured by an increase in revenue, products listed, participants, size and number of transactions, and a decreased reliance on initial members. Also address whether the primary revenue stream is through transaction or advertisements. Ultimately, the primary indicator is the percentage of industry revenue flowing through the exchange.

Use the following point allocation scheme for rating an exchange for the liquidity component:

0   Does not generate any transaction revenue

25 Generates substantial revenue, but is primarily advertisement based or linked to only a handful of customers

50 Successfully drives a majority of revenue off a transaction model

75 Generates revenue from multiple sources, including services, and revenue is not linked to only a handful of customers

100 Facilitates a measurable portion of the industry's overall revenue

Strategic Position

Depending on the industry, either neutrality or partnerships are key strategies. While most exchanges initially touted independence, they are rapidly moving into two distinct camps. One group is firmly holding on to their neutral positions. Another group is seeking third-party partnerships with established brick-and-mortar companies within the industry.

Use the following point allocation scheme for rating an exchange for the strategic component:

0   Has not capitalized on neutrality or partnerships

25 Is only beginning to explore strong brick-and-mortar partnerships, but is not driving revenue. Neutrality is to its detriment.

50 Maintains strategic positions with second-tier brick-and-mortar companies. Neutrality is established and publicized, but the jury is still out on the correctness of the position.

75 Has given up significant equity stakes to substantial brick-and-mortar companies, which utilize the exchange as a primary distribu-

tion or sourcing channel. Neutrality drives majority acceptance inside the industry.

100 Is either neutral or aligned, and is recognized as an integral part of the industry value chain

Rating the Functionality

The second dimension to rank an exchange on is its functionality. For this measure, consider four distinct levels of functionality (see Figure 3.6). The following points recap the different levels:

- Information: Successful exchanges convey a high level of industry expertise and relative information. The information takes the form of industry directories, product databases and catalogs, discussion forums and billboards, and professional development.

- Facilitation: Distinct from the first level of functionality, facilitation is the ability to match a buyer's specific need with a supplier's specific offering. However, the transaction is completed offline via traditional channels such as EDI, phone, or fax.

- Transaction: This level involves a higher degree of commitment from the exchange and participants. Buyers and sellers are typically registered with the exchange as well as with banking and industry institutions. The primary difference from the previous level of functionality is that trading partners can consummate the transaction online.

- Integration: Integration functionality allows exchanges to fit into a larger supply chain and application integration strategy. They greatly increase their value to organizations if they can help companies leverage investment in installed applications and established relationships. This spans four levels: data, form, process, and business community integration. A higher value is achieved as the integration moves up the stack (see Figure 3.7).

TRADING EXCHANGES' ROLE IN EXPEDITING B2B COMMERCE ADOPTION

Technologies and applications for improving intercompany processes predate the public network. The problem with these early efforts was the enormous cost for smaller suppliers and buyers to participate. The Internet has lowered these barriers and made electronic interaction much more inclusive.

Evolution of ITX Functionality

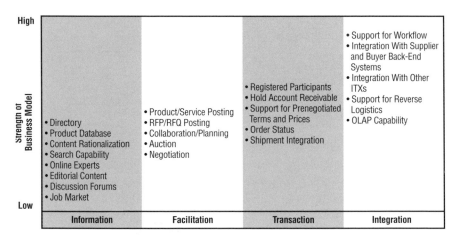

• Directory • Product Database • Content Rationalization • Search Capability • Online Experts • Editorial Content • Discussion Forums • Job Market	• Product/Service Posting • RFP/RFQ Posting • Collaboration/Planning • Auction • Negotiation	• Registered Participants • Hold Account Receivable • Support for Prenegotiated Terms and Prices • Order Status • Shipment Integration	• Support for Workflow • Integration With Supplier and Buyer Back-End Systems • Integration With Other ITXs • Support for Reverse Logistics • OLAP Capability
Information	**Facilitation**	**Transaction**	**Integration**

Functionality

Source: AMR Research

figure 3.6

Levels of
Integration Supported by ITXs

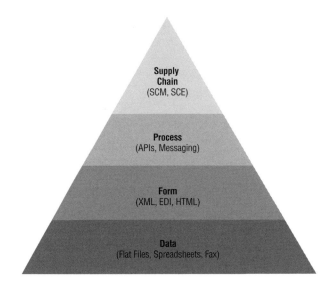

Supply Chain (SCM, SCE)

Process (APIs, Messaging)

Form (XML, EDI, HTML)

Data (Flat Files, Spreadsheets, Fax)

Source: AMR Research

figure 3.7

Early attempts to take advantage of this cost reduction revealed that inclusion efforts had to be followed by convenience considerations to resolve issues faced by smaller companies: The companies were facing the prospect of serving multiple masters because of each interaction being different, and integration issues were forcing redundant system entry of transactions.

Enter trading exchanges. By providing a conduit for transactions for an entire marketplace as well as providing the prospect of integration, the automation could be inclusive and convenient. Furthermore, with the free flow of transactions, companies could begin to use these exchanges for more complex collaborative processes. This promise has led to the funding of more than 500 independent exchanges. Large companies have initiated aggressive programs to establish them in their respective industry sector.

To date, realization of this promise has been minimal. AMR Research estimates that the best exchanges accounted for less than 1% of activity in their respective verticals in 1999. Once functionality, particularly integration, is established, adoption will be rapid. AMR Research expects that over 52.3% of B2B e-commerce transactions, or nearly $3.0T, will flow through exchanges by 2004 (see Figure 3.1). This is a composite number, and certain industries will see much higher adoption rates, including electronics (72%), aerospace (69%), chemical (68%), and discrete manufacturing (65%).

This level of activity has several implications:

- Trading exchanges will serve an important role in setting standards for semantics and business processes in the industries they serve. They will also be the arbiter of data ownership and distribution.

- Trading exchanges will accelerate the realization of benefits. Transaction cost reductions will lead to the ability to form more complex relationships, and the exchanges will want to be involved in these processes as well.

- Broad horizontal exchanges, such as those providing accounting, treasury, and human resource functions, will connect with those serving vertical industries. This combination will provide companies with a rich source of transaction support and allow a more intense focus on core competencies.

CONCLUSION

Trading exchanges, which will support over half of all B2B e-commerce transactions in 2004, will be the single most important catalyst of change. Those companies that are not assessing the potential impact of exchanges are risking extinction or becoming insignificant within their value/supply chain. As discussed in the next chapter, leading companies are already using or looking to use these exchanges, as well as some of the other tools and methods of e-business, to improve their position in the market.

chapter 4

Industry-Specific Business Models:
The Impact on Vertical Industries

It was an early decision that the state of e-business and its impact on supply chain and logistics across multiple industries would be a key focus of
this research. That meant we had to select a group of industries that could
adequately portray what is happening on the leading edge of progress and
where the future state would be. We also had to give the reader a sense of what
could be learned from these industries and applied to different business circumstances. For the industries selected for research, we decided they had to
meet the following key criteria:

- Exhibit knowledge and information that could be broadly applicable to the member companies of the Council of Logistics Management (CLM)

- Demonstrate best practices that were applicable to the CLM membership

- Considered as bellwethers for trends and lessons

- Include a mix of "old economy" and "new economy" companies, with an emphasis on old

- Contain firms that had an impact on practicing members of the CLM

We determined that the following industries met those criteria and would provide general business learning:

- Automotive

- Aerospace

- Chemicals

- Defense (U.S.)

- E-fulfillment

- Consumer goods

- High technology

It is important to note that the lessons and insights derived from our industry analysis represent a composite of what would be considered best practice and where the leaders are headed. Duplicating the applications and results should measurably improve the operations of any firm making such an effort. Unfortunately, many companies are reluctant to use lessons from other industries as a guide for improvement. We think that conclusion is shortsighted, as we found many of the insights are broadly applicable. In this chapter, we will elaborate on our industry analysis and begin to bring the findings into a framework for implementation that can be adapted for virtually any industry or firm.

A BROAD BASIS OF RESEARCH

Creating this book required a sizeable amount of research, both primary (actual interviews with companies and the use of focus groups) and secondary research (literature, books, and articles). This technique allowed us to document both the current state and in many instances understand what were the future plans of representative companies and industries. We also had the extensive databases of both AMR Research (www.amrresearch.com) and CSC (www.csc.com) to investigate. Through this process, the viewpoints and activities of thousands of individuals and companies were considered and the findings applied throughout the book.

Interviews were conducted with fifty companies, specifically to gather current state and future visions from leading firms and thought leaders. More than 200 books and articles were reviewed (see the Literature Review). The University of Maryland's Robert H. Smith School of Business provided another library of business studies and cases that helped our thinking and understanding of critical needs. Dr. Thomas Corsi and Mr. Yuliang Yao of the University of Maryland were instrumental in developing that research for this book. Several focus group sessions were conducted with logistics, supply chain, and e-business managers and executives and a survey of logistics executives was undertaken to deepen our understanding of the key activities in the chosen industries.

The research pointed to some key themes that were broadly applicable to multiple industries. Other findings were either industry specific or had an industry flavor to them. Our task became how to synthesize this broad array of information into a meaningful set of premises for the readers of this book.

FIVE THEMES

Following our initial analysis, five key themes emerged and were developed as we pursued our synthesis. These themes cut across multiple industries:

- The consumer has won the battle for control of buying. Industry leaders demonstrated a focus on the end consumer in their supply chains, even when the interrelated firms included companies that are removed from direct consumer contact.

- The move toward offering features of mass customization is having an impact on all companies, as they focus on doing their part to bring that dimension to the consumers of choice.

- Cycle time reduction is a primary aim—in both products and services—for those supply chains determined to gain an edge in future competition. Reducing the time it takes to understand the needs of a market and develop products and services, supported with an appropriate system of response, places requirements on all constituents of the supply chain for rapid response.

- New distribution channels have to be established to meet the needs of consumers, as they split their buying choices between Internet, telephone, fax, and in-store purchases. That circumstance requires the elimination of channel conflict for many companies. It also means the linked firms must realize that the new channels have to be supported and in some cases will either eliminate or reduce the use of older channels.

- E-Business supports further operational efficiencies— the electronic movement of information and the growth of online trading exchanges are about transactional efficiencies and increased leverage. They will be a factor in virtually all future business transactions.

Each targeted industry has specific interpretations of the themes that will be shown in the sections devoted to them.

GENERAL CHARACTERISTICS OF IMPROVEMENT PROCESSES

Along with the general themes that emerged from our research, some clear patterns emerged that cut across companies and industries. We quickly found a consistency in what had transpired and what the consensus thinking showed would have to take place to succeed and move forward. One point to be stressed at the outset helps in understanding the progression most firms made. Improvements to logistics systems and supply chain in general were started for two reasons: to bring efficiencies and cost reduction to the firm and to resolve some very long-standing problems. While almost all companies that embarked on such initiatives extolled the intention of becoming better sources for their customers as a primary reason, the reality seemed to have two much clearer directions: cost savings and defensive postures.

The defensive postures showed themselves as mechanisms to "ride" the wave of the Internet, often demonstrated by joining or participating in the startup of an online trading exchange. The cost cutting was usually undertaken with the intention of improving earnings by shaking out quick return savings from what appeared to be a fruitful area and to get rid of some old and lingering inefficiencies.

As we focused on cost cutting, we found the greatest attention and reinforcement of effort was still in that area. On the positive side, we also found strong evidence of significant gains. As firms mobilized talented people, gave them a specific focus and targeted objectives, and encouraged them with continuing support, the results were positive. An unusual finding was that few companies invested heavily in training these people for their new assignment. The typical scenario was to appoint a leader, often with little or no staff, and assign the responsibility of wringing savings from whatever would be defined as the supply chain. With dedicated internal resources (typically on a part-time basis) and with help from cooperating suppliers and customers, the leaders tended to pick a particular business unit headed by a visionary leader and embarked on a list of prioritized improvement possibilities. Despite the lack of a rigorous structure or well-defined approach, savings did result.

Generally, we found savings in costs of purchased goods that ranged between 3% and 10%. This range has to be explained. When analyzed carefully to determine whether there had been a translation of these savings to the profit and loss statement, the range of 3% to 5% appeared as the safe amount. Where a company fell in the range depended on its starting position or how well it had been buying in the past. There was also a fairly good correlation between how well a company worked with its supply base and was willing to share in the savings. Those firms that tended to dictate terms to suppliers, for example, showed large savings (typically from forcing suppliers to make price concessions) that tended to settle back nearer original positions. Firms that worked hard with their suppliers to apply mutual resources for mutual gains tended to be at the upper end of the real savings range.

We also found a 5% to 8% savings range in the area of logistics, most of which came from lower transportation costs, outsourcing the function to a third-party provider, and some reductions in warehouse and distribution costs. We offer a caution in the last area, because we see a surprising trend. While many large firms extolled the virtues of eliminating redundant warehousing and using pooled arrangements on joint facilities, the total amount of warehouse space has not declined. In fact, it's growing (see Figure 4.1).

According to a report published by Cass Information Systems and ProLogis, as documented in Table 4.1, the total supply of industrial warehouse space in the United States has risen steadily in the last 10 years. It certainly made a rise in 1999. In spite of the fact that many leaders in our study could point to

Total Supply of Industrial Warehouse Space

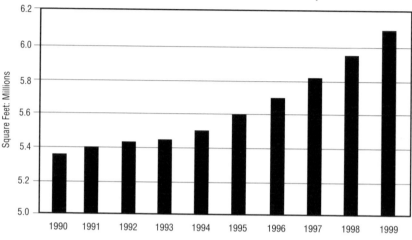

table 4.1

specific warehouse and distribution center elimination, the total space grows. Since there is an immutable law that as space is available it will be filled, we are dubious regarding many of the claimed inventory reductions. Indeed, we see this area of improvement as the leading challenge and opportunity in the next four to five years. The next frontier for bottom-line improvement lies in getting rid of the extraneous inventories that still clog most supply chains.

As we listened further to the conversation around inventory savings, we noticed most of the supposed savings tended to be pushed around the supply chain network rather than actually being eliminated. A safe estimate of real inventory reductions through improved communications and better handling of stocks seemed to be in the range of 10% to 15%, although some firms did show reductions up to 50%.

As these ranges of improvement are presented for general purposes, it must be recognized that the savings being cited for supply chain efforts are not net savings, as virtually no company deducted the cost of the effort put into getting the savings. A general finding that does stand up is that the leaders could show about a 1% per year bottom-line improvement, for each year they had been pursuing a combination logistics and supply chain effort. So an overall range of net savings would fall between 3% and 5% for a firm that had been pursuing an effort for 3 to 5 years. We concluded that most firms did make some real savings and have improved the processing and efficiency of their supply chains. They did so through focused pilot and project efforts with strong executive support and specific objectives. Virtually none of the large companies studied had accomplished such improvements across all business units within the firm.

As we enter the next phase of improvement effort, a general measure of logistics costs can be cited as a benchmark for gauging progress. Using the fact that the U.S. logistics costs in 1999 were equal to 9.9% of nominal gross domestic product (GDP), firms should first get themselves to that level as a percentage of revenues and then attack further reduction. The transportation portion of that figure came in at a steady 6.0% for the seventh consecutive year (Delaney 2000).

Regarding total supply chain costs, the national average is probably close to 12%. These figures offer some guidelines to calibrate your starting point for future actions. Our research indicates there are another 2 to 4 percentage points left to be extracted from logistics and supply chain costs that can be reflected in bottom-line performance, for the leaders. The amount you can extract depends on how you calibrate your performance with the leaders in your industry.

CHARACTERISTICS OF THE LAGGARDS

We mentioned that one of the major reasons for starting an improvement effort was to clean up old problems. Our research showed plainly that problems in supply chains are often the manifestation of very deep-rooted faults, some of which still exist. They certainly exist for those companies not keeping pace with the leaders. Across our sample of interviews, focus group discussions, and case analyses, we often found problems similar to those reported by Dr. Richard Wilding, senior lecturer in supply chain management at Cranfield University, as he cited what inhibits progress with supply chain improvement:

- Lack of effective use of available resources, evidenced by poor sharing of talent within organizational business units and the reluctance to accept offered external help

- Failure to recognize existing weaknesses, particularly by business units more concerned with image than performance

- Lack of shared visibility, especially of valuable data on actual consumption and current trends, and inventory throughout a total supply chain that could help other constituents of the supply chain

- Failure to analyze performance in detail, most dramatically when the analysis would lead to metrics not covered by management bonus systems

- Technology-driven solutions rather than solutions for customer needs, usually in companies where there was near total isolation between the IT department and operating units (Wilding 2000)

These are major problems confronting the laggards in our study. Overcoming these obstacles is one of the primary challenges to be faced. The degree of success varied greatly in our research, but it's important to note that none of our studied companies appeared to have conquered all of the challenges. Many seem to have business units able to move forward in spite of a house full of internal problems yet to be resolved. The conclusion we have drawn is that the impulse to move forward and the sustaining of momentum is consistently dampened in the trailing firms of an industry. The factors contributing to that unfortunate circumstance include the lack of a visionary business unit leader, no compelling business reason to make the effort, and a cultural imperative that protects the status quo. For companies with these symptoms, only a strong demand from a large customer to develop supply chain improvements gets any action, and it is generally short-lived. The desire to gain a commanding lead in the industry is also not present in these firms. They prefer to watch the landscape carefully with an often-misguided perception that they can quickly match any gains made by the leaders. With progress being made so rapidly in today's business environment, that thinking will leave a firm at a disadvantage as it tries to close an ever-widening gap.

CHARACTERISTICS OF THE LEADERS

We'll document specific leadership traits and actions as we pursue the industry analysis. In general, however, some characteristics tend to distinguish exceptional results:

- Organizations and cultures open to change and new ideas: Many companies who are successful have cultures where people are encouraged to submit new ideas and approaches.

- Long planning horizons: Cisco Systems, the arguable leader in e-business has constructed a whole operating model around it and has been doggedly pursuing that goal for several years.

- A compelling business reason for applying what will be significant time and resources for poorly defined end results: This reason is usually customer driven, but the potential positive and negative (for not reacting) results ignite all functions to the effort.

- A visionary business unit or corporate executive, who is determined to participate and to provide direct leadership of the effort: Sometimes this takes on the form of having an executive who is ready to listen and adopt input from within the organization. Much of the success at Cisco came about because senior executives were willing to listen to ideas. Microsoft made one of the most rapid changes in business direction in history because employees were able to get the attention of Bill Gates and convince him of the importance of the Internet.

- Cross-functional support and participation, particularly between the IT group and operations personnel: If energy is drained by internal conflict, there is little hope of overall success.

- An acceptance of using external resources to augment team efforts

- A willingness to share the savings with those organizations providing positive benefit to the effort.

Further information is available on what the leaders have accomplished. The Performance Measurement Group, LLC, in their December 1999 issue of Dimensions, presented on a "collection of metrics and business practices . . . collected from the Supply Chain Management Benchmarking Series: Deliver Survey." Among the survey results, they report the following:

Leading companies use the Web to fundamentally alter the nature of communications among trading partners.

- Seventy-five percent of Internet exchanges are unrelated to order placement. The Web is being used to transmit . . . shipment status, order status, and inventory status

- Best-in-class performance in perfect order fulfillment has improved 5%, since the mid-1990s, as industry moves to . . . a holistic view of complete, on-time, and accurate order fulfillment.

In their sample of best practices, the Performance Measurement Group showed that leaders sustain a quality dimension to their supply chain activities, saving money for themselves and their customers. They report the leaders do the following:

- Coordinate initiatives to improve delivery with initiatives to reduce shipping errors, installation errors, billing errors, and invoice errors.

- Leverage Web and electronic data interchange (EDI) technologies to receive and enter orders, thereby reducing the opportunity for error through manual entry.

- Use rules-based configuration; build in logic that prohibits incompatible configurations.

Our personal experience with both laggards and leaders validates these findings, and we would add that the laggards spend a considerably larger amount of annual dollars on errors and reconciliation than do the leaders. In another study, Covill and Knudson report on the challenges facing companies as they attempt to engage in e-commerce (as the effort pertains to delivery channel management). Their challenges tend to be managed much better by leaders than laggards.

> The promise of e-commerce channel management initiatives is real. The challenges facing senior business managers is to develop a strategy that addresses several concerns:
>
> - The complexity of managing multiple product lines for multiple channels
> - The mapping of products to channels in a way that enhances brand identity, increases the breadth and depth of markets reached, and lowers transaction cost
> - The building of successful long-term relationships with channel partners, whether real or virtual. (Covill and Knudson 2000)

Augmenting good progress among the leaders, we typically find a compelling value proposition that energizes the key people in the pursuit of improvement. Solid documentation of real progress with meaningful metrics helps maintain the energy and leads to higher accomplishments. This factor was explained in detail in a previous CLM book, entitled Keeping Score: Measuring the Business Value of Logistics in the Supply Chain (Keebler et al. 1999).

DIFFERING DEGREES OF PROGRESS

With these characteristics and associated caveats in mind, we'll present the result of our research, interviews, and case analyses in seven industries.

The Automobile Industry: From Rust to Silicon

The automobile industry is recognized globally as having a huge impact on the world's economy. It is also known as having a complex supply chain and sophisticated logistics, which uses almost all mechanisms available to be successful, including:

- rail transport,

- sea transport,

- over-the-road carriers,

- air transport, and

- cyber communications, whereby solid models and math data are shipped around sophisticated networks to reduce costs and reduce cycle time.

In the United States, one in seven jobs is linked to the auto industry. It is a technically advanced industry and has a very complex supply chain with multiple tiers of suppliers, distribution facilities, dealerships, and consumers who spend hundreds of billions of dollars annually on automotive products. The leaders have made huge investments in information technology and are leveraging their purchasing power, data investments, and knowledge of supply chain to forge ahead in e-business. Professionals in supply chain and logistics have to take notice of the automobile industry. Many companies are linked to this industry directly or indirectly; if your company is so connected, they will be calling you about e-business and what they expect from you. Here are some insights into those expectations.

The automotive industry is still coming to grips with all things "e." In the 2000 Automotive Industries Magazine and CSC Consulting study of Technology Issues in the Automobile Industry (see Figure 4.1), responses from senior executives showed they were still trying to figure out exactly what to do. Many initiatives are under way at strategic levels, but how exactly these will be accomplished and what impact they will have on overall business performance is still being determined.

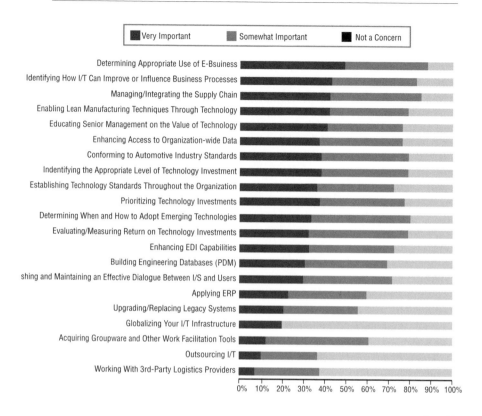

Legend: Very Important | Somewhat Important | Not a Concern

- Determining Appropriate Use of E-Bsuiness
- Identifying How I/T Can Improve or Influence Business Processes
- Managing/Integrating the Supply Chain
- Enabling Lean Manufacturing Techniques Through Technology
- Educating Senior Management on the Value of Technology
- Enhancing Access to Organization-wide Data
- Conforming to Automotive Industry Standards
- Indentifying the Appropriate Level of Technology Investment
- Establishing Technology Standards Throughout the Organization
- Prioritizing Technology Investments
- Determining When and How to Adopt Emerging Technologies
- Evaluating/Measuring Return on Technology Investments
- Enhancing EDI Capabilities
- Building Engineering Databases (PDM)
- shing and Maintaining an Effective Dialogue Between I/S and Users
- Applying ERP
- Upgrading/Replacing Legacy Systems
- Globalizing Your I/T Infrastructure
- Acquiring Groupware and Other Work Facilitation Tools
- Outsourcing I/T
- Working With 3rd-Party Logistics Providers

0% 10% 20% 30% 40% 50% 60% 70% 80% 90% 100%

figure 4.1

The manufacturers are the channel masters of the automotive supply chain. The goal of the original equipment manufacturers (OEMs) is full supply chain visibility and interaction. The first order is for visibility on order status, shipment data, and so forth. Then comes the need for interaction capability, as production scheduling and production capacity information become available online. Providing these capabilities will be enormously difficult but crucial to future plans that include moving from a build-to-stock (BTS) orientation to a build-to-order (BTO) consumer model. Taking more than half the time out of the current supply chain cycle is a requisite for this objective. When a consumer orders a vehicle, the order has to ripple quickly throughout the entire supply chain. The OEMs will want to understand the production and logistics capabilities of the entire supply chain and supply that information to consumers and dealers.

Two key themes emerge in the automobile industry: the move to a BTO versus BTS orientation and the movement that the OEMs are making into services (see Figure 4.2). The first theme includes the recognition that the sales and delivery model is changing. The recognition of the shift from push to pull, based on consumers and their changing needs, is causing a key strategic change across the industry. In particular, General Motors, Ford, and Toyota have acknowledged the consumer has won, and these firms are trying to move form being manufacturing companies to becoming consumer companies. "We are transitioning Ford Motor Company from a car company to a consumer company," states Jacques Nasser, CEO of Ford Motor Company.

Auto Supply Chain Old and New

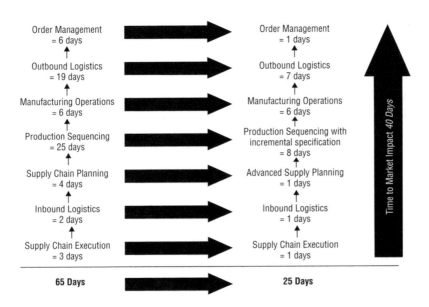

Source: AMR Research, CSC

figure 4.2

Those activities have taken on a single key theme, a shift toward the BTS or order to delivery (OTD) models (see Figure 4.2). Consumers will recognize these terms as forms of mass customization.

The challenges for the automobile industry in moving toward an e-business model are immense, including the following:

- Consumer apathy or downright hostility regarding the current sales and marketing system
- Dealer reluctance to change
- Regulatory issues regarding direct interaction between consumers and manufacturers
- Internal management processes and methods of the manufacturers
- Suppliers constantly whipsawed by demands from the manufacturers
- Infrastructure investments by suppliers that have yet to be recovered
- Complicated and long logistics cycles

Nevertheless, Ford, GM, and Toyota have announced large programs that include an e-transformation. Ford has introduced Customer Connect as GM rolled out its OTD process. Toyota is in full swing with a similar program. The movement to being a service company is less apparent but just as real and

Potential Impact of E-Business

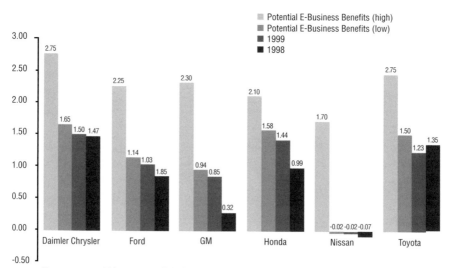

Figures are per vehicle average profit by Manufacturer.
Potential benefit is the application of E-Business processes throughout the supply chain.

Source: Harbour Research, Detroit Free Press and CSC Consulting

figure 4.3

perhaps more important in the long run. Ford is relying on a move toward becoming a consumer company. GM is looking to even more supply chain efficiencies, leveraging its success with OnStar to provide ever more value-added services to consumers. Toyota is looking to use its reputation for quality and its lean manufacturing processes as a foundation for a consumer-oriented effort.

Auto Industry Benefits Could Be Significant

What is the impetus for these movements? The financial benefits can be startling (see Figure 4.3). Most of the savings would come about via increased efficiencies in the supply chain. The North American auto industry could send between $16 billion (a conservative estimate) and $50 billion directly to the bottom line each year. Improved customer relations by being more responsive to the changing demographics is another key success criteria for the industry (see Figure 4.4).

Median Age of Consumers

GM	52		VW	36	
Ford	51		Audi	43	
DCX	53		Nissan	43	
BMW	44		Subaru	48	
Honda	44		Saab	46	
Acura	46		Toyota	46	
			Porsche	57	

Source: AutoPacific, Detroit News

figure 4.4

Another benefit could come from the reductions in rebates and discounts and traditional advertising expenditures. GM spends more than $10 billion annually on rebates to spur sales. Much of this is avoidable if consumers could custom-order a vehicle, getting exactly what they want it and when they want it. With potential efficiencies in supply chain, an order could be processed and turned around in between 10 days (similar vehicle sequenced for production) and 25 days. Another potential advantage could come to the dealerships. A dealer could reduce its stocking levels by approximately 75%, allowing huge savings in inventory.

The demands on logistics providers will be enormous in the implementation process. For these new models to work, outbound logistics (from manufacturing facility to dealer or consumer) will require a near 100% improvement. Currently, outbound logistics are one of the Achilles' heels of the BTO model. Outbound logistics time frames are so unpredictable that dealers can't predict the month a car will arrive.

Covisint: A Key Component

The use of private trading exchanges (PTXs) is a key to increasing operational efficiencies in the auto industry (see Figure 4.5). The auto industry's consortium trading exchange is called Covisint, and it was approved in principle by the Federal Trade Commission in September 2000. The key participants are General Motors, Ford, Daimler Chrysler, Renault, and Nissan. Delphi, Visteon, Lear, and ArvinMeritor; many other firms have joined at the urging of the OEMs. The use the firms will make of Covisint varies by company. Covisint will be both a buy-side and a sell-side exchange. Some predict that hundreds of billions of dollars annually will flow through Covisint. Suppliers in many categories will have to use Covisint to sell certain supplies to the OEMs.

Initially, it will be primarily maintenance, repair, and operations (MRO) supplies. The OEMs differ beyond that point, and suppliers will again be forced to understand various rules and operating models. Who will buy complex assemblies? Who will buy engineering services? Will the OEMs band together to have even more leverage to reduce costs and make groups buy? These questions need answers before the full impact of the new auto exchange will be apparent.

The automobile industry is in the early stages of a massive transformation. The shift toward the consumer is in full swing, and the OEMs' goal of full supply chain visibility will impact all that do business with them. It's likely that when the dam bursts and the key tier 1 suppliers provide supply chain visi-

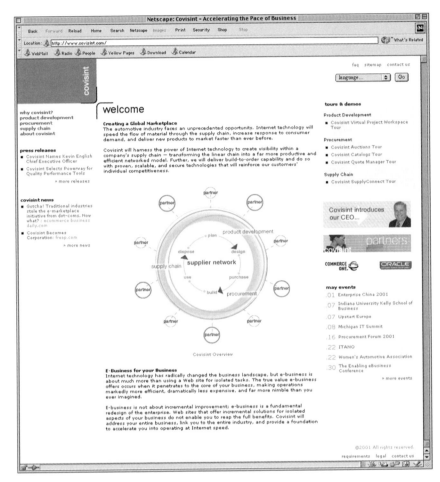

figure 4.5

bility, they and the OEMs will demand new capabilities throughout the supply chain. That will take several years to accomplish (see Figure 4.6).

Aerospace: Forging Ahead

The aerospace sector includes companies that manufacture aircraft and aircraft parts, guided missiles and space vehicles, land combat systems, surface and undersea vessels, defense electronics, and other aerospace/defense components and systems. The industry constituents are inextricably linked and also provide services such as repair and maintenance systems in the field. The primary business customers are members of the defense sector, including the United States Department of Defense (DoD), military and police forces around the world, and the major national and regional airlines.

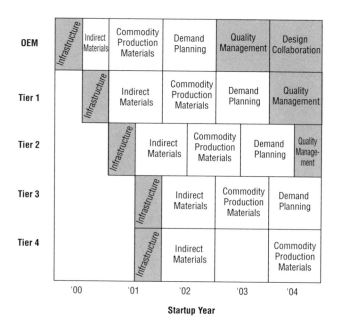

	Infrastructure	Indirect Materials	Commodity Production Materials	Demand Planning	Quality Management	Design Collaboration
OEM	Infrastructure	Indirect Materials	Commodity Production Materials	Demand Planning	Quality Management	Design Collaboration
Tier 1		Infrastructure	Indirect Materials	Commodity Production Materials	Demand Planning	Quality Management
Tier 2			Infrastructure	Indirect Materials	Commodity Production Materials	Demand Planning	Quality Management
Tier 3				Infrastructure	Indirect Materials	Commodity Production Materials	Demand Planning
Tier 4					Infrastructure	Indirect Materials		Commodity Production Materials
	'00	'01	'02	'03	'04

Startup Year

figure 4.6

A typical supply chain for an aerospace firm would proceed from parts broker to a primary supplier to an OEM to an airline. Intermediate steps could include parts distribution centers, service shops, airline repair facilities, and diagnostics centers. At all times, the Federal Aviation Association (FAA) acts as a watchdog on the industry. Multiple companies often work on large, complex projects that are difficult to manage. Product development time is long. A look at some of the techniques being applied will give you insights into how this industry is moving and how future best practices will be defined.

For a defense contractor, the process would begin with a procurement or specification from a branch of military service or the DoD. Then a complicated bidding and vetting process occurs that requires participation of many suppliers by legislative dictate. A particular opportunity lies in the huge amount of parts inventories that exist and the lack of inventory management in that area. Old airplanes never seem to die. They just show up in other parts of the world. These planes need parts, and parts seem to be everywhere. Manufacturers carry spares; distributors have their stock. The airlines carry a safety stock at their maintenance sites. One senior executive told us that if there were an accurate accounting of the current value of all parts versus the actual usage in a year, inventory turns for the industry would be less than 0.5 per year. To date, no one firm has offered an end-to-end solution that would be applicable for an integrated aviation community, although there is fevered activity to finally come to grips with the long-standing problem.

The problem is basic to what happens in the industry. When an airplane sits idle on the ground, it costs the airline between $5,000 to $7,000 an hour. Airlines and other users of planes need quick and easy access to spare parts to keep their fleets available for use. How fast and accurately they get the response they seek is also a measure of how they will remain loyal and satisfied to the parts source. Customers need up-to-the-minute information about the availability, location, and current price of the spare parts needed to repair and maintain the airplanes in their care. The goal for a viable source is to be so fast that customers can regard the inventory as virtually their own. The ideas of parts and maintenance will be a recurring theme in our aerospace analysis.

In general, solving this problem involves the same elements regardless of industry conditions. To begin, you have to know what and how much is in the existing inventory. In many of our interviews, we talked to organizations that simply could not identify exactly how much of various products were in stock. They could send someone to find out, but they lacked what the leaders had—online, real-time visibility with high accuracy of what was in stock. Next, you need to know where the inventory is, which includes the very large amount in some industries that is in transit or tucked away someplace by an overly cautious manager for "just-in-case" emergencies. Again, the leaders have this information online, while others simply send search teams at times of need to find important parts.

When you know what you have and where, you then need to be able to access the stock and ship it or divert it to the point of need. For the laggards, this task becomes very labor-intensive, with innumerable telephone calls and heroic expediting efforts. For the leaders, it is a calm online process of following decision rules and making an occasional diversion for a very special customer. Finally, with low reliability, the laggards keep stocks high and turns per year low. As one manager told us, "No one ever lost a job around here because inventory was too high, but some did because they shut down a manufacturing line." The leaders rely on their screen to tell them what they need to know and slash the safety stocks without compromising performance. Let's consider what the airline industry is doing to come to grip with its problem and make some significant savings in the process.

Boeing

Boeing is a national icon in the United States. It is the largest aerospace manufacturer in the world with a leading position in many facets of the industry. The only maker of big commercial jets in the United States, Boeing has divisions devoted to commercial airplanes, military aircraft and missiles, and space and communications systems. It is a company that prefers not to increase head count to serve its anticipated business growth. They want to leverage e-business technologies to keep costs down while ramping up volume and sustaining and improving quality.

Under the leadership of Tom DeMarco, senior manager in the customer service division of Boeing's Commercial Aviation Group, Boeing launched an innovative and successful inventory management system to tackle the problem mentioned—spare parts for its burgeoning fleet of aircraft. Called Part Analysis and Requirement Tracking (PART) Page, the Boeing Web site has the following features:

- Delivery cycles are shortened usually to next-day or same-day for emergencies.

- Orders can be modified right up to the time of shipment and can be tracked en route—the PART Page is linked to six major shipping companies' sites.

- It enables customers to perform ad hoc queries for parts pricing and availability.

- It contains four million parts recorded with detailed specifications.

- HTML pages are browser-independent.

- Multilevel security access control is achieved with a single sign-on.

Within three months of launch in 1996, 125 of Boeing's 700 airline customers were using the Web site on a regular basis, and customers were coming on board at the rate of 15 per week. The volume of transactions has grown more than 100% each year since its launch, and the Web site supports nearly 75% of the world's jet transport fleet in spares-related business. The site currently processes about 18,000 transactions on an average day. In addition, 85% of all spare ordering from Boeing is conducted electronically, including both EDI and PART Page transactions.

Another division of the company offers an insight into how collaboration between suppliers and manufacturers can bring significant benefit to manufacturing costs by reducing the amount of parts necessary for assembly. Boeing Rocketdyne supports the NASA Marshall Space Flight center with the design, manufacture, and support of the main engines for the space shuttle program. It also provides the electrical power distribution system for the international space station as part of Boeing.

Rocketdyne has adopted a collaborative working practice with other NASA contractors that includes a goal to reduce the development and manufacturing time frames, cost, and complexity of their offering. Their effort is a model of what is happening in advanced supply chain and e-commerce initiatives.

TRW Aeronautical

TRW Aeronautical, through its Lucas Aerospace division, was presented the UK Council of Electronic Business 2000 award on June 20, 2000, for the most significant implementation of e-business techniques. The Lucas division provides the industry with high-integrity systems and equipment in engine controls, flight controls, missile systems, power generation and management, cargo handling, and flexible shafts and couplings. The award was presented to its Web site, www.trwaerospares.com, launched on March 27, 2000. The site links directly to the company's spares logistics system and provides access to 166,000 TRW commercial aircraft spares, 24 hours a day, anywhere in the world. The Web page allows customers to check pricing and availability, place orders, and track order and delivery status any time of day (Business Wire 2000).

According to David Ashton, director of TRW Aeronautical Systems Equipment Service, the Web site and its use have been "successful in simplifying and streamlining spares ordering and processing and is a significant contributor to our e-business solutions for after-market support." TRW has been aggressively expanding its e-business solutions in spares trading, automated repair logistics, catalog procurement, electronic request-for-quotation, supply demand, and eliminating waste. The company has driven its e-business effort against these objectives, rather than using e-business for e-business sake.

Pratt & Whitney

Pratt & Whitney (P&W), a unit of United Technologies Corporation, is a leader in the design, manufacture and support of engines for commercial, military and general aviation aircraft, and space compulsion systems. P&W manufactures engines for more than half of the world's commercial fleet and the majority of U.S. Air Force fighters. This firm developed Supplier Direct Ship (SDS), a system created in 1995 that has contributed to increased productivity and lowers operating costs for both P&W and its supply chain partners.

SDS has dramatically increased communication by allowing P&W suppliers to obtain more accurate and up-to-date scheduling information so they may better plan their internal resources. It has also improved supplier cash flow by eliminating the standard invoicing process and providing payment upon receipt of material. Internal P&W SDS benefits have included significant reductions in inventory, operating costs, and material flow cycle time. SDS is a mission-critical system and can be considered the "material circulatory system" for the business, as no material can be moved either internally or externally without authorization from SDS. SDS manages close to $2 billion in purchases each year from 380 suppliers (a high 90% of external suppliers use the system).

The SDS system has this general description:

- Provides schedule visibility, contains early-over logic for managing inventory levels, prints bar codes at the supplier that identify approved shipments, allows suppliers to view and change purchase commitments, and contains supplier delivery performance data

- Is used for external and internal (interplant shipments) materials movement

- Is fed by thirteen to twenty legacy systems

Its business impact has been significant, as it has:

- increased fill rate from 95% to 96%,

- raised inventory turns from three to four,

- decreased receiving cycle time from 3 to 5 days to 4 hours,

- increased shipments from 175,000 to 350,000 per year without increasing head count,

- eliminated a warehouse,

- reduced inventory by $60 million per year,

- totally eliminated the invoicing and matching processes, and

- allowed customers to be immediately paid on receipt of material.

Raytheon

Raytheon is one of the world's leading diversified technology companies, serving customers in more than eighty countries worldwide. Raytheon's core businesses are defense and commercial electronics, engineering and construction, and business aviation and special mission aircraft. The high volume of requests for inexpensive materials used to meet both engineering and production requirements resulted in significant backlogs at Raytheon's local supply chain management offices. These requisition delays meant it took up to 20 days for a buyer to administer a purchase order. Large amounts of time were also spent on routine repetitive tasks that did not add any value to the end customer. By freeing up a buyer's time, they are able to focus more on the core business competencies such as designing strategic purchasing agreements. The goal was to push ordering capability for low-dollar materials from approved suppliers down to the end user or enable automated purchase order transmissions from corporate approved agreements.

Raytheon's Sensors and Electronic Systems Department's SCM Group developed an automated purchase order release system to support production program requirements. The SCM Group also worked with FASTXchange to adapt its automated and outsourced procurement solution to fit Raytheon's special needs. Features of the program include the following:

- Electronic catalog system for indirect purchases from a supplier base of 30,000 data sources with customized search capabilities

- Universal access to parts, real-time access to order status, and rapid response guarantee

- Customized ordering screen including all fields required for transactions

- Seamless interfaces to existing systems and after-hours electronic submission to Raytheon's back-office systems for reconciliation

- Weekly, monthly, quarterly, and annual reports for management reporting, planning, and auditing
- Supplier rankings based on Raytheon's established parameters for secondary source purchasing

Since the start of the FASTXchange relationship, the average purchase order cycle time of 2 days has been maintained for more than 2 years, which translates into a 90% reduction from the preagreement levels. Operating expense has also been reduced by as much as 40% since this solution has been initiated. In late 1999, FASTXchange was awarded a multimillion-dollar contract for specialized procurement services after having served several Raytheon sites in California. This 3-year agreement has been expanded to select Raytheon sites outside of California and is available to all Raytheon businesses worldwide.

Aerospace Spare Parts, Inventories, and Emerging Exchanges

An element of trading exchanges that is very popular in the airline industry illustrates one of the dominant features of the new supply chains, an element useful in getting rid of slow-moving and obsolete material languishing in aged inventories. Understanding how its use is emerging in the industry helps illustrate the importance of collaborative industry efforts and how the parts issue is being further resolved.

As an example, AirLiance Materials, LLC, was created in 1998 through equity ownership of three airlines: United Airlines, Lufthansa Technik, and Air Canada. It's a marketplace that essentially distributes used and surplus parts to airlines. By aggregating the surplus and excess aircraft parts of the equity owners, new liquidity and income were found for stagnant assets. AirLiance is a no-fee site that has an exclusive arrangement for sourcing surplus material for use by its parent airlines with the goal of increasing surplus content to 10% of total direct spend on maintenance material.

Just two years in operation, it already has a place among the top five surplus parts distributors. The value proposition for this exchange is to provide high-quality, traceable after-market parts to the airline industry. Its features include online order entry to more than 150,000 line items and inventory position transparency through a component-based architecture, allowing for future exchange integration. Future phases will include integration and business process alignment with surplus brokers and providers of secondary parts. The inventory shrinkage at the parent airlines has provided free cash of $60 million on an annual basis (reduced capital spending and cost of money improvements.

Another marketplace for aircraft parts, services, and general business supplies is represented by a consortium of thirteen major airlines called Aeroxchange. Air Canada, All Nippon Airways, Lufthansa, SASA, and Singapore Airlines launched this site. It has been joined by America West, Cathay Pacific, Federal Express, Japan Airlines, and Northwest. Additional equity partners include Air New Zealand, Austrian Airlines, and KLM Royal Dutch. Billed as the first comprehensive e-business solution dedicated to the aviation industry, the site works for buyers and sellers. Examples of items that will be traded through the exchange include airframes, avionics and engine components, and maintenance services.

PartsBase.com is the largest neutral, global exchange for the aviation, aerospace, and defense industry, with over 27,000 members in 135 countries. Auction categories vary from bearings, landing gears, and hydraulic components to interior equipment, airframes, and furnishings. It encourages sellers to dispose of slow-moving or excess products and buyers to use a reverse auction to buy needed components.

Not to be left out of the game, United Technologies, Honeywell, and i2 Technologies are combining to form MyAircraft.com. This site is designed to combine industry expertise with e-business solution software, hopefully to reduce cycle times, improve transactions, manage parts inventories, and reduce equipment downtimes.

A concluding comment should be made concerning the difference between the United States and other countries and the approaches taken to improvement and the use of exchanges. An early focus of the emerging exchanges has been on indirect procurement and movement of spare parts. The European aerospace industry is primarily a government sector of business. For most of those countries and their airlines, a fairly disciplined and rigorous process is in place for buying and transferring equipment and parts. While there has been strong interest in maintenance and spare parts, the Europeans will have to be convinced of the long-term advantage of an aggregating mechanism and trading exchanges that span the full industry. Collaborative product development is also a possible area of interest but will again take some time for offshore action to occur.

Chemicals: Advancing on Many Fronts

AMR Research and others cite the chemical industry as being toward the front of activity in advanced supply chain and e-commerce applications. Our study showed that much of the activity has been initiated by a few of the dominant players. The effort tends to be focused on lower logistics costs (basically transporting feed stocks and blended chemicals in dry and liquid states to manufacturers), having online inventory information, buying nondirect materials and supplies electronically, and aggregating needs to leverage e-commerce for reducing supply chain costs. In particular, the industry is taking a lead in the manufacturing sector in terms of handling of upstream feed stocks and commodity chemical inventories. Players are also shifting from the current batch ordering processes to online withdrawals or "turn-on usage" systems facilitated by an exchange or clearinghouse. Hopefully, this new technique will be error-free and eliminate a long-standing industry headache.

BASF

BASF is one of many chemical manufacturers using the Internet as a low-cost communications medium for vendor-managed inventory (VMI) systems. In their case, the desire was to have the supplier assume responsibility for control of the inventory, a business technique that has been active for more than a decade. This scheme has met with mixed results, particularly in the grocery industry where it is a common practice, but where there is pushback on the part of some manufacturers that see all the benefits going to the retailer. In a B2B situation between supplier and manufacturer, it seems to work better.

Because VMI lets the suppliers control the flow of goods, it changes the relationship and facilitates business processes such as just-in-time manufacturing. BASF is part of a supply chain network that starts with the purchase of feed stock chemicals from such suppliers as Monsanto and Union Carbide. They then turn those chemicals into compounds that go to manufacturers that make the paint for automakers' cars. Having enough inventories to always be sure of supply across the full supply chain has been a problem for decades. The classic solution was to have more than enough stock and never have an outage. If a company buys more chemicals than it needs, the surplus typically sits in its tanks indefinitely. In spite of precautionary conditions, sometimes a crucial ingredient still could be missing.

In an industry typified by emergency phone calls and heroic expediting, the Internet offers a better solution. By using a Web browser at the supplier's site, the feed stock suppliers can check BASF's current inventory of their chemicals. They can compare against historical usage patterns and calculate forecasts for consumption. The stocks on hand in the tanks now belong to the suppliers that get their payment upon usage. Monitoring the inventory on a daily basis via the Web-based VMI system is crucial to not having too much stock in inventory. The company gives its suppliers online forecasts of consumption and makes agreements with them about which levels will alert schedule refills. When the stocks drop below an agreed-on level, the suppliers call BASF to schedule a delivery. If the supplier decides BASF's forecasts are off, it can renegotiate. Regardless of the number of deliveries, one bill per month is transmitted to BASF for summary payment.

Progress with VMI (especially in the retail arena) was always limited by the wide variability in actual consumer consumption. It's becoming a practical application in the supplier to manufacturer arena where there is less uncertainty concerning usage and future needs. Manufacturers also have technology for accurately measuring the materials they use. They can track consumption of chemicals to the last ounce using tank telemetry systems, which employ sensors to measure the level of liquid in a tank and then store the data in a relational database. During the last year, several vendors have introduced systems that feed such data into web browsers (Hibbard 2000).

Stephen Fraser, CEO at GATX/CSI, sees an enormous opportunity to introduce VMI to manufacturers. "VMI has never been supplied to the industrial market," he says. GATX bought its CSI subsidiary (Clover Systems Inc.) to capitalize on the perceived opportunity. "For companies that are in chemicals," Fraser adds, "there is an enormous amount of value in inventory in their supply chains. If they have real-time information on what's going on in a complex of tanks, the ability to make a decision about when to make a delivery and in what quantity is significantly enhanced" (Hibbard 2000).

Shell Chemical Company
Shell Chemical Company in Houston offers its version of VMI to customers as an incentive to make Shell their sole supplier for chemicals. The value proposition is that customers use what they need without interruption, without buying and expense, and get a single monthly bill for that usage. Shell's system started in 1994 as a Lotus Notes–based application called Supplier Inventory Management Order Network (SIMON) and expanded it with an interface to its enterprise replenishment planning (ERP) system. Customers enter daily inventory levels, confirm receipts of shipments, and analyze historical inventory levels and consumption data. Shell service representatives receive the data and, if a shipment is needed, enter an order in their SAP R/2

planning and scheduling system. The order is sent back to SIMON, and the customer sees a notice that the chemicals are on the way. The latest version includes a feature that automatically calculates forecasts and a function that generates a resupply plan.

Dow Chemical Company

Dow Chemical Company is emerging as the Internet champion in the chemical industry, developing its own e-commerce strategies, including broadcasting information through its Web site, creating a direct dialogue with its key customers, transaction processing, and collaboration applications. The company plans to leverage the Internet to sell high-margin engineering and other services as well as chemicals and plastics. Dow has two main IT objectives: to leverage the Internet to improve decision making and to expand links with customers, suppliers, and supply chain partners. It's taking multiple, often overlapping approaches by developing internal applications, rolling out packaged applications, investing in existing e-business ventures, and teaming with competitors to create new companies.

Under its DowNet 2001 project, the company is working to build an integrated voice, data, and video network to support collaborative projects within and between divisions. Some 80% of Dow's customers buy from multiple Dow units, and the system is intended to assist internal excellence with state-of-the-art intra- and interorganizational data communication. Dow is also an investor in several marketplaces, as it studies and learns how to use these novel sites as part of its Internet strategy. One investment is in ChemConnect, a third-party exchange for spot purchases of chemicals and plastics. It's also investing with BASF, Du Pont, and others to create another online exchange for the sale of plastics-related materials.

Dow has been most aggressive in streamlining its supply chain/customer relationships. For example, Dow set up a company with Du Pont, Bayer, and twenty other industry companies to build an online exchange for buying and selling chemicals. Called Elemica, this global e-marketplace offers an integrated, end-to-end system that helps buyers and sellers to streamline their contract sales. Its logistics planning systems claim to reduce transportation costs, improve delivery, and provide online tracking and tracing of shipments. To purchase nonproduction supplies online, the company built Dow e-mart, an Ariba-based system, to buy $50 million worth of safety equipment, office supplies, and other indirect products from 100 sources selling 100,000 items.

Dow is involved in several specialty marketplaces. It buys lab supplies under an arrangement with SciQuest.com. It disposes of surplus business equipment under an agreement with ZoneTrader.com. It bids for everything from long-distance telephone service to marine transportation through a deal with auction site FreeMarkets. It is also currently evaluating marketplaces to buy transport, customs clearance, and logistics services.

The company also set up an extranet called MyAccount@Dow that provides registered customers with access to transactional functions and customer-specific information, such as order status, account history, repeat orders, and payment data. MyAccount has helped customers move from mail, phone, and fax orders to e-purchasing. The plan is to allow customers to place raw material orders directly from their ERP systems to Dow's ERP system over the extranet. It has also reduced Dow's cost of maintaining large archival files and mailing technical data to customers. To extend the site's use globally, Dow is piloting the use of double-byte languages, including Chinese and Japanese.

Eastman Chemicals

Eastman Chemicals has an e-supply chain strategy that includes three aspects: intranet within companies, online communities with customers, and open Internet logistics sites. Eastman disseminates real-time monthly sales forecasts over its intranet, giving users worldwide a clear picture of product demand. It also launched an online customer center to sell products, expecting that about 20% of its revenues will come through this center by the end of 2000. At the same time, Eastman has initiated ShipChem.com to bring together chemical manufacturers, distributors, carriers, and 3PLs. ShipChem has the ability to arrange orders automatically through registered carriers when customers enter orders. It has also started a pilot e-commerce program for its Asian market. Eastman is also working with e-chemicals Inc., a site that started as a catalog for chemicals and moved to more comprehensive services.

Emerging Trading Exchanges in the Chemicals Industry

Envera.com is a venture intended to be a hub for chemical Internet commerce, connecting buyers and sellers to all services involved in a chemical sale. The intention is to be a state-of-the-art clearinghouse with an in-depth menu of services. There are two intended markets: supply chain members within the network and third-party service organizations. The idea is to use the site without changing long-standing supply chain relationships. Once a buyer and a seller agree on a price, for example, they can go to Envera to find a company to deliver the goods. The site bills itself as a model for e-business-for-business (eB4B), through which trading partners can leverage their existing relationships in a neutral trading environment.

Most chemical companies have a large amount of interdivisional sales and sales to small customers. Benefits could accrue in both areas from integration into this type of clearinghouse. One member company told us they look for better decisions to result, "particularly on inventory management and movement. There will be a one-time reduction in working capital and less overall variation in stock levels." Borden Chemical, Occidental Chemical, Rohm and Haas, Sunoco Chemical, Ethyl Corp., and Lyondell-Equistar are early members. Companies participating in the clearinghouse do own the input data.

Most of the exchange progress has been in attracting corporate investors and potential users. Actual transactions, however, remain small. Most companies interviewed told us they see expanded use of the sites mushrooming in the industry for B2B purposes, but most said more work needs to be done on the routings and translation of data that have to move to standards that are not now present. One interviewee indicated she sees a long-term integration process that will take out many of the duplications in processing, speed up data flows, and cut errors—all problems plaguing the industry. Others said there is a need for the exchanges to get more efficient and that they see a shakeout in the industry as the better sites prevail over those that disappear.

Chemical users don't just need help with better pricing. They need to be guided through the maze of safety and environmental regulations, the handling of transportation, and delivery under virtual fail-safe conditions. Presently, more than fifty chemical-oriented marketplaces are either planned or operating on the Internet. The survivors will find their niche solving some of the long-standing problems in the industry as well as offering an e-commerce network for multiple players.

Department of Defense: A Special Insight
At the October 1999 meeting of the Association of the United States Army (AUSA), Army Chief of Staff Gen. Eric Shineski promulgated his vision for the 21st-century army. As he addressed requirements for deployment and responsiveness, he introduced some interesting objectives: to have a combat brigade deployed anywhere in the world in 96 hours, a division on the ground in 120 hours, and five divisions in 30 days. Meeting these goals will require a major transformation in military logistics, within the army and across the

Department of Defense (DoD) and sister services. This transformation is well under way and as we write this book is moving from the planning to the execution stage. As we look at what has been accomplished and what is yet to be done, we see a textbook example of how to transition from a current state into an advanced and much more effective logistics and supply chain environment.

Prodded by Congress to modernize and forced to meet specific deadlines by legislature, all the military services have analyzed their current conditions, and each has come up with a plan for improvement. Among the determinations made by all of the services is that they will "reduce their logistics footprint and replenishment demand." Footprint refers to the size, area, composition, capabilities, and stocks of the logistical support structure within a theater of operations. That means they want to cut the amount of stores held for operations to what is really needed. The idea is to invest in a systems approach to the weapons and equipment being designed and revolutionize the manner in which they are transported and used to sustain people and material.

Make no mistake, the services plan to satisfy the needs of their troops. There can be no diminishment in that aspect. Just as a commercial business cannot lower customer satisfaction and stay in business, so the military must support and sustain its customer—the battle-ready soldier. At the same time, they recognize that any extra materials and supplies, just as in the commercial world, take time, space, cost, and management. And in this industry, when the conflict is over, what remains has to be returned for storage or other use. Among the future considerations, a priority will be placed on "smaller, lighter, more lethal yet more reliable, fuel efficient and more survivable options when deciding on equipment design." (The quotations come from various government documents citing the progress being made by the military and DoD.) Another priority will be placed on rapid deployment and return of just the right amount of supplies, with the supplier taking some of the responsibility for inventory and logistics.

Another move was prompted as Congress has come to realize the critical value of visible logistics—being able to see just what is in stock—and wants to see that element and other best commercial practices reflected in future initiatives. As DoD analyzed itself and became determined to meet the demands made by Congress, while using best commercial practices wherever applicable, some interesting findings developed, most of which apply to industry in general. Use of the Internet requires owners to understand and differentiate their true requirements. It also causes all functional requirements to be reexamined. A major finding from such a review is that most current requirements are bound by the use of old technology and software. The result is a greatly suboptimized systems design, run by people who are reluctant to change, particularly if they were involved in the old designs. To overcome such resistance and make the most of the change process, it definitely helps to find well-positioned visionaries and make them the requirements champions. These champions find the greatest risk is not application development. It's the underlying infrastructure integration. One example was finding that traditional army programmers will have to be replaced by more varied technical staff, including designers, data engineers, systems administrators, and integrators (source: team notes from the 1999 Dayton workshop on DoD modernization effort).

To realize what's being considered for change, let's look at the sheer size and amount of transactions handled by the organization being reviewed. The DoD is a unique organization representing some of the largest logistics numbers in the world. It has, for example, 1.1 million logistics personnel. Logistics support equals 60% of weapon system life cycle costs, which are becoming extremely long and large, for old but valuable weapons. Twenty-five percent of that logistics cost is maintenance; including field maintenance, the cost is $80 billion or $200 million per day. Maintenance inventory is valued at over $63 billion. The current number of items managed by DoD stands at 4.9 million. The number of shipments from the Defense Logistics Agency (DLA) for fiscal 1999 was 11.5 million. How is it all handled? DoD operates with a network including more than 1,000 legacy information systems. How would you like to try and modernize that business?

The numbers are all staggering, as DoD tries to cope with keeping up with all the old stuff that's in good condition, while making necessary transitions to new weapons systems. For the old stuff, repair parts order lead time is 20 to 25 days, and because they keep so many parts stored, turnover on reparable parts inventory is less than 0.5 per year. Weapon systems have long lifetimes. Some aircraft, like the B-52, have an extended life of 94 years. In the military world, a problem of suboptimization occurs from the perceived need for individuality as various services maintain similar equipment in their way. The result is higher prices, heroic expediting (or what the military calls "drive-by fielding") across the supply chain—and lots of scrounging. The informal infrastructure has learned how to move what is needed to the point of need.

Best Commercial Plus Best Existing Practices Yields Big Results

In a change away from its traditional approach to sourcing and logistics, the DoD is trying to adopt those commercial best practices that will yield improved results. High on its list of priorities, the DoD is looking to form external alliances to meet its needs, just as major industry companies seek valuable external resources. That includes relying on some channel masters, such as Boeing or Lockheed-Martin for aircraft or General Dynamics and Newport News Shipbuilders for ships. Some of these channel masters are inextricably linked to DoD. For example, General Dynamic's Electric Boat division cannot define its e-business strategy without first having an understanding of what DoD is defining as its. Two themes impact this latter strategy: how to use new models from business transformation to have a significant impact on supply chain and logistics within the military, and how to use the Internet to improve operations.

Among the most important of its new strategies is Vision 2010. This vision is central to how to leverage technology, e-commerce, and use of the Internet. One of the major factors that has to be considered as they pursue their new strategies is that the size of the military is shrinking. In recent years, the armed forces have been reduced by over 600,000 persons. With fewer personnel to do the same job, there has to be a greater reliance on external resources, which means the suppliers have to pick up some of the slack. At the same time, some clear possibilities for improvement have developed. Using e-commerce techniques to create a glass pipeline showing accurate levels and positions of inventories can help the various services to take advantage of the total inventory instead of having everything they need in their own stores.

To summarize the factors driving change in the military and DoD and some expected results, we'd include the following:

- Joint Vision 2010—and the "Army after Next"—goal of "future logistics" will ensure that combat forces have the right equipment, on hand, at the right time. Advanced information systems and rapid transportation are keys to this success.

- Extended weapon system life cycles

- Logistics workforce reductions—40% funds reduction from 1989 to 1996, 42% civilian staff reduction from 1989 to 2003, and 36% military staff reduction from 1989 to 1996

- Pressure from Congress for further improvement and adoption of industry best practices

- Need to prepare for the "digital battlefield"

One effect of the changes has been that acquisition and logistics support have become one integrated process, sharing a pool of life cycle data. A second is the need to share information across boundaries between departments, services, government, industry, and a host of new alliance partners—about how data are managed throughout the life of equipment. An affecting factor is continuous acquisition and life cycle support (CALS) being applied by all services.

As the DoD moves from planning to action, these factors describe the primary target areas for what has now become the reengineering and management focus:

- Optimize cycle times—acquisition, supply, maintenance, transportation, and distribution

- Manage the total life cycle through integration of acquisition and logistics processes

- Meet deployment and sustainment requirements across the full spectrum of military operations

- Guarantee total asset visibility through fully integrated, secure information systems

- Meet or exceed DoD logistics metrics and cost reduction goals

The future U.S. Military Vision—Joint Vision 2010—means the military adapts to changes from protracted global conflicts with massed armies and massed logistics to localized skirmishes, information dominance, precision strikes, and focused logistics. The logistics requirements take on new meaning in terms of speed and agility. The expectations include deployment in 24 hours, sustainment in 7 days, reduced in-theater footprints to enhance mobility, and reduced overhead and support structures. One specific target is to be able to deliver bombs on target in 72 hours.

From the military perspective, the ultimate consumer is the war fighter. Having those one million–plus consumers as prepared as possible and supported is the primary objective. The second objective is maintenance of all of the equipment needed for defense support. That includes how to manufacture the piece in the first place and how to remanufacture it after use. To support war fighter needs for mobilization and sustainment, the DoD is transforming its mass logistics system to a highly agile, reliable system that delivers "logistics on demand," replacing a multiple-echelon infrastructure with rapid, affordable transportation and information. A typical question under the new scenario is, Do I have control of the replenishment system when the consumer is in battle or the replenishment officer is online looking for supply?

Four Stages to the Transformation

According to former Deputy Undersecretary of Defense Roger W. Kallock, the logistics transformation will result in real-time awareness and come in four stages:

1. By fiscal year 2001, the DoD will optimize logistics processes to minimize customer (the war fighter) wait time using variance-based metrics.

2. By fiscal year 2002, customer confidence will be secured in a simplified priority system with a time definite delivery schedule.

3. By fiscal year 2004, there will be total asset visibility through use of AIT, shared data environment, and other applications.

4. By fiscal year 2004, they will have real-time, actionable, Web-based logistics information system in use.

Logistics in the 21st century to the Department of Defense will mean:

- a lean infrastructure and workforce,
- optimized business practices based on world-class commercial operations,
- better utilization of commercial logistics providers,
- performance based on satisfying customer requirements at the point of need,
- large investments in infrastructure replaced by agility and rapid transportation
- significantly reduced cycle times to affect support,
- sustainment costs are minimized while high readiness is maintained, and
- highly integrated information systems that both control and provide visibility.

Part of the new vision is the Global Transportation Network (GTN), an operational system with more than 5,600 unclassified and 8,000 classified users delivering in-transit visibility of DoD-owned or -controlled assets and collecting information on moving DoD cargo from the top DoD commercial carriers through commercial EDI. GTN processes at least 1.8 million transactions of information a day about shipments of DoD material.

Under the new effort, vendors such as PYA Monarch for food and Merck for pharmaceuticals have prime positions to help in the integration effort. To save money in transportation costs, DoD is working on a centralized system called Transcon, which is much like the Schneider/3M consortium arrangement (described later). It could include putting dispatchers within the military operations to oversee transportation.

Another example of how the plan is progressing is provided by the army's Modernization through Spares (MTS) program. MTS is one part of the army's determination to reduce the life-cycle cost of existing systems. It means they will no longer buy spare parts based on outdated specifications and technical data packages. Rather, they will use performance specifications to take advantage of newer designs and technologies. One example increased the track life of the M1 Abrams tank from 1,200 miles to about 2,000. Additional improvements could raise that number to 5,000 miles. The new performance specifications include the track, road wheels, sprockets, hubs, rollers, and idlers as a system.

The army is also using modeling and simulation to reduce acquisition costs, total ownership costs, and time to operating capability. They capitalize on industry experience in using these techniques to conduct design and engineering, testing, and manufacturing during development of a new system. Another move is very similar to what is happening in industry as manufacturers assume a position on vendor-managed inventory. The army is discussing an arrangement with Boeing and Lockheed Martin to implement a prime vendor support management pilot for the Apache helicopter. This arrangement would transfer responsibility for complete support to a single accountable corporate entity. It would eliminate the need for government personnel and facilities to manage and store spare parts. Similar initiatives include self-propelled howitzers and field artillery ammunition support vehicles.

Common themes in the effort are a guideline for industry. They show the same type of requirements that an industry faces. These needs are a primer for those who want to overhaul their logistics and supply chain systems. These themes are as follows:

- There is a clear need for a visible champion, who can be instrumental in changing the cultural barriers.

- Creation and evaluation of the vision and deciding between core and noncore competencies has to be a deliberate, risk-evaluating process and requires the highest leadership in decision making.

- Those who would enable the changes require some capital commitment up front and must be able to sell their concepts.

- Metrics are critical to success. You become what you measure and change organizational behavior based on what the measures prove.

- Information becomes the heart of logistics improvement. It may never be a seamless pipeline of supply, but the information system will make it seem that way.

- Asset visibility makes it work, and both customers and suppliers need that access. It's critical to building confidence in the new system.

- You need to form strategic partnerships with best-in-class providers with mutual trust as the binding ingredient.

- Participants need to see and use an executable plan.

Fulfillment: Several Developing Models

Moving from the government sector to the private sector, there has been no greater story that documents the need for a supporting logistics infrastructure—if supply chain networks are going to be successful—than what happened during the holiday season of 1999.

Many new and traditional firms decided to offer their products over the Internet during this important buying period. Without a solid understanding of what might transpire, companies large and small told the Web buyers they could get products sent to the home after a click of the mouse. Many offered such response in 72 hours or less. Unfortunately, few were prepared for what happened.

In many cases, the companies received a larger than expected response, often several times what was planned. That response showed the growing magnitude of Internet use and how those sites offering toys were particularly hard pressed to react. As much as 40% of all sales for this category can be received during the holiday season, and Internet buying is apparently going to be a big part of the ordering process. As Web sites went live and the orders came in, most of these retailers were not able to respond adequately. Indeed, we heard one story where a major retailer was sending clerks scurrying up and down aisles of the its stores, trying to pick and aggregate toys to fulfill orders. The packages were sent to the back of the distribution center for packaging and transfer to a carrier, for home delivery. The result was chaos.

The first lesson learned was to promise a realistic time frame for delivery of cyber orders. This is a lesson for all business. In the new Internet age, the caveat should be very simple: make realistic promises. That translates to telling the customer when you can make a delivery and then keeping the promise. Most firms try to promise unrealistic time frames as a feature for getting the order, and nothing irritates the buyer more than being disappointed. Often, the time frame can be longer than that being suggested and still be in plenty of time to meet the buyer's need.

The second lesson is to understand the cost of packaging and delivery. In the early phases of the Web explosion, when new retailers and supply chain intermediaries were showing up on the Web on a daily basis, there was little pressure to make a profit. The aim was simply to gain consumers, hooked on the Web site, so future profits could be made on advertising and eventual volume gains. Our research showed clearly that most of the Internet retailers greatly underestimated or understated the cost of packaging and delivery. Many companies lost money on every delivery. In the second wave of Internet use, there is a greater demand to make a profit. That will require the Web retailer to have a system that includes packaging and delivery sources that are geared to the small individual package size and getting the "last mile" of the delivery (to the home) done efficiently.

This latter point is introducing an entirely new industry, which we term e-fulfillment. Many firms, particularly third-party logistics providers, have already been active in this field. But recent events have led to a proliferation of firms establishing subsidiary units focused on this industry or entirely new companies basing their future on being an integral part of solving the last mile requirement, for both business customers and end consumers. Some of these ventures use extensions of current business models, while others are formed around entirely new business concepts. We'll take a look at some of the leaders in this new industry as we point out how they are playing a key role in resolving the issue of fulfillment for the new e-business models.

Federal Express

Always on the front edge of new business applications, Federal Express has introduced its version of e-supply chain services. Senior Vice President of Worldwide eSolutions Tom Schmitt calls it the company's "e-business manifesto" and says it has affected over 70% of the company's business, as the firm has become "a product of e-business." The program was initially designed to save costs, but it became a tool to integrate Fed Ex services into its customers' processes. It has advanced into a process that becomes electronically imbedded in the relationship.

In the early effort, a business migration path was necessitated for the company, by virtue of an increasing number of customers (large and small) asking for help across new channels to market. That means the firm had to determine how to utilize existing capabilities and open capacities to assist firms in both physical and cyber channels of response. As an example, Fed Ex cites the e-business relationship with garden.com, a Web seller of 20,000 garden supply items, using seventy suppliers. This firm's connectivity spans an end-to-end supply chain system, from the seventy sources through the Internet retailer and its Web store, to its business customers and end consumers. Fed Ex handles the outbound portion of the deliveries for both customers and consumers, with 40% going direct to homes. Using existing equipment and facilities, the shipper handles both sectors effectively.

The firms' concept is to work from existing capabilities while bringing a new dimension to benefits for customers using its Internet solutions. The underlying premises are quite basic: Fed Ex works on the idea that collaboration can lead to savings through increasing profits on new business, lower operating costs, and reducing working capital and fixed asset investments.

By applying its services through a global e-solutions team, to find current routings with open capacity, that coincide with the business customer's needs on an inbound or outbound basis, Fed Ex can reduce freight costs. It uses a three-dimension system with best-of-breed software, some of which was supplied by i2 Technologies. It started with the premise that some companies have no internal connectivity and so need help with organization, metrics, and details on applications and integration.

Going further, the team looks at reducing the cycle times for delivery and raising customer satisfaction through quicker and more accurate deliveries.

New revenues could then be generated that result in higher sales for both the customer and Fed Ex. For example, if the typical 26 days from order to delivery becomes a targeted metric, the goal will be to reduce it to 10 days. In a complementary effort, eliminating the need to warehouse the products (by merging orders in transit or accumulating parts in the Fed Ex hubs) cuts the investment in those assets. And using Fed Ex's equipment cuts the need for buying, maintaining, and replacing trucks and trailers.

Since the concepts involved in what is a Web-based system are so new, Fed Ex helps its customers analyze the advantages through a "value measurement" process. Current state conditions are analyzed and the costs determined. These data are compared against industry benchmarking standards (from the Supply Chain Council's database and other recognized industry sources) and costs from similar businesses. Calculating the difference results in a report of the potential for improvement or a "net value proposition." Fed Ex's is a three-tier approach that goes from an initial assessment, through a situation-consulting phase, and into a solution implementation effort.

Logistix

Some firms use existing assets to take advantage of open capacity, like Fed Ex. Others use the assets of other companies and their open capacity to build a new e-business proposition. Customized Transportation, Inc. (CTI), recently changed its name to Logistix, to better represent what that company is doing. This business unit is a wholly owned subsidiary of TNT Post Groep that is essentially a lead logistics service provider using external resources for its delivery needs. Revenues are split evenly between transportation and value-added packaging and warehousing. For this unit, the "intersection of tactical business performance and use of the Web is a major subject the company intends to address," according to Executive Vice President Mark Morrison. He gave us an example.

A new marketplace called greentogo.com recently engaged Logistix as its e-fulfillment partner. This is a small vertical company in the "green" industry that matched growers and producers of green products with users—landscape architects, contractors, retailers, and large construction projects. More than 100 growers of everything from palm trees to shrubs and bushes post their inventories on the greentogo.com Web site. Future plans include listing hard goods, hand tools, and other products used by the customers. Buyers go to the site to order what they need, typically for large construction jobs or retail outlet beautification.

As the logistics provider to the site, Logistix balances orders and transportation needs and fulfills orders. Using software supplied by i2 Technologies, it reports back on shipments and delivery performance, basically managing the flow of information. Because of the extent of the deliveries and consistent with the theory that e-fulfillment is a system of virtual response, Logistix subcontracts the actual deliveries to about 150 carriers, as the firm has no assets tied up in trucks. A portion of its business is in south Florida, for example, where it uses 20 to 30 carriers with special flatbed equipment typical of that area of the country. Through its e-commerce system, the firm has complete visibility into these subcontract carriers, each of which is prequalified to be in the network.

USF Worldwide Logistics

One leader who sees a definite difference between the B2B and B2C channels and the need for different systems of response is Douglas Christensen, president and CEO of USF Worldwide Logistics. For him, after a lot of transition, e-business will be just another distribution channel with lots of logisticians involved, using the Internet for more efficient processing through two different supply chains. The biggest factor of importance in both channels will be that electronic connections have to be real time, because the electronic customers are pushing for quick response. A particular feature of his firm's Internet experience occurred when they decided to make a niche play and be a factor in quick, online returns.

The company formed an organization dubbed Ireturnit.com. The idea is basic to the new electronic environment. Buyers make purchases over the Web, and if they want to return the product (which a significant percentage do), they can take it to designated locations—for instance, the local 7-Eleven or White Hen Pantry store. There will be an instant return booth or kiosk waiting, where the buyer can deposit the item and get an instant credit. USF Logistics picks up the item and returns it to the manufacturer or diverts it to a usable location. The company is becoming the return arm for such firms as Safeway, Eckherd, and Walgreen's.

On the outbound side, the firm will make home deliveries for business customers, segregating the orders by ZIP code, and using two-person vans as the delivery vehicle. The idea in both cases is to use a nonasset infrastructure and become management agents. Its network of carriers is 1m700 strong with what USF claims are the best-of-breed cartage firms, van lines, and Internet delivery agents. In that sense, the infrastructure is really based on sales and marketing—using existing assets that belong to other companies for other applications. USF then becomes the logistics core for a special supply chain network, with an e-business model that works through a structured set of business alliances. Eventually the plan includes thirty global sites as the strategy is rolled out around the world.

Tibbett & Britten Group
Tibbet & Britten Group (TBG) is a multinational 3PL specializing in logistics for manufacturers and retailers of consumer goods, and it is expanding its services as a result of the impact of the Internet.

According to Mike Sprague, president of the Americas division, the company was already providing distribution for compact discs in Europe through a joint venture with Startle, a leading music distributor, called Track One Logistics. The original service was for "canned" music delivered to supermarkets and mass retail stores, as well as 56,000 regular CD titles delivered to independent retailers. However, the partnership was extended in 2000 to provide links to a catalog of more than 300,000 titles and direct to consumer fulfillment of CDs, for the Web sites of such established brick-and-mortar retailers as Virgin Megastore and Tesco.

In turn, TBG has leveraged this fulfillment experience into an capability to provide a full-line e-commerce service through TBG-led partnerships, which provide a one-stop service, from Web page design and hosting, through order management and customer relations (CRM) software, to fulfillment, payment, and delivery. A recent example of this is the B2B package created for lens-online, a fulfillment service for spectacle lenses now ordered and tracked over the Internet by optometrists throughout Europe.

In North America, another subsidiary, Connect Logistics, is the exclusive distributor of liquor, wine, and imported beer on behalf of the Alberta government to independent stores throughout that western Canadian province. Connect has established a B2B Web site for licensed retailers that enables them to browse inventory and place and track orders, in large part replacing the previous paper- and phone-based ordering systems. Within six months of its introduction, 55% of the entire business was being conducted via the Web site. This experience is being used as a template for other retail-distribut or applications.

Some leaders have approach e-fulfillment as a new business challenge, making their mark through the use of the World Wide Web.

Fingerhut

Fingerhut is an example of a company that made use of its existing infrastructure and strength to capitalize on the growth of Internet based business. In 1999, a Fingerhut customer typically ordered by mail 40% of the time. There was little to no interaction between the buyer and the fulfillment organization, and the product was typically shipped within 4 days via the U.S. Postal Service (USPS). Now it's a real-time game.

Today's customer, according to spokesperson Mike Murray, wants things quicker. He said expectations have gone from 10 days to 7 days and the possibility is to go to 5 days from order to delivery, unless the customer wants to pay for express delivery. With faster access to information coming from a transition from EDI to e-commerce, the possibility to make even further break through improvements could be feasible.

As the company evolves into this new environment, they have developed what looks like an 85/15 split between B2C, a traditional strength, and B2B business, with an information focus and attention given solely to e-fulfillment. To conduct business in the latter sector, they established Fingerhut Business Services as a separate business unit. Customers include Wal-Mart and Pier 1. In either case, the company follows an emerging model. It does no shipping with its own assets. Fingerhut lays out the possible delivery scenarios that could include ground delivery in anything from 2 days to a week or more. It could also include some express deliveries or a comingling of packages from multiple companies. All packages in a load pass through a "sortation center" for ZIP code segregation, to determine which "chute" it goes down. A Dallas ZIP code will divert the packages to the Dallas truck going to a Dallas-based hub. At that location, a designated carrier, such as USPS, will sort the packages and make the actual business or home delivery.

Modus Media International

Another firm that has capitalized on the new business environment to establish a lucrative e-business model with impressive results is Modus Media International (MMI). This firm is in transition from being a division of printing giant R. R. Donnelley, with a 90% physical and 10% cyber distribution methodology, to being an independent resource for business customers seeking e-fulfillment solutions. When its transformation is complete, the ratio could flip-flop, as it carves out a strong position in fulfilling cyber-based orders. MMI's is a lesson in building an e-business model to match the needs of a changing market.

President and CEO Terry Leahy believes the secret to being successful with e-fulfillment is to combine logistics, supply chain, and e-commerce capabilities at the bill of materials level. "If you don't have skills there, you will fail," he states. His view of the future includes an "integrated supply chain, in which the supply signal is connected directly to the demand signal, as received from the consumer." At the time of our discussion, he saw such integrated supply chains as being less than 5% of the potential.

The MMI model is to globally solve any supply chain management issue with a fulfillment engine that is reliable, flexible, and cost-efficient. It uses an outsourced model, in which the branded company has control of the product while others manage the delivery infrastructure. Leahy says the fulfillment engine is a system that takes the order directly, is reverent to the brand, handles a complete transaction anywhere in the world, including management of receivables and government requirements, and is integrated to the branded company's systems.

Beginning in the high-technology sector, MMI has blazed a trail with its model. In 1999, the firm dealt with on billion part number transactions for their high-tech customers, handling order sizes from 1 to 1,000. Leahy likens the problem to magazine fulfillment, which has an existing infrastructure, but with the coming of the Internet has to integrate that infrastructure into an e-business model. Creating the connection points with customers and dealing with changing expectations in a dynamic business environment are among the firm's biggest concerns. Therein lies the need for flexibility in the e-business model. One example includes the need to receive batch orders via an EDI system from a major business customer and transfer the data to the MMI Web-based system, without a glitch.

In an online demonstration, we saw orders coming to the Palm Web site—Palm Computing Online Store. There we scanned the material and decided to purchase a hand-held device, the Palm VII. It was a typical procedure, but when we got to entering the order, the address had changed on the page we were viewing. The header now read http://palmorder.modusmedia.com. That meant we were into the MMI system for fulfillment.

MMI's is a leading format, through which the Web orders are transferred automatically to the MMI fulfillment center, where the inventory of hand-held and other branded products reside, along with the instructions, packaging, labels, and so forth. MMI takes the orders, batched or single, and does all the packaging and delivery. That could be in units of one or dozens. It uses about 15 shippers, with USPS, UPS, Fed Ex, and Emery among the primary firms; in Europe, it's the local post office and DHL, in addition to UPS and Fed Ex, that make the final delivery. To seal the point, before we were finished with the demonstration, we went to the Sun Microsystem Web site, and sure enough, when we placed an order, the site changed to http://sun.modus media.com.

Supporting Software as a Key Technology Ingredient

As companies discover the importance of e-fulfillment and make moves to shore up their logistics infrastructure to cover this element of supply chain, they find another opportunity. They begin to realize that doing a better job of fulfillment offers a chance to aggregate their shipments with other firms to optimize the use of transportation assets. What they need is software that displays the shipment needs of a group of firms in a similar geographic sector and the pickups and deliveries that have to occur between these firms and their suppliers and customers.

General Mills and Nistevo offer a great example of what can be done in this area, as the two firms work together to integrate e-business applications with normal business processes and practices. One concept showing great promise occurred as the firm looked at better asset utilization to meet its transportation needs. General Mills has been working on a number of high-tech initiatives, but none looks more promising than the one worked out with Nistevo.com and a cadre of other supply chain partners. "Our transportation people are now the dot.com folks at General Mills," says Kevin Schoen, director of strategic alliances for the Minneapolis-based food company (Inbound Logistics, July 2000). "We've formed an alliance with eleven other companies to use Nistevo.com, which enables strategic procurement and management of strategic services."

The objective is to take advantage of the open space on trucks moving between the alliance partner sites and delivery points, creating benefits for the carriers and customers in the process. At the time of our discussion, the partners included ConAgra Inc., Fort James Paper, Graphics Packaging, Hormel Foods, International Multifoods, Ivex Packaging, Land O'Lakes, McCormick and Company, Nabisco Inc., Nestlé USA, and Pillsbury, in addition to General Mills. This consortium will use Nistevo's Web-based software solutions to communicate with carriers and between companies to manage documents and tender freight.

General Mills and its alliance partners have piloted the model, beginning with manually developed tours. Inbound Logistics reports on one such experiment with one of General Mill's new partners:

> *A driver may pick up a load of paper in Chicago and haul it to Cedar Rapids for Fort James, take a load of interplant freight back to Pennsylvania, pick up a load for a General Mills customer in Maine, deadhead to the Fort James paper plant 60 miles away, pick up a load of paper and deliver it to Buffalo, reload the truck with cereal at the General Mills plant in Buffalo and return to Chicago. Such a loop slashes deadhead mileage to less than 5%—a fraction of the 15% to 20% national average.*

Nistevo President and CEO Kevin Lynch says the key element is to use the Internet not only for faster communication but also as an effective way to change a business model. In the case cited, the use moved an existing system that was mildly effective to a collaborative system and shared information from common databases. The result will be a win-win for the participants. The basic premise behind his firm's software is that there are always "packets" coming into some form of data exchange looking for delivery. Currently, solutions are available, but the processing is not optimal. Nistevo provides a quick search mechanism that results in better asset utilization, lower total costs, and shorter cycle times. By matching real-time data on demand and supply, and providing what Lynch terms "time-forward visibility," a new dimension is brought to supply chain efficiency.

Consumer Products Firms: Sorting Out the Options

For a decade or longer, the consumer products industry has been trying to optimize supply chain costs and efficiencies. Working particularly with the grocery sector and other retail markets, many large consumer products firms have participated in multiple focus groups, share groups, and other partnering efforts to find the savings heralded by a landmark Efficient Consumer Response (ECR) study that predicted $30 billion of potential savings. Now, after much effort and the finding of some of that potential, the effort seems to have stagnated except for a few focused team efforts involving specific suppliers and retailers. Part of this ongoing effort is to reduce the stockpiles of inventory and safety stock that exists in most consumer products supply chains.

Procter & Gamble

One of the leading companies is this effort is Procter & Gamble, the Cincinnati, Ohio–based consumer goods giant. Ralph Drayer, a vice president for P & G, says the company first employed a version of VMI with Schnucks Markets, a regional grocer in St. Louis, to find enhancement opportunities. This effort was extended later to Kmart Corp. and then to Wal-Mart Stores. "We started with soap products and then added diapers," Drayer said. "Today, over 40% of our products are sold via VMI" (Cooke 1998).

In our interview, Drayer said that e-commerce will have a significant impact on further advancements on supply chain, particularly because of its ability to speed the decision process through better information handling. Intent on handling both of its targeted markets, P & G is developing an e-business strategy for both B2B and B2C. In an interesting twist with their effort, the focus is on process step effectiveness rather than cutting cycle time. This thinking is based on relations with their "trade customers," and it gives them an opportunity to leverage off their ECR efforts, in which P & G took an early lead.

At the heart of the P & G B2B effort is collaborative planning, forecasting, and replenishment (CPFR®), another area where the company took a lead. This effort is concentrated on pilot work with twelve key customers, a central feature being Web-based order management. P & G is actively using point-of-sale (POS) data and bringing supply and demand information into one process. The concept is to have one planning method, with weekly changes made to the demand forecast. Now, the company has a 12-week window it calls "visibility forward." With the planned system, staff have set up pilot tests using their CPFR® experience, and they have seen a 20% improvement in forecast accuracy. The biggest values, according to Drayer, are understanding what the demand is and what is the result of the response.

In the B2C sector, P & G's Connect.com is its new portal, intended to bring new products and brand management techniques to consumers. This portal reflects a deliberate strategy called "Organization 2005," with intentions to move from geographic profit centers to seven global business unit centers. These units will have local market development efforts, with ideas tailored to specific consumer groups. The firm has always had a strong tie with the UCCNet effort, and that is the foundation for its information use in the new format. Showing the extent of the company's scale and influence, P & G is also a board member in the Transora consortium trading exchange effort (discussed later).

To measure success, the company uses a model called the "perfect order." On-time, complete, and accurate orders, with no returns and perfect invoices, are examples of the parameters of the model. The idea is to gain process reliability—of the manufacturing process and supply chain processing. A tangible result has been the better handling of promotions with selected retail customers, where the firm jointly worked on using the benefits of joint improvement efforts to attain more perfect orders and to respond more effectively to the results of promotions.

Nestlé USA

Nestlé USA has approached e-business through a number of channels. On the one hand, it is partnering with other major consumer goods suppliers to form a huge online consortium trading exchange called Transora.com. Among the forty participants are Procter & Gamble, H. J. Heinz, Best Foods, Unilever, and Kraft Foods. At the same time, it announced the formation of an electronic trading exchange in the European food sector. Known as CPGMarket.com, this venture was begun in April 2000 with cooperation between Nestlé of Switzerland and Danone of France. The marketplace, to be based on the mySAP.com e-business platform developed by SAP, also includes German manufacturer Henkel KgaA. The venture is intended to pool purchasing power and automate a myriad of accounting functions. On the other hand, the firm is launching NestléEZOrder, a Web site that lets small and midsize retailers order products online.

High Technology: Leading the Way

The high technology and financial services industries are generally thought to be the leaders in using e-business and having adopted sophisticated approaches to supply chain and logistics activities. Our research did not touch on financial services but did look at key companies in the high-technology sector: Cisco Systems, Sun Microsystems, Oracle, Intel, Hewlett-Packard, and Adaptec.

"I Saved a Billion Dollars" was the headline article on the cover of the November 2000 issue of eCompany Now. Referring to the savings that Oracle Corporation achieved through the use of e-business, it is a quote from Oracle's CEO, Larry Ellison. While our findings showed that the high-technology sector was the leader, these savings demonstrates three other things:

- The high-tech industry offers many innovative approaches that other industries can use as best practices.
- Many areas in the industry still exist where e-business and advanced supply chain management can have a tremendous impact.
- The lean supply chain and just-in-time inventory models have their drawbacks.

During the 2000 preholiday season, the high-tech industry had been beset with stories of production delays on the eagerly anticipated Sony Playstation II (Reuters 2000). Production delays halved the scheduled delivery to the United States of what was one of the most eagerly anticipated products for the 2000 Christmas holiday shopping season. This has opened a market opportunity to a competitor of Sony's Playstation, the Sega Dreamcast. According to CNET, Dreamcast sales soared 156% as retailers rushed to fill the gap in product for the holiday season. It wasn't just video games that suffered production delays due to poor forecasting and extended supply chains.

Palm and San Disk had also reported shortages of components that delayed production (*Wall Street Journal*, October 10, 2000). Prices of flash memory doubled as demand has outstripped supply. Carefully crafted negotiated prices skyrocketed as companies rushed to find alternative suppliers. Poor forecasting tied to unexpected demand led to production delays, unfilled orders, lowered margins, and the abilities of competitors to steal a march on companies. Supply chain and logistics are two key tools for competitive advantage in today's high-technology business environment.

An Industry in Transition

Much like the automobile industry, many elements of the high-technology sector are in a state of transition. Much of the computer industry, both hardware and software, are transforming themselves from a computer-centric model to a network-centric model. The semiconductor industry is moving more and more into the venue of communications processing. The most visible changes to most members of the CLM are in the computer industry, where companies are changing business models and new players emerge nearly daily.

Don't think that you can't learn from this industry sector because it is high-tech! For example, Intel now conducts more than $2 billion in business monthly over the Internet. Looking at Intel as a global manufacturer in a highly competitive and changing industry, and with complicated logistics and supply chain needs, allows us to see that it uses the Internet to improve current supply chain practices, gain more operational efficiencies, and open new channels to market. These are lessons that any industry can use.

The high-technology sector offers other lessons to include managing a complex global logistics and supply chain network. Adaptec, Inc., a manufacturer of computer peripherals based in Milpitas, California shows how a complex supply chain can be managed and how cycle times can be reduced. Adaptec is a company that offers a clear example of how to exploit an opportunity with the help of supply chain partners. This $700 million manufacturer makes sophisticated computer subsystems, such as input-output (I/O) boards, to transfer information flowing through a PC from the hard drive. Central to these boards are application-specific, integrated circuits that embed proprietary software on silicon chips. The company operates in a very competitive environment and is challenged by constant price pressures, rapid changes in the markets it supplies, and accelerating changes in the sophisticated components needed for its products.

Adaptec met these challenges through the creation of a virtual factory and an Internet-based communication system, in partnership with Taiwan Semiconductor Manufacturing Corp. (TSMC), which makes the silicon wafer containing the chips. Their arrangement takes advantage of supply chain optimization and Web capabilities as illustrated in E-Supply Chain: Using the Internet to Revolutionize Your Business (Bauer/Poirier, December 2000) Dolores Marciel, vice president of materials management, took an early step in the process when she began treating a select group of suppliers as partners. Using new computer software supplied by Extricity and the Internet, engineers from Adaptec and TSMC work together electronically to design and integrate new components through a combining of their e-commerce intranets. Before the process improvements, at each stage in the supply chain, information was entered manually, most into different computer systems. Adaptec was using an SAP's ERP system, while TSMC's system was largely homemade. Moving all the necessary information through the interenterprise system via the Internet became the obvious solution.

By connecting their computer-aided manufacturing and design systems, the two firms were able to dramatically speed up the data interchange and shrink typical cycle times. Orders and information now move over the Web with drawings attached. This linking of internal systems, using the Internet as the mode of connection, speeds the development process and provides the means to gain an advantage for Adaptec in its market. TSMC's manufacturing capability is made available direct to Adaptec product developers immediately, reducing the art-to-part cycle by as much as 50%. This improvement gives Adaptec a strategic advantage in development and introduction time and the cost of supplying its computer subsystems from a virtual factory across the Pacific.

Production of the Adaptec board starts at TSCM's plant in Hsin-Chu, Taiwan, moves to an assembler in Hong Kong or South Korea for chip packaging, and ends at an Adaptec plant in Singapore. There, the I/O boards are assembled and shipped—half to the United States and half to other countries. Other parts are shipped from Japan to the assembler or to Adaptec in California. With their new systems, the partners can track any of the inventory or semifinished product online, in real time.

Starting with a delivery cycle of 110 days, the organizations worked collaboratively to apply optimization techniques (internal best practices) to their connected supply chain to dramatically reduce that time. By seamlessly integrating information flows critical to the process steps, the linked firms were able to reduce the cycle to 55 days, with a reduction of work-in-process inventory of 50%. Their experience points the way to the next evolution in partnering within supply chains—an external connectivity made possible through the use of the Internet.

There are many more stories in this business sector, as high technology was not constrained by existing business models but designed strategies and e-business formats to match the needs of the industry. We strongly recommend that any firm interested in constructing an e-business model take a look at what's going on in this leading business sector.

CONCLUSION

Many industries are reaping the benefits of e-business. The high-tech sector, with its newer business models and fewer legacy practices and systems, is the leader. All industries stand to benefit from this revolution. Manufacturing companies—in particular, have an opportunity to streamline their supply chains, gaining full views of inventory from the acquisition of raw materials through outbound logistics and consumer purchase and use.

Other high-tech leaders such as HP, Cisco, and Dell, as well as others—will be covered in the next chapter, as they emulate some of the future e-business models. The leaders' use of trading exchanges, Internet connectivity, and partner integration portend future supply chains that marry physical goods flows with cyber-based electronic funds and information flows.

chapter 5

Future State Hypothesis:
A Compelling
Case for Understanding
and Application

T here is a basic requirement for establishing advanced supply chain and logistics excellence. A seamless, virtual network of companies must be established and linked so the constituents have integrated their supply chain communication systems. This linkage has to occur at a level where data transfer is online, costs and availability of products and services are known, and the value proposition for customers and consumers is understood by all participants and is compelling to the end customer. With such a network, interenterprise efficiency will peak and near optimized conditions will be achieved through the effective management of shared information. A further benefit is reduced or zero information lag. All participants will receive the information at the same time, in a rapid fashion.

Higher levels of performance will be introduced through Web-based buying and selling, lower transaction costs, interactive design and planning, and more effective inventory and transportation management. Asset utilization will reach new levels of efficiency as sharing of equipment and resources is carried out across the network. External benefits will accrue to all network members through the deliverance of just-in-time-of-need value-added information to suppliers, manufacturers, distributors, and customers. None of this will be truly effective, however, without the physical services needed to fulfill promises made by the network. Logistics across the value chain will be of paramount importance.

In a marketing sense, business will move from touch and feel to visualizing and imagining in a virtual world. Markets will be enlarged in most industries, by getting products to consumers faster, extending product life, and creating use for refurbished units. Market trials will be conducted quickly and inexpensively, guaranteeing a higher degree of success with new introductions. The growth of B2B commerce, in particular, will not be some type of cosmetic refurbishing but a complete transformation of the supply chain and logistics mechanisms that support order fulfillment, whether the order is received by mail, fax, telephone, or electronically. And clearly, logistics professionals and providers will benefit, as they become enabling agents of this transformation.

While the old ways of receiving input—phone, fax, mail, and so forth—will be with us for some time, there will be a massive swing to electronic communications of orders and order status. This will be dictated by the changing demographics as those growing up today enter the business world and transform their companies' way of doing business.

In this new business world, supply chain will move from one enterprise supplying the needs of many processes, to one holistic process that drives many enterprises. At the heart of this process, e-fulfillment centers will appear, as adjuncts to existing physical distribution centers or as stand-alone centers dedicated to satisfying electronic orders. These will feature capability to service multiple-type clients, handle assemble-to-order products, provide vendor-managed inventory capabilities, and offer a host of personalized delivery features.

In this chapter, we'll take a futuristic look into this new business world, as we describe a set of future state hypotheses. We'll also introduce a model describing how these hypotheses will impact supply chain, logistics, and e-business across a full network of response and replenishment.

How Will an Organization Fit into a Future Supply Chain?

Questions many of the companies we interviewed were trying to answer included "Where is my organization, where is it going, and where should it be in the future?" Figure 5.1 depicts the emerging supply chain environment and asks, "How will I fit into the future Internet-connected supply chain?" From the drawing, we can see that the supply chain arena is not getting less cluttered as firms strive for optimization. It's becoming more complex as new intermediaries are introduced into markets, exchanges and marketplaces proliferate, and new and existing players assume traditional roles. In the past, almost all players leveraged brick-and-mortar operations to play a role; in the future some will be pure infomediaries that never own, make, or even touch a physical good.

How Will I Fit Into the Future Internet-Connected Supply Chain?

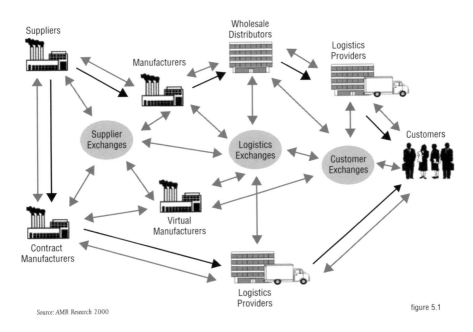

Source: AMR Research 2000

figure 5.1

To decide properly where a firm should be going, it's important to know where it is today. In a previous chapter, we introduced a four-stage transition through which we see most companies progressing on their way to a leadership position. Figure 5.2 brings a similar supply chain-focused perspective to this consideration as we draw our future state vision and try to help a company position itself in the emerging environment. A firm should study this chart and determine its current and projected position, as strategies are formulated for future progress. An approach for doing this as well as a further explanation of the chart is detailed in Chapter 7, "Developing an E-Supply Chain Strategy."

Supply Chain Evolution Model

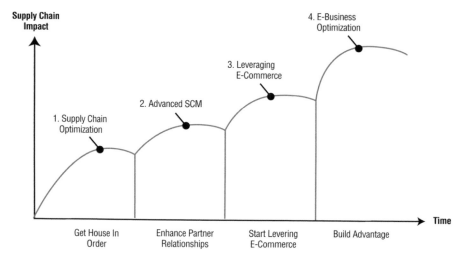

figure 5.2

In the first stage, characterized as "Get the house in order," the organization works at optimizing its supply chain operations, applying many of the e-business tools and methods discussed in Chapters 2 and 3 and elaborated on in Chapter 8. Using such traditional e-business tools as transportation and warehouse management systems, the firm seeks internal excellence across its supply chain. This is a crucial first step in the supply chain evolution, and most firms we studied had made some documented progress as a result of their efforts. Some were still trying to assimilate the most appropriate tools and reduce their costs to acceptable industry levels.

In the second stage, characterized as "Enhance partner relationships," the firm moves out of its internal shell and selects external partners with which it can move into the realm of advanced supply chain management. Now the firm works more collaboratively with suppliers, distributors, and other external partners. Rather than concentrate on leveraging sales volume for continued lower prices, the focus moves to applying advanced tools to jointly manage product development, production, distribution, and inventories. With this enhancement, the supply chain can offer customers and consumers access to reliable information on exactly what the system can deliver through its combined e-fulfillment capabilities. Our study found many firms experimenting in this stage or trying to capture what a few industry leaders had demonstrated was possible.

In the third stage, called "Start leveraging e-commerce," the network of supply chain partners begins to coalesce and truly exert the capabilities offered through the application of e-commerce. Here, the firms connect their computers and systems into an interenterprise network of communication. Web-based selling becomes a reality. Internet procurement flourishes. Trading exchanges define their potential and provide services where appropriate. And logistics exchanges mature as one of the enabling factors behind delivery of the goods and services in the new Web-connected business world. It was in this stage that we found most of the soon-to-be leaders in most industries. There is currently much experimentation and pilot tests proceeding, so the participants can perfect their future e-commerce enabled business models. Most companies surveyed as part of this book are not at this stage.

Finally, the fourth stage emerges as the "Build advantage" sector. Now the leading network constituents are hard at work to achieve e-business optimization, the ultimate manifestation of supply chain management, advanced logistics, and the application of e-commerce techniques. In this final stage, a conglomerate of trading partners or a virtual keiretsu is formed where all are bound in a common set of purposes relating to customer satisfaction, asset utilization, revenue growth, and profitability. This also allows virtual manufacturing and distribution business models to prosper, as links are established from beginning materials to consumption and handling of any and all returns. The collaborative supply chain scenario becomes very clear in this stage. We found very few firms at this level of progress, so the playing field is open in most industries for companies and their allies to secure the high ground and become the entrenched e-business masters.

We should be clear regarding an important aspect of our thesis before proceeding with this analysis. A firm can be anywhere along this continuum, and it may or may not chose or need to make a full progression. Small businesses may be satisfied to remain in stage 1, where they have their house in order, have some measure of supply chain skills and optimization, and can work with larger business customers or a niche group of consumers to make a comfortable living.

Contract manufacturers may be content with a stage 2 existence where they are more advanced and have the capability for online cooperation with their more sophisticated business customers. Manufacturers, suppliers, and distributors in a primary resource industry, providing feed stocks or basic ingredients to an industry, may also not feel the need for full network connectivity. Nonetheless, we see an inexorable movement toward the final stage and our future state hypotheses are formulated around the attainment of that level of progress.

WHAT WILL THE FUTURE SUPPLY CHAIN LOOK LIKE?

Today, the keys to success revolve around brand and scale for the large companies. For firms of all size, having a core competency is crucial. Design and engineering superiority always help as does having a unique product in demand. Some of those characteristics will still be important in 5 or 10 years, but they will be augmented by four new capabilities:

- supply chain and logistics excellence,
- IT expertise with a supporting infrastructure,
- interenterprise management process leadership across the value chain network, and
- formulation and use of value chain business processes.

We found these traits present in most of the leaders we researched. Firms such as Boeing, Dell Computer, Eastman Chemicals, Enron, Defense Logistics Agency, Kraft Foods, Nokia, Procter & Gamble, Solectron, Toyota, and Wal-Mart are hard at work refining their skills at the four new requirements. These firms are moving into the third and fourth stages of the evolution described in Figure 6.5. They have provided impetus to other supply chain partners, on whom they depend, to come together and forge new e-commerce connected networks. By working in a collaborative environment, these are the kinds of firms creating the fourth stage and highest level of progression.

They begin by combining best practices and sharing vital information on how to improve processes so supply chain and logistics excellence moves across the interenterprise actions needed for fulfillment. During this experience, they also share ideas and techniques on how to create the IT systems and infrastructure that they understand all of their partners need to have an effective e-business-oriented supply chain network. Throughout the effort, there is strong evidence of management process leadership, as they seek whatever external advice and help is needed to fashion a superior system of response to today's customers and consumers.

One best practice that is still needed is the use of value chain business processes. A value chain business process, or network business process, is a standardized business process that is used by all participants in the value chain. The process will have a business owner among the value chain participants, but it will be one process used across the value chain. An example of this would be a single remediation process, led by one participant that would cover the entire value chain. If a product was returned, a single return authorization and credit/debit mechanism would apply to all participants.

The transition to the future will vary by industry and between players in the industry, but it will follow a similar pattern if success is to be achieved. Our study showed plainly that there are leading and following industries, with variation across sectors of the world. The leaders simply move more quickly to embrace the techniques and processes inherent in the advanced efforts. The United States may lead in aerospace and defense, energy, and high technology, for example, because these industries in general have seized the initiative and are far along the progression described. Asia is not behind, however, in electronic components, consumer electronics, and communication equipment. Europe has closed the gap in books, entertainment, and travel services.

It's a mixed field of results and different competencies will determine leadership in different industries. Today an Amazon.com, for example, garners the headlines for introducing a new e-business model and competency into a traditional industry. Tomorrow it could be Borders or Barnes and Noble (traditional leaders with scale and brand) working in collaboration with Yahoo! or

AOL. New alliances being formed around the globe could erase gaps in a matter of months. In any event, the new leaders will have a dominant position in supply chain and logistics excellence, worked out with partners across their network. They will demonstrate superior capability in IT expertise and will have a supporting infrastructure that spans the network. In addition, they will continually demonstrate their leadership in managerial processing.

INTERNET USE: AN ENABLING FACTOR

As use of the Internet becomes more of a factor in the supporting infrastructure, another element enters the determination of who will lead and who will follow. Members of each industry will have to gear themselves for handling cyber transactions. They will be forced to move from mail, telephone, fax, and EDI and utilize an e-commerce system of communication. That system will be used for everything from entering orders, to tracking inventory, collaboratively developing new products and services, creating better demand management abilities, planning and scheduling across organizations, and fulfilling the orders received. The amount of usage moving to this new medium of communication will vary by industry and application, but it will rise geometrically until steady state conditions are achieved. The new consumer will dictate this change.

We see Web-based ordering, for example, spanning another industry continuum from low to high impact and use. On the low side, in such an industry as grocery, predictions—on how much of the buying will eventually be done over the Web—never seem to reach more than 7% to 10%. Construction and heavy equipment companies talk about 5% at best. One executive remarked that customers simply won't order airplanes or highway equipment over the Internet. (Curiously, we found one example where Gulfstream did receive an electronic order for two new airplanes via its Web site.) The U.S. government cannot be expected to buy weaponry via the Web, but the Web could enable the design and specification of weapons systems. All of these industries will, however, be making great use of the Internet for other transactions.

At the upper end of the continuum, the high-technology industry anticipates 50% of future orders will be received via the Internet, with such companies as Cisco and Dell looking at 80% to 90% of orders coming through the Internet and World Wide Web. Across this continuum, each industry will have to prepare for handling whatever amount of cyber ordering emerges. That will require having a system not only to receive the orders but a network of allies to process and fulfill the orders. Now the percentage of Web use rises dramatically for all industries, as the B2B part of the system kicks in and the linked firms use information from cyber or physical orders to determine how to produce and deliver the goods.

This sequence of events includes cross-enterprise communication on securing parts, planning and scheduling production, manufacturing, transportation, storage, final distribution, and the handling of any returns. Most companies are currently lacking in these skills. Success in the future will require a network that can respond from beginning to end with a supply chain and logistics system that is accurate, flexible, and quick. That will require transferring the important information electronically across all member companies in the value chain constellation that expects to dominate an industry.

FUTURE STATE HYPOTHESES

Figure 5.3 captures the essence of our future hypotheses, as they apply to creating and sustaining such a constellation. In the next 4 to 10 years, we see an evolution to the point where the model depicted in this exhibit will be the dominant form of supply chain and logistics interaction across most businesses.

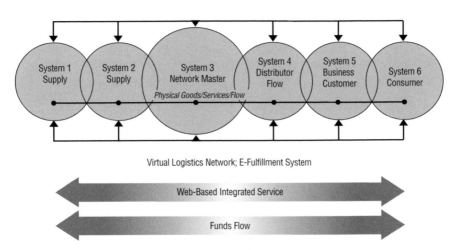

Web-Based Integrated Service

figure 5.3

The Network Master at the Core

At the center of the value chain constellations, we see as the logical extension of supply chain networks, we position a network master, or nucleus firm. All of our research points out that the formation of a group of firms linked in a common objective across an interenterprise supply chain system will be dominated by such an entity. Today we are accustomed to referring to the central player in a supply chain system as a channel master. This position will evolve as this type of central player develops its external partners into a value chain focused on specific market or industry dominance and as it assumes the role of forceful driver.

Admittedly, we can cite instances in which two or more parties could combine their resources and efforts to produce very impressive collaborative results. The work being done by Hewlett-Packard and Wal-Mart to better develop and execute promotions is one example. Nestlé and Tesco are doing similar work in Europe. Sometimes two firms may share the role of network master, although we predict the predominant situation will have one network master acting as the nucleus firm to the value chain. As we analyzed the cases and stories involving the creation of leading networks, it became apparent that one of the players typically became the impetus behind the effort. For that reason, we'll proceed with the concept of one firm assuming the position of network master to drive the formation being described.

As a company, such as Cisco, Sun Microsystems, Ford, Du Pont, Nestlé, Eastman, Kraft Foods, or Procter & Gamble, assumes the lead in forming future networks, their role takes on more importance than that of the other constituents. That's why, in Figure 5.3, the network master's circle is drawn larger. If a collaborative effort is truly equal between players, the circles can be drawn in similar size, to represent a peer-type arrangement. In the model drawn, the network master will know how to design, develop, and produce what the business customer or end consumer wants and will be central in determining how to deliver it in the best format and most efficient cycle. It will have the scale and brand recognition to establish a consistent demand for its products and services, and it will most likely provide most of the resources required for building the value chain constellation. These firms will be adept at selecting and nurturing key business partners to enhance total capability and respond to market needs and changes.

Be prepared, as the new model matures—some unusual names could be appearing in this network master position in some industries. Wal-Mart could become such a master in the grocery business, while Du Pont could appear in the carpet business. Hewlett-Packard could do the same in business consulting. Large firms could also be at the center of several models, because of their dominance in several markets. DuPont, for example, certainly has enough business units that its presence could be seen in many networks.

The Networked Value Chain Constellation

Also in Figure 5.3, the linked circles represent what has generally become an acceptable depiction of a connected supply chain network, beginning with the first raw material supplier and ending with either a business customer or the end consumer. A typical network could include raw material supplier 1, sending supplies to supplier 2 making subassemblies or components. These products could go to the network master for manufacturing or conversion into finished goods and services. We see distributors continuing to play a role in most supply chains, as the best will have defined their added value as they move goods to the appropriate retailers or to small and remote sales outlets. Some deliveries will, of course, be direct to the stores. The connection is complete when the consumer makes his or her selection from the store or Web site of choice. In the future all such systems will have a portion of consumption moving through an Internet-based order process. If returns need to be included in the model, the firms will have a system that accommodates that part of the supply chain and tracks movement online.

Connecting these constituents will be a physical flow of goods and services, represented by the connected line through the circles. Whether the order is received through the mail, over a telephone or fax, or through a computer connection, materials will still have to flow from company to company toward consumption and the occasional return of finished goods. Most organizations are already hard at work trying to bring optimization to this central requirement. That is the ante in the future game of logistics and supply chain excellence. The ante must be covered with a larger investment in an e-commerce communication system. Our hypothesis is that firms not equipped with an effective interenterprise value chain communication and delivery system will be left out of future sales, particularly from those of the younger generation, who will simply not know they exist.

Communication Extranets

Another hypothesis is that in the future, the best of these supply chain networks will be inexorably linked by an Internet system that provides Web-based integrated service across the entire value chain of companies. This extranet of communication will extend from end-to-end of the network, linking the information systems of important constituents, and is depicted by the line of connection at the top of Figure 5.3. Our research indicates that virtually every company we studied is developing some kind of Web-based information system. Hence, we show systems 1 through 6 in our network.

Unfortunately, today most of this development is done in isolation from supply chain partners. With so much software and so many systems in development, very little integration exists at present. Using Internet technologies to drive standards will reduce the cost of development and speed deployment of integrated systems.

As organizations develop the necessary external connectivity, they will need to introduce the means to integrate these disparate systems. We see that trend accelerating until the leading networks have the full connectivity indicated by the model, most likely coming through the joining of enterprise systems, like ERP. We see these systems finally becoming debugged and operational, so they become the glue that binds members of a network together electronically. With such capability, any member of the network will be able to access crucial information on supplies, inventories, planning, scheduling, shipments, and returns. The integrated service will require the network master to take a central role in development, testing, and integration as this extranet is established.

Through the future Web-based integrated service network, firms will offer a variety of responses to customers and consumers, with equal efficiency. This capability will create top-line growth in the form of new revenues secured for the network through vision, innovation, and a seamless system of total response to the buyer. In the next decade, business processes can't help but be impacted and designed by use of the Internet. Securing future customers who are determined to buy over the Web is just one facet of this new business environment.

The Virtual Logistics Network

Another hypothesis is concerned with the transfer of goods across this fully linked network. In the future, there will be a logistics network that spans the supply chain as well. This network will be virtual in the sense that the members will have formed a consortium that has online access to a transportation capability that is multimodal, global, and capable of extremely high utilization rates for the drivers, handlers, warehousing, and equipment involved. It will not be necessary with this logistics network for individual firms to own traditional assets. Most companies do not currently own ships, airplanes, or railroad cars, although many think they have to own trucks to control their destiny. Most of the warehousing and distribution space is currently leased or managed by a third party.

With the linkage shown in the model, the firms will have all of the required assets under contract to the network, and use will be determined by the current fulfillment needs. A needed supply could start in Asia and move by ocean freight or air service to an awaiting hub in the United States. An awaiting trailer could be loaded and sent on to the first destination, a manufacturer that will convert the supplies into a product. The trailer could then proceed to pick up a load from another network member and move to its distributor, and so on throughout the day. Back hauls optimize under such a condition as there is always a load waiting for delivery. Warehousing and distribution center space declines in this system, as there is mutual use of space in critical areas, and the member firms are sharing space rather than building new capacity.

Across this future electronic and physical system of collaboration there will also be a human resources network, as firms will be sharing employees, particularly truck drivers and logistics personnel. A funds flow will be established, as funds transfer will be electronic.

ILLUSTRATIVE SCENARIOS

Let's consider an evolving example being developed by Redwood Systems and Cisco. Through their new system, Redwood (a business processing outsourcer [BPO] division of Consolidated Freightways) holds inventory for more than fifteen Cisco suppliers. Redwood assembles to order Cisco products and provides inventory visibility and connectivity to Cisco and its suppliers. Costs have been reduced by 50% by linking suppliers and Cisco in a virtual fulfillment environment. Cisco designs and sells the products. Contract suppliers make the products. Redwood assembles and delivers the products. This is the kind of future interenterprise connectivity we predict will be common among the industry leaders.

In another developing scenario, General Mills and ten partners have formed what will be an example of the model being described. General Mills is a $12 billion food manufacturer with a broad range of branded products, a perfect example of a network master. In this case, the company moved beyond that role to establish a consortium of channel masters to bring optimization to the delivery portion of the value chain. Unlocking the power of the Internet, General Mills began collaboration across its supply chain network some time ago. Its success is reflected in the improvement in gross margin from 55.2% in 1990 to 58.5% in 1999.

As the fruits of collaboration proved beneficial, the firm began to look at the potential to collectively build a transportation system that would further enhance its progress. Working with software provider Nistevo, an alliance was formed with eleven other companies, including ConAgra, Fort James Packaging, Hormel, Land O' Lakes, Nabisco, and Nestlé. These firms are now linked through the Nistevo software so they can view online the possible delivery, transfer, and back-haul capabilities offered by all members of the alliance. Dividing the United States into sectors, one firm could start a load from its manufacturing facility toward a distribution center or a customer site.

Once unloaded, the truck could then be sent to a supplier for another company. Loads could be added until the truck is full and sent to the next unloading point. With visibility to the available equipment and drivers, the involved companies would have options regarding their pickups and deliveries. Instead of arranging a special truck for an emergency delivery, for example, there is often a possible routing that makes sense for the network system. Early results of the testing of this new arrangement show outbound and back-haul utilization rates in the 95% or better range.

THE TWO CHANNELS: PHYSICAL AND CYBER-BASED CONVERGE

In the future, firms will have sorted out their channels to markets and matched the appropriate channel with their offerings to maximize the throughput and efficiency of each system. Supply chains may still be complex, but the best will be nearing optimization as the partners work out their roles and end objectives. Hewlett-Packard offers an example of a leader on its way to this state.

HP is a global company with a very diverse product line that includes more than 110,000 suppliers around the world. The firm maintains one of the largest parts databases in the world, with 205,000 part numbers across 258 categories of products. Some of these products are sold exclusively through channels, including computer resellers, retailers, wholesalers, and original equipment manufacturers (OEMs). Others are sold direct to both consumers and business via two HP Web sites: HP Shopping Village for consumers and HP Business Store for business customers.

Manufacturing aspects are equally complicated, as HP printers are manufactured at the rate of one every second by a network of contractors in thirteen separate worldwide locations. Cartridges are manufactured in-house. Managing multiple outbound distribution flows becomes more complex by the growing need to have final options completed as close to the customers for the printers as possible. Channel partners at eighteen assembly sites complete final product configuration. Add in seasonal events, such as year-end and back-to-school promotions, and you have one of the most complex supply chains we encountered.

To cope with this complexity, HP used a two-prong supply chain approach that combines improved processing with use of technology, a model we see duplicated by those who will succeed in the future. On the technology side, use of the Internet led to the construction of platforms, tools, and solutions that let partners across the HP supply chain network share information. According to Robert Wayman, chief financial officer, "Rather than having to make totally independent decisions on critical issues such as forecasting, production schedules, inventory levels, and distribution plans, companies can now share information with partners and make the best choices."

TECHNOLOGY CONVERGENCE AND CAPABILITIES TO RECAST INDUSTRY SUPPLY CHAINS

A host of e-commerce services, trading places, net markets, special portals, and value chain collaborations are defining the new business models. As the evolution matures, we see a changing business world, in which technology has converged with the best of today's supply chain and logistics practices and applications, to establish a new e-business model that will dominate commerce. Across the world, linked constituents in value chain constellations will feature more agile, functional, and capable systems of response to customer and consumer demand. Those companies and value chains that are able to use technology most effectively will have a critical competitive edge. Participants in these extended supply chain networks will have convenient access to the information needed to make optimal supply chain and logistics decisions. What is required is moving from the world of industrial age communications to the world of e-business.

This movement can occur in any industry to any size firm. Consider the case of a small firm in an industry not known for its leading applications of the systems being espoused. Cemex is a company in Monterrey, Mexico, operating in the mundane world of providing cement and concrete. It is an asset-intensive, low-efficiency business with unpredictable demands and changes that are made up to the last minute of any shipment. Dispatchers at the company traditionally take orders for 8,000 grades of mixed concrete and forward them to six plants, previously by telephone, for delivery to a host of customers. Plagued by low margins and the constant shifting of schedules and deliveries, Cemex decided to go digital.

With an electronic system, Cemex eliminated the typical friction and errors that occur between process steps, saving the time and extra costs normally incurred. The company's customers, distributors, and customers can now use the Internet to place orders, find out when shipments will arrive, and check payment records, without having to access a customer service representative. The firm's delivery trucks were linked to a global positioning satellite system so dispatchers could monitor the location, direction and speed of every vehicle. Average delivery times were reduced from 3 hours to 20 minutes. Cemex now uses 35% fewer trucks to deliver the same amount of concrete and can charge a premium price.

Supply Chain Management in the Future Value Chain

The Internet has provided the means to connect future supply chain and logistics networks. Now the job is to fashion the business models that take the greatest advantage of this enabling tool. We see a world emerging beyond e-commerce or e-business. As competition moves more and more away from individual companies and more to competing networks, we see Web-based integrated services being the distinguishing factor between these networks. Interenterprise collaboration is the catalyst that will enhance the best of these networks. Future supply chains that include such conditions will provide for intercompany planning and delivery, the exchange of money, the online sharing of valuable information, and the conduct of crucial business processes across the linked firms. We even see the sharing of critical human resources among the constituents of the value chain constellations that will make up the leading networks.

The next step for those companies already pursuing such a position is to bring the necessary infrastructure and supporting Web-based communication system from concept and plan to operating reality. This system must be able to support the transactions that must occur across a seamless and virtual network of full electronic connectivity, what we have been calling a value chain constellation. Only through the mass proliferation of Internet services can a firm expect to keep pace with what is emerging in the new business scenario. These new e-services will become as valuable as the current capital assets and will be the factor that distinguishes a network or dooms it to a secondary position in future markets.

As described by Larry Carter, Cisco Systems' chief financial officer, in the June 26, 1999, issue of The Economist, "It's no longer about the big beating the small; it's about the fast beating the slow. The future belongs to the agile, and the proper use of e-business tools will enable the necessary agility."

chapter 6

The Fundamentals of
E-Business

A fundamental learning from our research is that while a myriad of activities are at work in e-business, as companies and industries pursue the application of this new tool, those activities are fragmented. Few companies have e-business strategies that integrate with their business plans. Some firms have e-business projects under way, others can point to specific e-commerce initiatives, a few have active Web sites where orders are taken and deliveries tracked, and so forth. In addition, a few companies will have a rudimentary e-business strategy developing. But we found no company that had a complete e-business strategy integrated with their overall strategy or supporting business plan.

Since every part of a modern company will be affected by e-business, it's important for supply chain and logistics managers to be able to understand and help guide their companies through the tumultuous times ahead. Without a clear understanding of this necessity, and in view of the absence of supporting strategies to guide implementation, there is an obvious need for some fundamentals to serve as a road map to success. In this chapter, we'll delve into this need and explain the basics necessary for supply chain and logistics leaders to help forge the pathway to the future.

THE IMPACT OF E-BUSINESS

At the heart of building a viable e-business platform and strategy is being able to articulate the overall impact on a company and its supply chain partners. As we describe the characteristics of that impact, we'll also present arguments on the importance of developing an e-business strategy for your company. We'll pay particular attention to the context of what was described in prior chapters, what leaders are doing, and the future vision offered in Chapter 5. We'll also provide readers with a formal framework and calibration tool for assessing their company's stage within its evolutionary e-business development. This will help business strategists develop an overall e-business strategy for their companies and value chain partners. Chapter 7 will offer a detailed approach to specifically developing e-supply chain strategies based on the use of the Internet and the World Wide Web. These strategies will need to integrate and support a company's overall e-business strategy.

That necessity will grow in importance as the use of the Internet continues to pervade business practices. Our research and insight would indicate that a company having disparate e-business and traditional business strategies is a short-lived phenomenon. Soon e-business strategies will no longer be stand-alone parts of a firm's plan; they will be integrated into business strategies. We depict this situation in Figure 6.1 as we place the e-business strategy on top of the needs of each major business discipline. This part of the new business model then underpins the overall business strategy and resulting business plans.

Some firms understand this simple reality; others are either unaware or have decided to ignore its importance. Our research showed that almost every company studied had some form of e-business activity under way. A few have formed alliances to further develop this activity. For example, Toys 'R' Us has launched a new strategic relationship with Amazon.com, giving Toys 'R' Us a

Components of a Business Strategy

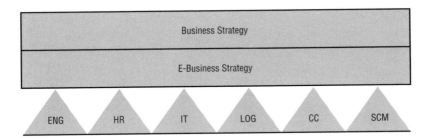

ENG: Engineering Function
HR: Human Resources
IT: Information Technology
LOG: Logistics
CC: Customer Care
SCM: Supply Chain Management

figure 6.1

new Internet-based delivery channel. The toy company is adding its already strong brand name to Amazon's well-known Web presence. Both firms take advantage of Toys 'R' Us's buying power and inbound logistics skill, and Amazon's customer service and distribution (outbound logistics) capabilities. While the alliance appears to contain an excellent tactical approach, it only covers certain aspects of their supply chain, not the end-to-end perspective that we advocate be taken. Missing is an integrated business strategy that positions both companies for building new revenues in a network fashion.

Companies in a value network can work together to find their current position and develop a mutually rewarding roadmap for the future. To help prepare this road map, we'll provide insight into the impact of e-business on all functions within a corporation and how those functions will evolve as businesses become members of a value chain. A diagnostic will be provided to calibrate your company's position and what steps can be taken to move ahead.

Figure 6.2 indicates there are relative levels of maturity as computing skills increase. As an organization becomes adept at internal applications, they develop the requisite skills to take on an external orientation. With that progress, the firm can begin building the value chain alliances so important for future success.

The S-Curve

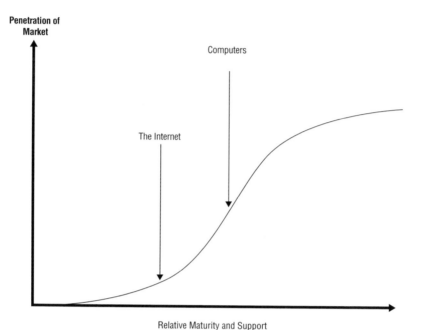

figure 6.2

KEY SUCCESS FACTORS

We feel it's important for everyone to understand the impact of e-business on their firm and to understand the necessary next steps to move ahead. An e-business strategy does not necessarily mean just having a Web site. It means having an interenterprise structure that creates a market advantage. Consider Spain's Inditex and its Zara brand. Inditex is a vertically integrated clothing company, producing most goods in Spain, with a small percentage of products coming from Asia, a very unusual circumstance in this industry. What distinguishes Inditex is not just its clothes but its approach to logistics and manufacturing (along with clever designs).

Inditex has a maximum 21-day supply chain, as they can design, produce, and deliver to retail stores within that time frame. They produce 20,000 new items each year, and every store is linked to the design department so consumer preferences, hot items, and inputs are delivered to the design department every day. Inditex has more than 1,000 stores in Europe and South America. A key element of their business strategy is changing styles every 2 weeks, in contrast to the normal company in the fashion industry that changes styles four times a year. By using the power of logistics and being in touch with suppliers and consumers, Inditex can change styles much more often. The company's computer communications is the e-business backbone of its approach to its market.

E-Business is having an impact on nearly every business, even if those impacts are driven by companies wondering what to do or concerned with reacting to competitor activities. Our research showed that many e-business announcements were defensive in nature, with companies or executives feeling something had to be done. We also found that business drivers and strategies will be changing soon. Several key success factors are what will differentiate businesses in the future. Execution of these factors will allow a company to distinguish itself in the new economy. The new economy is not a myth, nor is it an economy where profits don't matter. The new economy is about speed and customer focus. Two leading executives have aptly positioned this reality: Brian Kelley, a Ford vice president and president of Ford Motor Company's CustomerConnect, said in the July 10, 2000, issue of Automotive News, "There is no such thing as an old economy company or a new economy company. . . . Rather, the winners in the global business competition will be the companies with new economy thinking." According to Larry Carter, Cisco Systems' chief financial officer, in the June 26, 1999, issue of The Economist, "It's no longer about the big beating the small; it's about the fast beating the slow."

Listed here are five critical success factors businesses should keep in mind as they progress along a path toward becoming "new economy thinking" companies, focused on speed:

- Business strategy: A business strategy has to combine the consumer point of view, the value chain, e-business, and traditional business plans.

- Focus on the end customer: All participants in a value chain will need to focus on the needs of the consumer and how they can help meet and create those needs.

- Value chain: A value chain needs to be formed to target specific markets.

- Fulfillment—Logistics and Remediation: The "last mile" will be the key to success—efficiently putting goods and services in the hands of consumers and end-users.

- Internal management structure and organization: An entire value chain needs to focus on two things: business success and consumer satisfaction. ("Internal" in this case refers to the value chain.)

LEVERAGE FACTORS

These five critical success factors in combination with corporate leverage factors will help put companies well on the way to their e-business, new economy future. Leverage factors are the assets companies use to better their position in the market relative to other companies. While many of these factors are still viable, some have been subjected to criticism, as others have been added, as detailed here:

- Old leverage factors:
  Brand identity
  Cost advantage
  Market leadership
  Management and leadership skills
  Quality
  Physical assets
  Capital
  Logistics expertise

- New leverage factors:
  E-Business strategies and capabilities
  Information technology capabilities and supporting infrastructure
  Supply chain/value chain capabilities

A case in point is the aforementioned alliance of Toys 'R' Us and Amazon.com. This alliance combines old leverage factors, including the brands of the two companies plus the market leadership of Toys 'R' Us in toys, with Amazon's new leverage factors, which include e-business strategies and capabilities, and IT capabilities and infrastructure. The two companies have formed the beginnings of a value chain that targets a specific market—the affluent online shopper who is driven by convenience and home delivery.

Successful value chains will be able to combine such leverage factors. Executives planning to develop strategies for their businesses will have new methods to use that include the ability to leverage new factors and combine new and old factors with value chain partners.

INTERNET IMPACT

Has the Internet had an impact on your business? If you answered no, you are in the minority. For example, a recent CSC and Automotive Industries magazine survey (August 2000) of more than 200 senior executives in the automotive industry showed that 62% of them felt that the Internet had changed their business, with another 59% expecting more change.

With all the talk about e-businesses, NetMarkets, and dot-coms, many people have missed something. The greatest amount of activity, and the activity that will have the most profound impact on most businesses and individuals, will be focused on the transformation that conventional, old economy businesses will undergo. That activity is still developing and in many individual companies is occurring with an eye not toward transformation but toward improving efficiencies. No one disputes the phenomenal growth of the Internet; nevertheless, it takes a long time for the widespread adoption of technology and even longer time for us to see the impact of the effort. Think of this: More than half the world's population has never made a telephone call, yet the telephone was invented in 1873!

In his most recent book, Leading the Revolution, Dr. Gary Hamel says, "The age of progress is over." His point is the age of revolution is beginning. The Internet is revolutionizing supply and value chains and is beginning to revolutionize business in general.

THE IMPORTANCE OF AN E-BUSINESS STRATEGY

There is little doubt that the Internet and the Web will be one of the inventions having the greatest impact on business transformation—a huge amount of activity and impact is already occurring. Still, most e-commerce pursuits have been about improving efficiencies: make things better, faster, and cheaper. But is that truly revolutionary? Is it truly transformational? The answer is no. E-Business will revolutionize business practices and models. The difference between e-commerce and e-business is huge, as our stages of e-business will show. E-Commerce is about wringing the last efficiency out of your business—a great goal, but not the end. Interestingly, the majority of companies are still trying to improve their internal business operations, before they start transforming their value and supply chains.

Many of the recent major announcements around e-commerce are still about improving efficiency, yet some industries and a handful of companies are thinking about transformation. Companies feel compelled to act, even without knowing what the full impact of the changes will be or what shape that transformation will bring. In this book, we're not against the reduction of unnecessary expenses. Rather, we believe that as a differentiator, cost reduction is where quality was at one time, a necessary and expected part of your business model. This book is about the next wave, the networked organization and its allies, driving for a differentiated image in the chosen market, with new revenues as a major measure of success.

Why is it important to transform your company into an e-business? Figure 6.3 shows some projected economic value of e-business for the automobile industry. Look at the average profitability per vehicle from some of the world's leading manufacturers in 1998 and 1999. Then see what some potential benefits of e-business might be—a significant bottom-line impact, improving not only profitability but also competitive positioning by increasing flexibility. We'll look at the automotive industry later in our scoring and calibration section.

Potential Impact of E-Business

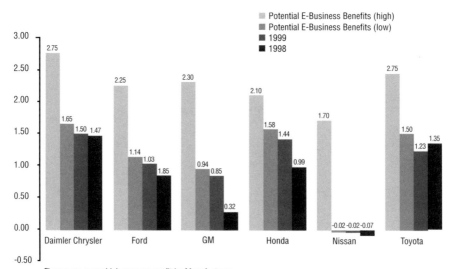

Figures are per vehicle average profit by Manufacturer.
Potential benefit is the application of E-Business processes throughout the supply chain.

Source: *Harbour Research, Detroit Free Press and CSC Consulting*

figure 6.3

Thinking about an E-Business Strategy

Few current e-business strategies are comprehensive enough. A comprehensive e-business strategy needs to cover all aspects of your business, addressing the business benefit of the plan, the affected areas, and the areas that are not affected. That has an upside and a downside. Current e-business planning activities tend to focus on one area such as sales, marketing, procurement, customer service, engineering, or supply chain.

Your business strategy has to also comprehend the impact of the Internet. A generation growing up right now has been born with the Internet in place. Their expectations will be different: How they communicate, learn, and, perhaps most important to you, how they buy and sell, and whom they buy and sell from. That generation will be succeeded by yet another generation that will only have known a new way of life. The first wave of transformation has to understand and comprehend that new way, beginning now and lasting for the next 30 years or so. At the same time, the transformers need to understand that there could be a downside to the new wave. Organizational complexity will increase dramatically.

Figure 6.4 relates the complexity of e-business with the stages of evolution a firm will go through. In the beginning, the complexity is low as all the focus is on fixing internal practices. As the firm moves to higher levels of evolution, toward the value chain and collaborative organization being espoused, the complexity rises dramatically. The economic benefit increases as well, but the firms building the value chain have to accept the need to work through the complex issues that will surely develop.

In developing an e-business strategy, a variety of the following factors influencing all businesses will need to be considered:

- Business will be global. Influences and competition will be global, even if you are a small, or local or regional business; there will be a global influence.

- Everyone will be connected. If your company is not visible electronically, it won't exist. Even specialized "craft" businesses will have an electronic presence for contact and payment. Part of your delivery will be digital.

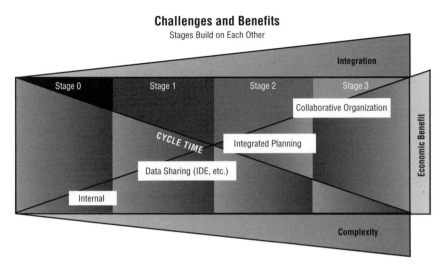

Challenges and Benefits
Stages Build on Each Other

Integration

| Stage 0 | Stage 1 | Stage 2 | Stage 3 |

Collaborative Organization

CYCLE TIME

Integrated Planning

Data Sharing (IDE, etc.)

Internal

Economic Benefit

Complexity

figure 6.4

- Strategic differentiation will be similar to today, but understanding your customers and rapidly adapting to change will be the key to success. There will be more knowledge available about products and services than ever before. Each year it will increase by an order of magnitude, at an amazing rate. Rising above the din, tracking the changes and responding will be your keys to success. In our new e-business model, everyone must know the latest trends and business conditions.

- Understanding how to work with diverse social and business cultures around the globe will be very important.

- Firms have to ensure that an Internet infrastructure is available for use.

- Companies must understand the state of suppliers' and other trading partners' physical infrastructure.

- Linked partners will need to change internal management processes and points of view.

THE E-BUSINESS EVOLUTION MODEL

The remainder of this chapter presents the e-business framework from an external, or value and supply chain, perspective. The framework is an evolutionary model that includes four major e-business stages that your company can achieve over time. (The original model was developed for the book

E-Supply Chain: Using the Internet to Revolutionize Your Business, by Mike Bauer and Charles Poirier, published by Berrett-Koehler in 2000.) It is depicted in Figure 6.5 and more specifically explained in Table 6.1 as a matrix that details the evolutionary path a business will need to take toward becoming a new economy company. Definitions of all the cells in the matrix are provided so you can understand where your company is and where its business environment is going.

Evolutionary E-Business Model

Progression / Business Application	Market Laggards — Stage 0 Supply Chain Optimization	Majority — Stage I Advanced Supply Chain Management	Current Leaders — Stage II E-Commerce	New Economy — Stage III E-Business
Design Development Product/Service Introduction	Internal Only	Selected External Assistance	Collaborative Design- Enterprise Integration and PIM linked CAD/Cam	Business Functional View- Joint Design and Development
Purchase, Procurement, Sourcing	Leverage Business Unit Volume	Leverage Full Network Through Aggregation	Key Supplier Assistance, Web-Based Sourcing	Network Sourcing Through Best Constituent
Marketing, Sales, Customer Service	Internally Developed Programs, Promotions	Customer-Focused, Data-Based Initiatives	Collaborative Development for Focused Consumer Base	Consumer Response System Across the Value Chain
Engineering, Planning Scheduling, Manufacturing	MRP MRPII DRP	ERP - Internal Connectivity	Collaborative Network Planning - Best Asset Utilization	Consumer Response System Across the Value Chain
Logistics	Manufacturing Push - Inventory Intensive	Pull System Through Internal/External Providers	Best Constituent Provider - Dual Channel	Total Network, Dual Channel Optimization
Customer Care	Customer Service Reaction	Focused Service - Call Centers	Segmented Response System, Customer Relationship Management	Matched Care - Customer Care Automation and Remediation
Human Resouces	Regulatory Issues/Hiring Recruiting, Training	Network Models, Training	Inter-Enterprise Resource Utilization	Full Network Alignment and Capability Provision
Information Technology	Point Solutions Internal Silos	Linked Intranets Corp Strategy/ Architecture	Internet-Based Extranet Shared Capabilities	Full Network Communication System Shared Architecture Planning

figure 6.5

Following a description of this matrix-based framework, we'll offer readers an e-business scoring tool that includes suggested next steps for a company to take based on its scores. The scoring tool is just a blank matrix in which you can enter your company's position and quickly add up the score. Then you'll have a ready-made gap analysis of where your company is versus where the future state of business. Each column in the evolutionary model's matrix represents where a company might be. However, it's important to realize that some companies will have activities in one or more columns. When you begin your scoring exercise, score yourself where the preponderance of activity is. Read the chart from right to left, with the leftmost column being the future, or transformed, company.

Stages of E-Business

In this section, we'll explain what each element in the E-Business Evolution Model's matrix means (see Table 6.1), plus you will see the scoring table and some sample next steps. The far-right column, "E-Business," will be the logical progression of the stages of e-business.

Each column represents where a company may move to or is currently positioned. Some companies will have activities in one or more columns. When you begin your scoring exercise, score yourself where the majority of activity resides. Read the chart from left to right, with the right-most column being the future or transformed company.

In each instance of the "E-Business" column, business processes such as purchasing, engineering design, and scheduling are presumed to be networked business processes. A networked business process is a consistent way of performing a business activity across the value chain. For example, an engineering change request is the same across all the companies involved. In addition, each process has a business leader who is responsible for the process and whose responsibility cuts across corporate boundaries.

A note of caution is in order. A business's desired position in the market will determine where it needs to be. For example, if your company is a contract manufacturer, then creating the infrastructure to do collaborative planning may not pay off. However, some of the characteristics of an e-business will still be appropriate.

Reading the Table

The "Business Application" (left-most column) is the functional element in your company: planning, human resources, logistics, IT, and so forth. The stages are a progression based on a view from a supply chain perspective: how your suppliers and customers see and interact with your company.

Transforming an Industry: Examples from the Global Automotive Industry

Seeing a future state is not helpful unless it leads to three things:

- Understanding how the future state will impact your business

- Knowing where you are in relationship to the future

- Moving toward that future in the most effective manner.

The first part of this chapter shows and defines a future state. This section will address how to understand where your company is today and some steps to move toward the future. The automotive industry will be used as an example of an industry trying to transform itself. Several manufacturers—General Motors, Ford, and Toyota, for example—are all moving toward the e-business column as aggressively as they can.

The savings of many days of inventory combined with meeting the demands of the revolution in consumer retail is an ideal e-business strategy. The combination of the efficiencies of e-commerce with the transformational aspects of becoming an e-business are compelling. The automobile industry is one of the industries attempting to transform itself. It is faced with many barriers: its own internal processes, investment in capital goods and technology, regulatory issues, extraordinarily diverse markets, global overcapacity, changing consumer expectations, and more.

Even with all those barriers, key executives realize they must change the way they do business. For an auto company to become an e-business means adding a build-to-order (BTO) capability, allowing a consumer to customize a vehicle order, receive a firm price and delivery commitment, and reduce the time to deliver a vehicle. BTO is a change from the push model. The push model is what we experience today—it fills the distribution channel with vehicles and influences buyers to make a purchase using extensive ad campaigns, rebates, low-cost financing, and more. An ideal pull model means the consumer will order a vehicle, and it will be produced after the order is placed. The consumer gets exactly what they want, and the manufacturer and all the rest of the supply chain are assured of a sale.

Business Application	Internal Optimization/Supply Chain Optimization	Advanced Supply Chain Planning (some external optimization)
Design and development of products and/orservices[1]	Products and services are developed using internal resources only. Engineer-driven focus on best product design. Quality is often put in via excessive rework after product or services are produced.	Some selected outside resources are used such as consumer clinics or contract design firms.
Purchasing, procurement, and sourcing	Volumes of purchases are aggregated at a business unit level and discounts are sought using purchasing volume.	Purchases are understood and leveraged at a corporate level. Sometimes suppliers/customers are included to raise volume level for larger discounts.
Marketing, sales, customer service	Internally developed programs and promotions—account ownership as a sales strategy.	Customer-focused database initiatives, marketing clinics, and strong knowledge of customer buying patterns with your firm. Advanced telemarketing systems* and boiler rooms.
Engineering, planning, scheduling, manufacturing	These functions are discrete, without formal linkages and collaboration.[3] Tools such as MRP may be used, but the focus is primarily on a single function. Multiple processes and /or organizations can originate change requests.	Sharing of scheduling for manufacturing is done. Engineering specifications are shared, sometimes electronically. First-tier suppliers know manufacturing plans for new products. Suppliers often use (or are forced to use assembler tools).[3]
Logistics	Logistics functions are primarily in-house. Inventory drives a "push" strategy (driven by incentives for manufacturing based on high utilization of manufacturing capacity) that rewards a "full truck" even at the expense of delayed shipping for customer benefit.	Still often driven by manufacturing capacity, the beginnings of a pull strategy emerge. Linkages (manual, phone, fax) in place to link orders to shipments (not necessarily end orders—orders to the next stage in the supply chain). Some digital channel in evidence.[4]
Customer care	Complaint reaction. Statistical information is kept on customer complaints; product or service updates are done on those complaints with the greatest volume. Rebates and incentives are often used to promote sales.	Customer care was primarily delivered by call centers. Call centers were a mechanism to provide some level of service to customers seeking information or redress. Call centers were primarily cost centers inside a company. Some made attempts at sales (Telco's) to offset expense. Product complexity and attempted improvements in efficiency and (staff reductions by another name) shifted customers to call centers from inside sales forces.

table 6.1

E-Commerce	E-Business
A team including selected suppliers develops products. Designs are shared via a network.	A truly collaborative endeavor—each constituent does what they do best, and all participants bring a view of the marketplace. Consumers are a key part of the design team, and a collaborative environment is established. Processes extend across the value chain.
Supplier expertise is sought out, and Web-based purchasing is used, sometimes combined with electronic catalogs and/or online auctions.	Best constituent—letting the most capable[2] member of your value chain purchase goods or services for the entire value chain. Full electronic (Web-based) catalog available to all value chain members.
Collaborative development of solution sets for customers. Joint marketing with key suppliers and utilization of supplier insights. Unsolicited fax and e-mail campaigns (spam)*.	Marketing and sales plans developed collaboratively across the value chain, focusing on the end consumer. Implement a consumer response system across the value chain. Processes extend across the value chain.
Team-focused approach to engineering and production planning. Suppliers have visibility and access to CAD/CIM and PDM tools and information. Companies have visibility into the supply chain, to include customer orders.	Collaboration across the entire value chain: customers, suppliers, and other key constituents. Market insight and analysis are shared; the best constituent takes the lead on planning, scheduling, design, and so forth. All companies have full visibility of entire chain with the ability to see what changes will impact the entire chain. Processes extend across the value chain
Best constituent provider—can be outsourced partially or totally, or logistics can be led by the company in the supply chain that is best able to perform operations. The dual channel starts to come into the forefront.[5]	There is complete network visibility, including consumers or end customers. More and more content is digital. The build-to-order model is in the forefront for manufacturing. Logistics planning is done centrally and consists of in-bound, intrafirm, and outbound. Processes extend across the value chain
Primarily the same as advanced supply chains planning characteristics except help was often available on the company's web site. Also, tremendous advances have been made in autoresponding e-mail systems to answer questions. Again, many of these activities are in support of cost reduction. Companies have been formed to preform remediation and returns for e-businesses. In fact, the creation of another industry segment has resulted.	Customer care will transition into a profit center. Customer care activities will work across the entire value chain, with at times a single contact being responsible for the entire value chain. Customers will have full access to a customized customer care experience delivered via individualized systems and people. Full access to a customer's records and transactions will be available to all value chain participants for support (privileged information is an exception). Processes extend across the value chain

Business Application	Internal Optimization/Supply Chain Optimization	Advanced Supply Chain Planning (some external optimization)
Human resources	Screening and regulatory compliance. Internal functional views for staffing and resources. Little involvement in business plans, strategies.	In addition to internal optimization, responsible for new work models and seeding academic programs with business requirements. One big US issue was telecommuting as employee lifestyles changed.
Information technology	Point solutions and data silos are the norm. No consistent use of technology resources. Companies often outsource with little or no strategic benefit at this stage. No corporate technology standards in place; divisions and/or business units set own directions. Architecture[6] is normally product based. If there is a corporate architecture, it is from a centralized team and is often an academic exercise that is not used.	Corporate architecture is in place and adherence is voluntary but often used. Migration from silos is underway and intracompany communication is improved. Some published standards are in place to assist in communication with suppliers.

E-Commerce	E-Business
Work streams extended across the enterprise.	All resource loading and acquisition will be done across the value chain. Processes extend across the value chain.
Corporate architecture is in place and adherence is mandatory. Initiatives are made in establishing intercompany technology standards.	Value chain architecture is in place. Resources (strategy and implementation) are extended across the value chain. Internet tools and technologies are the dominant technology infrastructure. Intercompany communication is the norm. Processes and standards extend across the value chain.

footnotes:

1. Engineering is also comprehended here, but this is collaborative design for new products and is a strategic function. This is differentiated from collaborative design, engineering, and manufacturing, which is a mechanism for operational efficiency.

2. "Best constituent" is the partner in the value chain having the best resources, skills, insight, or whatever to purchase goods or services. There are two key elements: purchase aggregation for the entire value chain and fully Web-enabled procurement to reduce transaction costs and make the value chain consortium easier to do business with.

3. Formal collaboration is not the traditional product planning meetings. Engineering and design comprehends the full product life cycle in a collaborative environment. Suppliers are often forced into using the design and planning tools of the channel master. This often results in some higher costs due to training, version control problems, network capacity, and so forth. Larger suppliers will often have to use multiple tools—one for each channel master.

4. Much of today's supply chain is in a digital form already—for example, a CAD design transmitted to a manufacturer, a formula for an additive, and an ad campaign for television. Costs are reduced tremendously and production is sped up dramatically when components are in a digital format. Just-in-time inventory is merged with just-in-time manufacturing (JITI/JITM).

5. Some companies will have a dual channel, one that has a physical and digital nature. A current example is record companies that still press CDs but also allow people to purchase digital copies of recordings. Another is the movie business: some films are sent out in a physical format. However, now many movies are being transmitted in a pure digital format, drastically lowering production and shipping costs.

6. Here we will consider three types of architectures: (a) product—largely based on the proprietary products and services of a key supplier or suppliers; (b) standards—using architectural standards derived from national or international organizations (WC3, IETF, ISO, etc.); and (c) hybrid—based on product and standards organizations. Product architectures leave your company at a disadvantage in case of significant shifts in momentum, e.g., the Internet's impact on ERP solutions. Product-based architecture can usually be implemented more quickly. Standards-based types are often too slow and unrealistic, due to lengthy deliberations and technology focus. There is some protection against fading proprietary standards. Hybrid architectures use the best of both worlds. It can be difficult to find people who can properly formulate an architecture of this nature.

*dvanced telemarketing, fax, and spam (unsolicited email) have become so widely disliked they have spawned legislation to protect consumers.

Calibration and Scoring

Now it's your turn. Where is your company? Go through the matrix in Table 6.2 and put a check mark in the section that best describes your company's position. As a rule of thumb, if you are undecided about which cell to choose, choose the cell on the left.

Business Application	Stage 0 Internal Optimization/ Supply Chain Optimization	Stage 1 Advanced Supply Chain Planning	Stage 2 e-Commerce	Stage 3 e-Business
1. Design and Development of products and/or services				
2. Purchasing, Procurement, and Sourcing				
3. Marketing, Sales, & Customer Service				
4. Engineering, Planning, Scheduling, & Manufacturing				
5. Logistics				
7. Human Resources				
6. Customer Care				
8. Information Technology				
Column Totals				

table 6.2

Totals

Determining Your Score

Read the definitions and the notes of the E-business Evolution Model. Determine your company's position in each of the categories by placing an "X" in one cell per row. Again, if you are in doubt choose the left-most column.

The scoring is as follows:

  1 point for each cell in column 1

  3 points for each cell in column 2

  5 points for each cell in column 3

  7 points for each cell in column 4

The maximum score is 56. Refer to Table 6.3 for an explanation of the possible scores.

Rule-of-Thumb Scoring

0-15	Internally focused. You are lagging in the market; look into advanced supply chain management tools.
16-29	Some external focus. Your company is with the majority of firms. You are likely well positioned to move quickly ahead; for example, examine the possibility of providing vendor-managed inventory/scheduling via a secure extranet.
30-40	Good external focus. You are well positioned as a potential market leader. Examine the possibility of taking the next step of forming a value chain with key customers and suppliers to focus on and fulfill the needs of a particular market segment.
41-56	You are a market leader. Look into your one or two areas of improvement.

table 6.3

chapter 7

Developing an
E-Supply
Chain Strategy

One does not plan and then try to make circumstances fit those plans. One tries to make the plans fit the circumstances.—General George Patton

As General Patton recognized, plans needs to fit the circumstances. Patton felt that planning is extremely important in war and that it must be done in the context of current and future circumstances. A plan becomes the foundation for moving forward with intent, purpose, and a clear direction and a road map for victory over time. While today's business battles take place among individual companies pitted against one another, it is expected that future competition will be among electronically connected supply chain communities composed of networked trading partners. To prepare for these future battles, companies need an e-business strategy along with a corresponding supply chain strategy—to "fit the circumstances" expected.

This chapter describes an approach that can be used to develop a supply chain strategy that leverages e-business. As covered in Chapter 6, it will first be important to note the difference between a supply chain strategy and an e-business strategy. In our mind, an e-business strategy deals with the use of electronic means, e-commerce, and the Internet in all aspects of a company's business, including all functional departments, such as finance, human resources, customer service, sales, and marketing, in addition to supply chain. A supply chain strategy is a key supporting component of an overall e-business strategy, basically supporting it along with all other functional strategies. In the context of e-business, a supply chain strategy is one component of the overall e-business strategy that needs to support two purposes:

> Internet leverage—leveraging the Internet, Web, and electronic connectivity to support and enhance supply chain management processes and practices

> New business model support—aligning supply chain operations in support of the new e-business models available for conducting business over the Web

This chapter builds upon the foregoing ones to provide guidelines and a blueprint for developing a supply chain strategy for moving forward with plans that leverage e-business and that are tailored toward a company's needs within its industry. Chapters 2 through 4 offered detailed coverage on the generic tools and methods of e-business and described what specific companies are doing in their supply chains to leverage it. These chapters discuss examples as to what things might be done and what tools could be used to move a company toward achieving future strategic supply chain visions. In Chapter 5 a future-state hypothesis was postulated to give readers a glimpse of what future value and supply chains will most likely look like. This should help readers develop a vision for their company that optimally ensures its future competitiveness, survival, profitability, and prosperity.

In Chapter 6 the development of an overall e-business was discussed and a wake-up call was sounded for logistics professionals. It warns most that their companies are already falling behind relative to their competitors and e-business leaders in other industries, especially given the speed at which things are changing and the quantum leap in competitive advantage e-business will provide. Being behind in many cases is compounded by the fact that most companies are operating disjoint processes, organizations, and systems that will hamper their ability to move at the Internet speed needed in some industries and to conduct future supply chain activities that will be necessary.

Chapter 6 introduced the e-business evolution model that will help companies understand the e-business stage they are at in comparison to some of the leading innovators. It was also pointed out that in support of an e-business strategy, a company might very well choose to implement a supply chain strategy that is more or less advanced than the company's overall e-business strategy. A company will tend to be more advanced within its core functional competencies and competitive differentiators. A company like Cisco Systems, for example, operates an electronically connected supply chain ecosystem with their trading partners that is the envy of many. The ecosystem, using real-time Internet messaging, allows Cisco to take a multiline item order over its Web site and automatically assign and coordinate its fulfillment among internal and external suppliers to ensure that everything reaches a customer's destination in time for installation. Cisco chooses to lead with a strategy that focuses on its supply chain competency, while other functional areas of the company may lag behind in e-business sophistication. In contrast to Cisco, a company might decide that its supply chain strategy can lag behind to gain competitive advantage in another functional area, such as selling and marketing. Such was the case with Amazon.com, which got its start by first establishing a sophisticated Web presence that was responsible for building up its brand name as an Internet retailer. This company focused first on marketing and sales, order management, and personalization and has waited until recently to start building supply chain competencies.

However a company chooses to position its supply chain capabilities vis-à-vis its overall future e-business competencies, it is important that a strategic supply chain strategy be developed that supports future operations. This chapter offers readers the Strategy Development Process that represents a structured, prescriptive approach toward developing a supply chain strategy, similar to those espoused by many supply chain strategy consultants, such as CSC Consulting. It prescribes four major steps that need to be taken during the supply chain strategy formulation process:

Step 1: Determining the as-is state

Step 2: Developing a to-be strategic vision

Step 3: Creating the road map of change

Step 4: Getting the organization ready for change

Chapter 8 will provide ways for companies to use the tools and methods described in Chapters 3 and 4 to support a company's move to an e-business stage. These provide practical next steps for supply chain professionals to follow to help successfully enable future supply chain processes.

To support supply chain strategists with a tool to use for nomenclature as they go though the four-step Strategy Development Process, we first offer an e-business evolution model in this chapter that is supply chain–specific—the E–Supply Chain Evolution Model. This supplements the e-business evolution model described in Chapter 6.

THE E–SUPPLY CHAIN EVOLUTION MODEL

Conceptually, the E–Supply Chain Evolution Model should be used by supply chain strategists to assess and categorize their company's current competencies. Allowing them to leverage e-business concepts and tools to improve their supply chain operations. It can also be used to help articulate and define a future-state supply chain vision. Recall in Chapter 6 that the E-Business Evolution Model is designed to help a company assess where it is in comparison to where it can ultimately go by leveraging e-business to improve its overall business operations. As discussed, that model is used to assess all functional operations within a company, including marketing, sales, human resources, and finance, in addition to supply chain operations.

The E–Supply Chain Evolution Model focuses exclusively on functional operations that are supply chain related, including procurement, manufacturing, logistics, and customer service. It is designed to be specifically supply chain oriented to support logistics practitioners as they assess where their company's supply chain operations are, in comparison to where they need to be, if enabled by leveraging e-business tools and methods. As per the E-Business Evolution Model, this model also has four stages of development:

Stage 1: Supply chain optimization

Stage 2: Advanced supply chain

Stage 3: Leveraging e-commerce

Stage 4: E-Business optimization

Achieving each of these succeeding stages beneficially impacts a supply chain greater than the preceding stage (see Figure 7.1), so that moving from a supply chain optimization stage to an advanced supply chain stage offers less impact than moving from the latter to the leveraging e-commerce stage. The ultimate stage, stage 4, e-business optimization, offers the greatest opportunity for benefits, by orders of magnitude over the preceding stages. While it might be enticing for a company to attempt to achieve this stage right away, it is often impractical to do so. To achieve it requires some level of competency in all prior stages, since each stage builds on the supply chain process competencies established in its preceding stage. For example, moving to stage 2 requires a level of competency in stage 1 processes; hence, moving to stage 4 requires some level of process competency in stages 1 through 3. This will become evident once the supply chain processes that are included within each stage are understood, and described next.

Supply Chain Impact of E-Supply Chain Stages

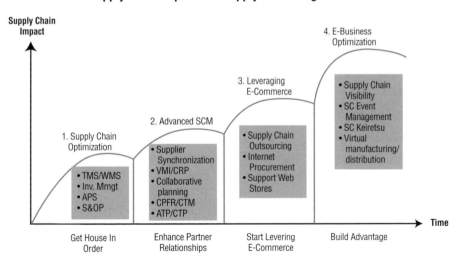

© 2000 AMR Research, Inc.

figure 7.1

Stage 1: Supply Chain Optimization

The supply chain optimization stage is one that many companies have been working on for the past several decades to improve their internal supply chain operations. This has included supply chain management improvements from a functional perspective as well as a cross-functional perspective.

Functional Process Improvements

To accomplish functional improvements or achieve functional excellence, companies have implemented more formalized methods and systems within their logistics organizations. Transportation management systems (TMSs) and corresponding processes have been installed that support optimized freight consolidation, routing, scheduling, and mode/carrier selection, as well as core 3PL programs, aimed at substantially reducing logistics expenditures by partnering with fewer, tightly integrated logistics service providers. Warehouse management systems (WMSs) and corresponding processes have been installed in company-owned and public warehouses to automate processes that improve efficiencies from a perspective of operating costs and customer responsiveness. Lastly, from a functional perspective, companies have implemented more formal inventory management processes and methods that include sophisticated inventory tracking and target setting—such as using statistical safety stocks methods that formally optimize the alignment of inventories to customer service and order fill rate targets. These early TMS, WMS, and inventory management initiatives have been focused primarily around improving the performance of a single functional area. At times, they did so at the expense of other functional areas, a factor that contributed to the creation of the functional silos operating within many companies today.

Cross-Functional Process Improvements

To improve internal operations even further and break down the functional silos, companies have more recently implemented cross-functional processes and systems. One such type is a sales and operations planning (S&OP) process that fosters a formal matching and reconciliation of supply and demand plans. The process involves regularly scheduled meetings that bring together a cross-functional team of employees from marketing, sales, operations, customer service, and finance. At these meetings participants agree on a set of demand forecasts and supply plans that detail how demand will be supplied, including what will be manufactured, inventoried, and procured in support of a demand plan. In addition to S&OP processes, other advanced planning and scheduling (APS) processes and systems have been recently implemented by many of the largest companies—often under the banner of integrated supply chain management. These processes develop plans and schedules across multiple functional areas, typically using sophisticated systems that incorporate business intelligence, such as constraint-based optimization algorithms and methods.

One such process is advanced production scheduling, one of the earliest APS processes. It supplements a manufacturer's MRP process by helping develop a more realistic material plan via the creation of a production schedule that jointly considers all production resources, including labor, equipment, and materials, to ensure an accurate plan in a constrained-resource manufacturing environment. Another cross-functional APS process is integrated supply chain planning that concurrently develops demand, distribution, procurement, and manufacturing plans for a multifacility supply chain network, potentially composed of a company's plants, distribution centers, and other supply chain resources.

Stage 2: Advanced Supply Chain Management

The advanced supply chain management (SCM) stage is one that a limited number of larger companies have focused on for the past several years to start to improve their supply chain operations that span across trading partners and themselves. This involves supply chain relationships or interenterprise programs a company has with its suppliers and customers that begin to reach out beyond the four walls of their enterprises. These programs are aimed at enabling a company to have some awareness and influence on their customers' needs and external suppliers' capabilities.

Jointly Managed Inventory Programs

Jointly managed inventory programs, such as vendor-managed inventory (VMI), continuous replenishment process (CRP), quick replenishment (QR), and CPFR® fall into these types of programs. Under the VMI, CRP, and QR programs a manufacturer manages its customer's finished goods inventories and a supplier manages its manufacturing customer's inventory of production materials. A newer process, CPFR®—predicated on widely published findings from a Warner-Lambert and Wal-Mart pilot, released in mid-1995—supports the joint development of forecasting and the replenishment planning of inventories among trading partners. Since 1996, the Voluntary Inter-Industry Commerce Standards (VICS) Committee has been leading the charge in this area with its retailing and consumer goods manufacturing member companies. (See the VICS CPFR Web site at www.CPFR.org for updated information.) Successful CPFR® pilots have been conducted by companies, such as manufacturers Sara Lee, Kimberly Clark, and Nabisco and retailers Kmart, Wegmans, and Schnucks. The results demonstrate that these types of programs offer the opportunity for benefits to all trading partner participants in the form of reduced inventories, improved availability of products on retail shelves, and increased sales. The success of CPFR® has led the VICS Committee to spawn another program called Collaborative Transportation Management (CTM) that involves joint planning among a shipper and its suppliers and transportation carriers.

Collaborative Planning Programs

In addition to the jointly managed inventory programs already mentioned, a few advanced companies are now starting to consider implementing collaborative planning processes with their trading partners. AMR Research has identified four general types of these collaborative processes: synchronized production scheduling, collaborative product development, collaborative demand planning, and collaborative logistics planning (see Figure 7.2). The programs described earlier, the joint inventory management and CTM programs, fall into the last two types of these programs, respectively. Under a collaborative production scheduling program, a manufacturer works with its multitier suppliers to align production schedules to ensure production materials reach each trading partner's production facilities in a just-in-time (JIT) fashion, thereby minimizing material inventories and the risk of disruption to final production operations.

Over the past two decades, OEMs have been using EDI to support programs, better termed supplier synchronization programs. OEMS in the high-tech, automotive, and discrete manufacturing industries have been providing forecasts, production schedules, and material releases to their tiered suppliers as a step toward synchronizing operations. However, these efforts have been less than collaborative with OEMs basically dictating their needs, unilaterally. This is in contrast to a collaborative relationship that entails working multilaterally with suppliers to jointly align demand and supply plans, a process that supports achieving what is best for all parties from an overall supply chain perspective.

A collaborative product development process deals with efforts by a manufacturer to work with its suppliers on the joint development and planning of

Major Collaboration Opportunities Within a Supply Chain

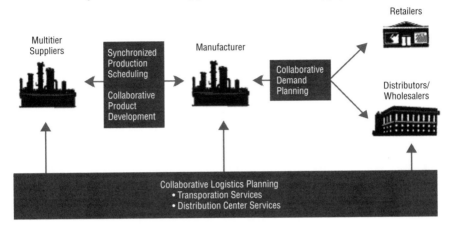

Source: AMR Research, 1998

figure 7.2

new products. This includes collaborative project management and engineering, as well as the development of new product designs. Many OEMs already have this process in place but have been improving it over time to help streamline and automate what has been a very manual process involving phone, fax, and mail.

Improved Order Promising

A last type of advanced SCM program involves improvements companies have been making in order promising processes, termed available-to-promise (ATP) and capable-to-promise (CTP). ATP involves committing a potential customer order to finished goods already available or scheduled for production. In contrast, CTP deals with whether a company will be able to commit to fill a customer's order with productive resources available, such as production machine time, materials, and work-in-process. With these programs, companies are trying to reduce the time it takes to provide customers with a promise date, moving these companies toward being able to quickly quote—potentially in real time—an accurate, realistic promise date, rather than a pre-specified manufacturing lead time. To support these order-promising improvements, a cross-functional process needs to be in place to quickly assess capabilities among supply chain functional departments, such as manufacturing, logistics, and procurement.

As with these ordering promising improvements, all the other processes described in the advanced SCM stage are contingent on having achieved a level of proficiency in the functional and cross-functional processes described in stage 1, supply chain optimization. Functional excellence in each functional organization is needed to ensure that each can execute on what they plan for and have made commitments against. In addition, cross-functional processes are necessary so that a commitment made to an external trading partner by one functional organization can be aligned to commitments made by other organizations within an enterprise. For example, if the sales or marketing organization jointly develops and commits to satisfying a customer's replenishment plan, they have to be confident that the manufacturing and logistics organizations can satisfy the plan. This is why stage 2 competencies cannot be worked on until some level of proficiency in stage 1 is achieved—in effect, stage 1 is the foundation on which stage 2 is built.

Stage 3: Leveraging E-Commerce

This stage is most closely affiliated with why this book was started in 2000. The Internet is hot, and CEOs are driving their organizations toward leveraging e-business to improve the way their companies sell and conduct business operations. When the annals of SCM are written, 1999 will go down as an inflection point year in which CEOs started to understand the potential of the Internet to enable interenterprise supply chain integration and selling via new business models. That year many started to understand that the Internet was a tool, much like the phone system, except it was a medium to be used to communicate among computers as well as people. Also, it could be used to support and supplement, not always supplant, their current ways of conducting business.

Much of the revelation that took place to foster the inflection point was due to a series of Internet-related events in 1999. There was the phenomenal success of e-business-based companies such as Amazon.com that were so successful that mighty retailer Wal-Mart threatened to sue it over its hiring of several key Wal-Mart IT executives. There was also the firing of Compaq's CEO, Eckhard Pfeiffer, ostensibly over his failure to implement a successful e-business strategy in light of the fact that Dell Computers catapulted to the top spot in the PC market, largely fueled by its Internet-based business model. All this created an exuberance to explore all the business opportunities the Internet could offer.

Three processes that leading companies are working on are leveraging e-commerce capabilities within their business operations.

Supply Chain Outsourcing

The first is supply chain outsourcing, a practice that many companies in the United States have been increasingly doing. This is part of a move to focus on their core competencies, such as marketing, sales, and new product development, by outsourcing supply chain operations to others that can do them more efficiently, leveraging a multitude of customers. In the high-tech industry, for example, manufacturing outsourcing is starting to become the norm as companies continue to use standard components and modularized architectures to build products. This has led to the fast growth of contract manufacturers such as Flextronics, Solectron, and Celestica. In addition, 3PL businesses have been growing rapidly as more companies get out of running their own distribution centers and transportation fleets. Lastly, the outsourcing phenomenon is evident in the emergence of lead logistics providers (LLPs)—assetless service providers that coordinate the logistical activities of their corporate customers, coordinating fulfillment processes that span from taking the order to getting it shipped, invoiced, and settled.

E-Commerce is being used to leverage this outsourcing phenomenon, further fueling its adoption in the industry. Recently, for example, Eastman Chemical announced that it would outsource its logistics operations to Shipchem.com, a new company formed by Eastman and Global Logistics Technologies, a software vendor. In a similar fashion, Ford announced that it would outsource its international customs operations to Vastera, an international trade logistics software vendor.

Internet Procurement

Internet procurement is another process companies are implementing that leverage e-commerce capabilities. Almost all companies that have started are using the Internet to procure indirect production goods. They are now showing an interest in being able to purchase direct production goods over the Internet to help reduce the cost of, streamline, and speed up their replenishment processes. IBM, for example, has already custom-built a sophisticated procurement system that leverages e-commerce capabilities to procure direct production items from thousands of its suppliers. The company recently announced that it would replace the system with software to be developed with two software vendors, i2 Technologies and Ariba.

Support of Web Selling

A last type of process companies are enabling via leveraging e-commerce is selling to customers over a Web site, on a B2B or B2C basis. With the success of Amazon.com in the B2C business, many dot-coms started selling over the Web for a variety of consumer goods items, looking to replicate Amazon's success. In addition, traditional brick-and-mortar companies such as Wal-Mart and Toys 'R' Us opened Web stores, basically moving from a bricks-and-mortar to a clicks-and-mortar business model—and effectively opening up an additional sales channel to consumers and defending against startup Internet retailers. With the success of Dell, which now takes in over half its revenues over the Web, and Cisco, which currently takes over 80% of its orders over the Web, many B2B companies have been attracted to selling over the Web to open a new sales channel. In addition, mature traditional distribution companies such as Marshall Industries (now owned by Avnet), which sells electronic components, and W. W. Grainger, which sells MRO items, have opened up successful Web stores of their own. These Web stores provide their customers with year-round 7-day, 24-hour service and reduce the manual, paper-based activities performed by their customer service organizations. W.W. Grainger has extended its offering by opening up OrderZone.com with five other MRO companies, including Marshall Industries.

While the new Web-selling business models show great promise, they require that the Web store be tightly integrated into a company's supply chain operations. A consumer complaint during the 1998 holiday season in B2C was the lack of adequate fulfillment. Consumers were not getting what they ordered or when they expected it—with some receiving Christmas gifts after Christmas. This was partially corrected during the 1999 holiday season. An AMR Research survey conducted among B2C consumers of the 1999 holiday season showed that while consumers rated their overall satisfaction with their Internet shopping experience at an average of 9 out of 10, once free shipping was taken out, the average rating plunged to 7. It was concluded that Internet retailers were running losing operations to ensure satisfactory fulfillment, largely due to inadequate order fulfillment processes. The Web stores were not being supported by efficient, integrated back-office supply chain operations.

To correct this, companies are working on reengineering their supply chains to support Web selling. Support comes in two ways. The first is to provide supply chain-related information, such as ATP/CTP and order status information, on their Web sites. The second involves seamlessly integrating supply chain operations to support orders taken over the Web with the same quality fulfillment service as orders taken by more traditional means, such as phone, fax, and mail.

The support of selling over the Web, as well as the other stage 3 processes that leverage e-commerce (namely, Internet procurement and outsourcing), all require a level of stage 1–level integrated internal supply chains and stage 2–level extended customer/supplier relationships. Because of this, companies need to have some level of proficiency in stage 2 before they can leverage e-commerce effectively, making stage 2 processes contingent on achieving stage 3.

Stage 4: E-Business Optimization

Achieving e-business optimization involves using e-business tools and methods to monitor, coordinate, and control the supply chain activities among all trading partners in a supply chain community. Much of it is predicated on establishing a sharing of real-time information among suppliers, manufacturers, distributors, retailers, logistics service providers, and their respective business systems. This is why the Internet holds great promise for this stage of e-supply chain evolution.

Supply Chain Keiretsu

The ultimate end-state of e-business optimization involves emulating an e-supply chain ecosystem or virtual supply chain keiretsu, which is defined as a conglomerate of trading partners in which each party provides unique value for the group's collective good. Under this end state, each trading partner is immediately made aware of customer orders and their role in the fulfillment process, and all are aligned to meet expected future demand. To do this requires the real-time sharing of coordination information that includes the details on and the status of orders, as well as demand-supply collaboration information (see Table 7.1).

Only a few companies have made substantial progress toward achieving this end state. As mentioned, Cisco Systems, for example, operates a virtual private network over the Internet that ties together its trading partners to enable real-time information sharing, in what is termed its supply chain ecosystem. This system has helped the company successfully acquire and assimilate more than fifty companies into its supply chain operations over the span of 7 years. A phenomenal feat, especially with the fact that many acquisitions are fully integrated into the ecosystem within 60 days, including fulfilling an order taken over the Cisco Web site.

Information Required to Enable a Virtual Supply Chain Keiretsu

Real-Time Coordination Information (Joint Order Fulfillment and Status)	Demand-Supply Collaboration Information (Joint Supply Chain Planning and Scheduling)
Configuration information Inventory availability (raw materials, WIP, finished goods) Sales order quotes Promise Dates Sales orders with changes Acknowledgements Shipping Dates Delivery Dates Advanced Shipment Notices In-Transit Status	Production schedules Sales forecasts Inventory availability (raw materialss, WIP, finished goods) Replenishment requirments Material requests Logistical resource availabilities Shipment plans Promotional plans Product design and specifications New product introduction plans Merchandising plans

table 7.1

One of the key building blocks needed to achieve this supply chain end state is the need to establish supply chain visibility. This involves visibility into where are all the goods, and where are they headed, as well as where are they supposed to going and by when. Full supply chain visibility includes high-level information on the procurement, inventory, production, and distribution plans of trading partners, as well as the status of customer and purchase orders. In addition, it would also include detailed information on the status of an order on the plant floor, within a warehouse, or in transit.

While supply chain visibility is important to stage 4 supply chain process-es, it eventually needs to be wrapped within an overall supply chain event management (SCEM) process. An SCEM process is one that monitors events (planned and unplanned) to notify supply chain decision makers and systems that a supply chain is responding as planned or it is not. When intervention is needed, it goes further, automatically executing prespecified contingency plans or providing "what if" support to decision makers responsible for taking action.

Support of Virtual E-Businesses

Another supply chain process that companies are implementing within the e-business optimization stage involves evolving toward becoming virtual manufacturers and virtual distributors. Under the virtual manufacturer e-busi-ness model, an organization does not manufacture anything and has no plants. A virtual manufacturer does, however, control new product development, marketing, and sales, as well as coordinates customer service for its products.

It hires contract manufacturers and logistics service providers to make, assemble, and ship final products to its customers.

Sun Microelectronics, a division of Sun Microsystems, is a case study of this type of organization as it outsources the manufacture of electronic boards to contract manufacturers and has orders shipped directly to customers from its suppliers' plants, eliminating any handling of the product by Sun. The company views its core competency as board design and development, not manufacturing or distribution. Another example of a virtual manufacturer is Dell. Best known for its success in selling computers online via the Web, it has also been successful in moving to a build-to-order manufacturing model, while holding little to no inventory. For some products, Dell emulates a virtual manufacturer by contracting with a logistics service provider to do final product assembly. Dell also operates a negative DSO cash flow business model, whereby it is paid on order, but suppliers are paid days later. This is supported by Dell requiring suppliers to hold consignment inventories close to its manufacturing plants in warehouses (operated by Ryder Logistics Systems) that are located within a 15-minute drive of Dell's plants. To enable a JIT assembly environment, Internet orders are sent every 2 hours to the warehouses for final assembly there or for component delivery to a plant within 2 hours.

Another e-business model that some companies are implementing is that of a virtual distributor. This type of organization does not distribute anything nor have any warehouses. It markets products and takes and sources orders to multiple suppliers. The virtual distributor usually controls marketing and sales as well as coordinates order fulfillment. However, it relies on its suppliers to make, assemble, and ship final products directly to customers. Ingram-Micro is an example of a virtual distributor that sells to more than 140,000 high-tech resellers in 130 countries, involving around 200,000 products from more than 1,500 suppliers. Real-time order information is transferred to suppliers, which allows Ingram to play a "middleman" distributor role, without holding inventory and, more important, adding virtually no delays to the order fulfillment process.

Similar to the other stages of the E-Supply Chain Evolution Model, to make these stage 4 processes work efficiently, companies need to have a foundation of processes built during stages 1 through 3. For example, to truly emulate a virtual supply chain keiretsu, an order taken over a Web store will need an accurate commitment date from every trading partner involved, which will need to be obtained from them in real time. In addition, each trading partner will need to be aware of the present and future status of an order, also in real time. For all this to happen, the trading partners will have to have leveraged e-commerce, reached outside their four walls to customers and suppliers using advanced SCM processes, and optimized their internal supply chains.

STRATEGY DEVELOPMENT PROCESS

As discussed at the beginning of this chapter, a major role of supply chain strategy development entails gaining an understanding of your company's current supply chain competencies before it can move forward toward a future vision. The E-Supply Chain Evolution Model described earlier is a framework in which readers can describe their stage of supply chain competency, as well as to provide a view of the process competencies companies should consider implementing over time. The model provides the nomenclature to go through the strategy development process. In addition, since companies can't skip over e-supply chain stages, a strategy process predicated on it must first start with an understanding of current competencies, before developing a future vision. With this in mind, supply chain strategists should use this model in conjunction with the following recommended four-step strategy process to develop their company's supply chain strategy.

Step 1: Determining the As-Is State

The first step in conducting a strategy development process entails determining a company's current state, the as-is state, used as the baseline from which to build toward a future to-be state. One purpose for developing a detailed as-is state is to identify potential areas for improvement and reengineering. Since the as-is state is the foundation upon which a company builds toward a future to-be state, a company must first assess whether its current processes are sound enough to support future supply chain operations. For example, to what extent should a company focus initial efforts on reengineering its internal processes and systems to fully integrate them before starting to connect to its customers and suppliers electronically—"getting its house in order" per stage 1, before developing process competencies of stage 2?

Another purpose of determining the as-is state is to help a company develop a practical, feasible future state to aim toward. This deals with being realistic in terms of what can be done and over what period of time. In many industries, for example, it is unrealistic for some companies to try to achieve an e-business optimization stage in the short run, since their internal supply chains need to be improved. This stage requires tightly integrated processes and systems with trading partners; thus, it is impractical to believe a company can jump to it skipping over stages 2 and 3.

An important step in determining a company's as-is state is mapping out its current supply chain processes. One well-known tool for doing this is the supply chain operations reference (SCOR) model, a product of the Supply Chain Council (www.supply-chain.org), an independent, not-for-profit corporation, cofounded by consulting firm Pittiglio Rabin Todd & McGrath (PRTM) and AMR Research. The SCOR model is used by companies to describe and redesign their processes to support SCM practices and systems.

While mapping out detailed processes is an extremely important component of determining a company's as-is state, it needs to be used in conjunction with a method for assessing what e–supply chain stage a company is in. In this book we provide a survey instrument for doing this composed of questions that will help uncover what stage a company is in. Here we discuss step 1, "Determining the As-Is State," in two substeps that address the two components that make up this portion of the strategy development process.

Using the SCOR Model to Map Processes

The SCOR model is a hierarchical model that focuses primarily on three levels of business processes—in contrast to functions that are normally looked at in many mapping exercises. This is why this model is recommended as a blueprint to use when trying to assess processes, as it helps to better understand the cross-functional process competencies needed to support SCM practices.

The SCOR model is organized at its top level around four major SCM processes: source, make, deliver, and plan. At its second level, called the configuration level, the model encompasses 26 process categories that further break down the top-level business processes (see Figure 7.3). At this level many companies start to profile and configure supply chains to meet demand needs, such as how to manage stocked, make-to-stock, and engineer-to-order product lines. In the SCOR model's third level, termed the process element level, processes are decomposed even further and a company can start to map out and identify more detailed process elements, information inputs/outputs, performance metrics, and applicable best practices.

SCOR Version 4.0 Level 2 Toolkit
Has 26 Process Categories

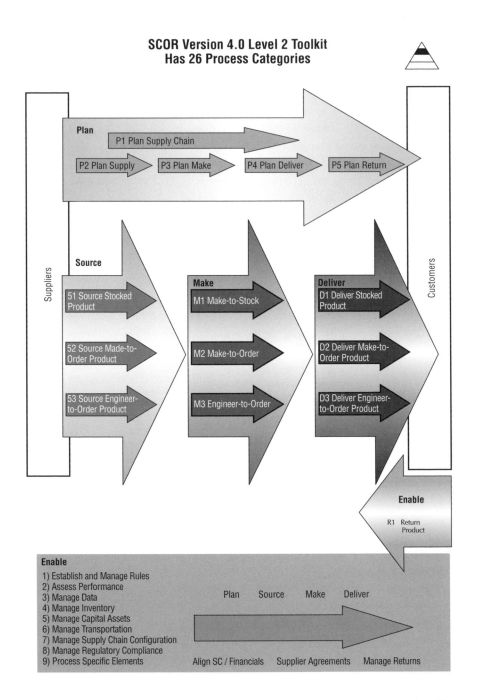

figure 7.3

It is at this third level that companies can start to identify any process gaps, redundant processes, and unnecessary process delays. For example, in mapping out an order-to-cash process, it can help address such questions as "Are there any unnecessary handoffs of an order among functional departments?" and "Are there too many levels in the order approval process that are causing needless delays in fulfilling orders?" Companies also typically use this level to fine-tune their supply chain operational strategies.

While the SCOR model is a useful guide for mapping out enterprise-wide supply chain business processes, it does not formally, as yet, address interenterprise processes. To work around this, readers are advised to view an interenterprise process as one that is similar to a cross-functional enterprise process, except that its subprocesses will be distributed and carried out among trading partners, rather than among functional departments.

Assessing the E–Supply Chain Stage

Assessing your company's as-is state, from the perspective of its e-supply chain stage, is more difficult and qualitative than mapping out its SCM processes. This is because there are no hard and fast rules or guidelines to follow, and many of the inputs will be subjective. A company needs to be honest with itself and on its position in the industry if it is to assess its actual stage. For example, many companies keep secrets from one another because they believe their practices give them competitive advantage. We've often found many of these secret practices to be less than best practice.

In this book we offer an interview guide that can be used to help assess a company's e-supply chain evolution stage (see Figure 7.4). The guide should be used to interview executives and thought leaders within a company. For example, it will be important to interview not only supply chain executives but also your CEO, CIO, and other C-level executives. Vice presidents in other functional areas, such as marketing, sales, customer service, and finance, should also be interviewed. In addition, often there are usually a few middle-level managers who, although not successful in climbing the corporate ladder, are viewed as movers and shakers in thought leadership. These types of individuals should also be interviewed. Some of them now carry newer titles with an "e" in them, making them easier to spot!

E-Supply Chain Interview Guide

CURRENT USE OF SCM BEST PRACTICES

1. I What best practices has your company already implemented?

2. Does your company have a sales and operations planning (S&OP) process?

3. Do you internally do collaborative operational planning. Who gets involved? Is there field input?

4. Does your company have an available-to-promise and capable-to-promise process in place? How long to quote a promise date?

5. Do you have any comanaged inventory programs in place? Continuous Replenishment or vendor-managed inventory (VMI) with customers/suppliers? How many customers/suppliers?

6. Have you piloted collaborative planning, forecasting, and replenishment (CPFR) concepts? With customers, suppliers, or both? How many?

SUPPLY CHAIN MANAGEMENT (SCM) INITIATIVES

7. What SCM initiatives is your company working on?

8. What SCM initiatives is your company working on to improve operations planning and scheduling?

9. What SCM initiatives is your company working on to improve procurement and sourcing?

10. What SCM initiatives are there to improve manufacturing operations? Are you moving toward build-to-order or assemble-to-order manufacturing?

11. What initiatives are there to improve logistics operations including warehousing, transportation, and inventory management ? Which of these activities are being or have been outsourced?

12. What initiatives are you working on to improve order management and fulfillment activities? What about the one order/one shipment concept? Do you or are there plans to outsource your fulfillment activities?

CURRENT ELECTRONIC CONNECTIVITY

13. Does your company use EDI via a value added or privatized network? What components? What percentage of supplier/customers is connected via EDI? What percentage of customer/supplier unit transactions? What percentage of dollar transactions?

14. Does your company use the Internet to do business with customers? To do what? What percentage of supplier/customers is connected via Internet? What percentage of customer/supplier unit transactions? What percentage of dollar transactions?

15. What is your company's primary use of its internal Intranet? Information and research? Business processes including Benefits, HR, Administrative, Customer/Supplier information/transactions?

MAJOR E-BUSINESS INITIATIVES

16. How do you see e-business affecting how you do business in the long run? Internally? With customers? With suppliers? With logistics providers?

17. What is senior management's view of e-business for your company? Critical to future success? Aid to business? Minor impact? Not applicable?

18. How has your business strategy from 2 to 3 years ago been altered to deal with e-business? Does your company have a formal e-business strategy?

19. How will your supply chain management activities change to support any e-business strategies?

20. How has or will the company's organization be changed to support the strategy? Any new job titles?

21. Are specific e-business goals and metrics formally included in the 3 to 5 year strategic plan?

22. What are your company's current specific e-business strategy projects? Are they designed and managed within business units or departments or centrally? Are they tightly coupled to any supply chain management initiatives?

23. Are these e-business initiatives primarily driven from U.S. operations? What is going on from a global perspective?

24. Does your industry segment have a trading exchange (NetMarket) to support it? Is your company using it or plan to use it?

25. What benefits does your company hope to achieve from e-business? From an internal perspective? Customer perspective? Supplier Perspective? Logistics provider perspective?

26. What are the greatest barriers you foresee to implementing your company's e-business strategies?

27. Does your company currently sell to or service customers via the Web – that is, directly from your company's Web site or through a trading exchange (NetMarket)? How do you support these sales from a supply chain management perspective?

28. Does your company currently buy from or exchange with suppliers/logistics providers via the web, i.e., directly from your company's website or through a Trading Exchange (NetMarket)? How do you support these purchases from a supply chain management perspective?

29. Have your customers, suppliers or logistics providers proposed e-business cooperation? If so what is it? Vendor managed inventory, catalog/product information?

30. Does your company use an internal electronic catalog for procurement? If so, which category of purchases – MRO, direct production, and transportation?

31. Do you act as a virtual manufacturer or distributor? Which manufacturing operations do you outsource? Which distribution operations do you outsource? To whom?

figure 7.4

As can be noted from the guide, interview questions address the following four areas:

- Current use of SCM best practices: These questions help identify what is already working from a supply chain best-practice perspective. When considering answers to these questions, distinguish what is planned from what is real and what is implemented versus what is just being piloted. Greater weight should be given to those practices that have been working and have already started to show benefits. These questions will be important in assessing whether a company is in stage 1 versus 2.

- SCM initiatives: These questions relate to what the organization is currently working on or is planning to start work on. They help identify where the company is moving from a SCM perspective. When considering answers to these questions, it is again important to separate the real from the planned. Give greater weight to initiatives that are funded from a budgetary perspective. This will help determine those initiatives that have already been through an executive approval cycle and stand the best chance of coming to fruition. If an initiative involves a pilot, also give greater weight to ones that have a follow-up plan once the pilot demonstrates success. These questions will also be important in assessing whether a company is in stage 1 or 2.

- Current electronic connectivity: These questions are aimed at getting objective information about the extent to which an enterprise is going beyond its four walls, reaching out to its customers and suppliers. Of itself, a company's ability to answer these types of questions that require real numbers (e.g., the percentage of suppliers connected via EDI) will be important in assessing the willingness and capability of a company and its trading partners to share information, electronically. Give greater weight to those trading partner connections that involve more than just a few customers and suppliers. Ones with just a few tend to be the ones that were implemented by fiat from your trading partners or at your own company's insistence. Answers to these questions will be important toward objectively determining whether a company has achieved proficiency in supply chain processes reflected in stage 2 and whether it has truly embraced leveraging e-commerce.

- Major e-business initiatives: These questions address where a company is moving with respect to an e-business optimization stage. One of their aims is to help strategists determine how ready a company is to move forward on future e-business initiatives. If a C-level executive is not yet committed, it is unlikely that much will be done. In a similar way, if executives believe a company must do everything itself and are unwilling to outsource to focus core competencies, most attempts to move to virtual business models will fail. Lastly, if no one is at least thinking of doing e-business by now, it is unlikely that much will happen in this regard over the next year. Answers to many of these questions will help determine whether a company is ready to move to stage 4 of the E-Supply Chain Evolution Model.

Putting It Together

Results from the interviews done with the interview guide need to be compared and contrasted with the process maps developed before a supply chain strategist can determine the as-is state and think about supply chain improvements that leverage e-business. The process maps document the supply chain processes already in place so they are best used to assess potential process improvements and also a company's current e-supply chain stage. The results from the interview guide, while supplementing the process maps to some extent, are more useful in determining whether a company should move on to the next stage or continue to focus on its current stage.

Step 2: Developing the To-Be State

While step 1 is useful to assessing whether a company can progress beyond its current stage, before developing a to-be state, it is extremely important to understand the planning horizon you are dealing with. Are you looking to execute on a supply chain vision that is 2 years, 3 years, or longer? This decision will be important, as it will provide the bounds on how much change can be realistically implemented.

Identifying a Supply Chain Strategic Theme

Another important issue to consider is strategic intent. This point directly relates to the company's business and e-business strategy. For example, does the company want to focus on being the low-cost provider in its industry or the best at customer service, and how will this be fundamentally accomplished. Strategic intent translates to a strategic supply chain theme or goal that supports a company's business strategy and that supply chain initiatives need to address. These themes are usually operational, channel, or customer service oriented, and they can vary by industry as noted from the following strategic themes being considered:

- Perfect order: In the consumer products industries, leading companies have been focused on attaining a perfect order process that involves the flawless execution of every order from order quoting to invoicing and settlement.

- Mass customization: In many of the discrete manufacturing industries, such as high tech and industrial equipment, companies have been focused on moving to build-to-order manufacturing models to offer unlimited product configurations to their customers (a lesson learned from Dell).

- Ten-day order-to-delivery process: In 1999 Toyota announced that for some models it would build cars to a customer's order within 5 days and then deliver it within 5 days. This came to be known as the "10-day gauntlet" in the industry, as it reflected many of the automakers' strategic intent to substantially reduce their order cycle times. While Toyota eventually backed off the reduced cycle time commitment, the industry is still focused on it. GM recently announced its order-to-delivery initiative aimed at significant reductions in its cycle times.

- Three-month airplane: To assemble an airplane currently takes 9 months from the time the order is placed, because each order is uniquely configured. Much like the automobile industry, the aerospace and defense industry is moving toward drastic reductions in their cycle times, eventually trying to potentially bring them down to assembly of a plane within 3 months.

- Defend against dot-coms: With all the hype of Internet retailers in 1999, many brick-and-mortar retailers countered by starting their own Web stores, including retail heavyweights such as Home Depot, Staples, and CVS. Major retail initiatives are now focused on implementing multiple channels to reach the consumer, including stores, Web sites, and even kiosks.

- Bombs on target in 72 hours: With the massive change in the world's political scene, the U.S. Department of Defense (DoD) has repositioned its logistics mission to be able to deploy military resources to anywhere in the world in 72 hours.

In many cases these strategic supply chain themes will never actually be achieved. They do, however, form the basis and the "rallying cries" to energize supply chain initiatives and to help keep them focused toward achieving a consistent long-term vision. As plans are laid out, these themes become the anchors for change, through constant checking of the extent to which initiatives impact and move a company toward the strategic theme.

Choosing the Future E–Supply Chain Stage
Many believe that reaching an e-business optimization stage is the right

answer for their company and industry. This is not the case. Most trading partners need to ensure that they are team players in a supply chain community, rather than trying to control it—which is normally left up to the channel or network masters. Hence, a major part of developing a future state is identifying the value-added roles your company will play within a supply chain. It is important to know what the overall supply chain strategy is for your community. Clearly future supply chains or value chains (Bauer and Poirier 2000) will make new demands on a company and set new expectations for success. As shown in Figure 7.5, "The Future Internet-Connected Supply Chain," while traditional brick-and-mortar roles such as supplier, manufacturer, distributor, and retailer will still exist, there are also virtual manufacturing and trading exchange roles, which act more like pure information intermediaries. In this regard, relative to the four-stage E–Supply Chain Evolution Model, different companies and industries will choose to focus their efforts on achieving different stages as follows:

Future Internet-Connected Supply Chain

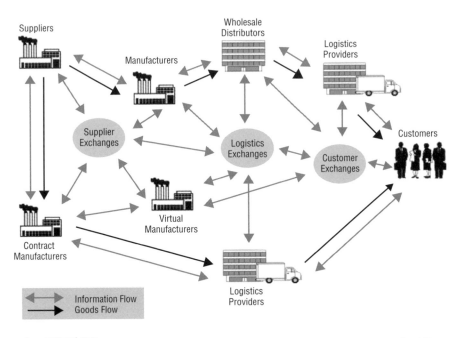

Source: AMR Research, 2000

figure 7.5

- In a future supply chain, small to medium-sized businesses (SMBs) will primarily focus on stages 1 and 2 processes because they will need to respond to their supply chain needs as dictated by the channel and network masters. These companies will need to be able quickly commit to and fulfill orders from their downstream supply chain trading partners. This will also be the case for many CPG companies that will continue to operate in make-to-stock businesses that will also continue to focus on these two stages. Upstream process industry manufacturers that operate heavy fixed capital manufacturing assets on a 7-day, 24-hour basis will also focus on stages 1 and 2 because they won't control their supply chains and need to book orders rapidly against ongoing production.

- Contract manufacturers and midtier suppliers will primarily need to focus on stage 2 processes since to stay in business, they need to add value by being as efficient as possible, focusing on optimized internal supply chain operations that align with customer needs and supplier capabilities.

- Tier 1 manufacturers, logistics service providers, and larger distributors exert more control and influence on a supply chain, but typically not as a channel or network master, although one could argue exceptions such as Ingram Micro and WW Grainger. These types of companies will primarily focus on eventually achieving stage 3, moving toward leveraging e-commerce to streamline their supply chain operations, connect to their trading partners, and expand their sales channels. Many companies in discrete manufacturing industries will also move toward stage 3 for the same reasons. They are moving further to lean build-to-order manufacturing models that require suppliers to be electronically-connected to enable JIT component deliveries to their assembly lines driven by dynamic customer demand.

- Channel and future network masters, such as large retailers and OEMs, will need to coordinate and control their supply chain ecosystems. As such these types of companies will need to continue to move toward stage 4 supply chain processes. Master companies of this type will be found in the high-tech industry, which experiences short product life cycles and long multitier supply chains— for example, silicon-to-computer supply chains.

In summary, developing a to-be state requires a company to understand the supply chain processes they will need that add value to their supply chains, and these will depend on the industry they are in and the roles they play. To develop a future to-be state, this understanding then needs to be weighed against a company's supply chain strategic theme and its current state.

Step 3: Creating the Road Map for Change

Once the as-is and to-be states are developed, the next major step to take in formulating a supply chain strategy is to develop a blueprint or road map for change that drives the strategy's implementation. As in all major endeavors, full strategic change will need to evolve over years rather than months and will need to be made incrementally. In this book we offer readers an approach called the business release approach that has its roots in a methodology developed by i2 Technologies to implement systems and processes with their customers and consulting partners, such as CSC Consulting.

The Business Release Methodology

The business release methodology advocates that an implementation plan be developed that has multiple phases, with business releases numbered from 1, 2, and so forth. Each business release is designed to be implemented and start providing real benefits within a 6- to 9-month or less time frame. Each phase has three major subphases: plan, implement, and assess. During the plan phase, an implementation work plan for the business release is developed with detail on tasks and activities. This plan drives activities during the implementation phase. The last phase of a business release is an assess phase during which an assessment is made as to whether the phase was successful in making changes and whether these are showing benefits based on performance metrics established during the plan phase (see Figure 7.6).

The multiphased business release approach ensures that a strategic initiative has a self-funding nature, in that value is provided at the end of each phase, also potentially making the whole initiative pay for itself over time. This also minimizes the chances of an important strategic initiative being stopped in the middle due to a lack of perceived benefits. More important, the multiphase approach allows project management at the end of each business release to review whether the next scheduled business release is still worth doing or whether it should be replaced by another.

Business Release Methodology

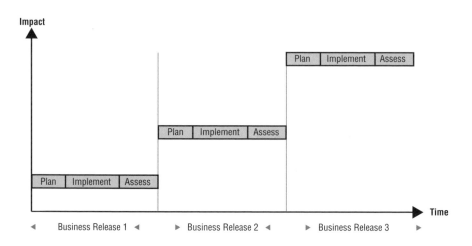

figure 7.6

Determining Process, People, and Technology Changes

During each business release, a project team needs to work on changes not only on supply chain processes but also on implementing the technology needed to enable it and the people and organization changes needed to operate it. In this book we offer AMR Research's first e-business model, depicted in Figure 7.7, as a tool to help project teams walk through the process of identifying the process, people, and technology needed to achieve the required changes. As shown, central to an e-business strategy is its alignment to a company's business strategy. Technology supports the e-business strategy with application software and enabling technologies that are composed of four major types:

- Relationship applications software directly impact but do not necessarily interact with trading partners, such as customers and suppliers. It includes logistics and fulfillment, as well as customer, supplier, and demand management applications.

- Back-office integration software work within the four walls of an enterprise and include administrative, planning, and asset/inventory management applications.

AMR Research E-Business Model

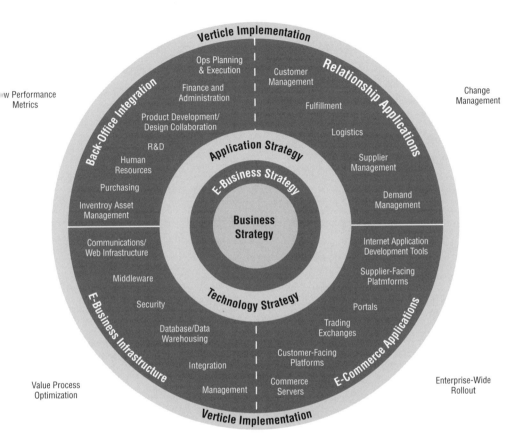

Value Process Optimization

Enterprise-Wide Rollout

Change Management

w Performance Metrics

Source: AMR Research, 2000

figure 7.7

- E-Commerce applications directly interact with trading partners, including supplier-facing technology platforms, trading exchanges, and commerce servers.

- E-Business infrastructure includes enabling technologies such as middleware, data warehouses, messaging/communications, and security software.

All these technologies need to be configured to support supply chain processes. Surrounding the core technologies in the AMR Research e-business model are processes that support business process and people changes, including a change management strategy that is required. In addition, performance metrics need to be developed to measure the impacts of planned changes, consistent with an enterprise-wide rollout plan.

Getting Started

With regard to an enterprise rollout plan and the business release methodology, important questions to consider are:

- where to get started and

- how to proceed.

Specifically, "What processes do I change first, second, and so forth, and in what ways?" While the answers to these questions will vary company to company and industry to industry, we do offer some advice.

1. Given the nature of e-business changes and the dynamic nature of the technology, companies are advised to implement an evolutionary, flexible set of processes. Be prepared to test as you go and modify/rectify as you roll them out across an enterprise, in contrast to attempting to implement a monolithic, fixed inflexible enterprise process. What works in some environments may not work in others.

2. A second guideline is to implement processes that yield immediate benefits, even if these are smaller than implementing other processes that would provide higher benefits but take longer. Given the dynamic nature of e-business, it is entirely possible that the technology will change drastically once or even twice during the longer implementation, anyway.

3. The last guideline is to try to work with internal organizations and external trading partners that are the most receptive to e-business changes. However, be careful not to develop solutions that are too specific to their organizational needs. Solutions need to be flexible enough to be implemented with other organizations with few modifications. While this approach runs the risk of having to do major modifications as processes are rolled out on an enterprise-wide or interenterprise-wide basis, it is better to get something

going that is successful. Once successful, others will naturally gravitate to a winning, proven strategy, even if it does not exactly fit their needs.

Step 4: Getting the Organization Ready for Change

Human nature is such that it is easier just to leave things just as they are. Why change if I don't have to or if things are going well? Because of this viewpoint, a supply chain strategist needs to place a lot of effort around getting organizations ready for change.

The Importance of a Business Case

A critical element of this readiness is the development of a business case that is credible enough to convince people that change is needed versus doing nothing is acceptable. The most important component of the business case is a statement of the value proposition for change in terms of tangible and intangible benefits. These fall into three major categories:

- Improvements in customer service involve being more responsive to customer demands. These include reduction in order cycle and promising times, improved order fulfillment, broader product choice, more appealing products, improved customer convenience, and better-quality products. In the long run these improvements lead to increased revenues, market share, competitiveness, and customer loyalty.

- Operating efficiencies might include reduced manufacturing, distribution, purchasing, and customer service expenses. These could also include a reduced cost of goods. In the long run, these reductions lead to improved operating margins and cash flow.

- Increased asset utilization might entail increased plant and warehouse capacity utilization, better return on inventory investments, and reduced capital requirements (such as in warehouse and plant space and equipment). In the long run increased asset utilization leads to an improved return on assets.

In preparing the business case it will be important to translate these improvements into financial terms to ensure support from the financial organizations as well as the CEO, CFO, and other C-level executives. Another important aspect to keep in mind is to tie each process change directly to specific benefits to help identify business releases, assess where to get started, and establish key performance metrics to track progress.

Communication Is Also Key in E-Business

Strategic supply chain initiatives should not be implemented in the dungeons of a company, to be brought out when they are ready—especially those that can widely impact an e-supply chain. These need to be marketed to internal employees, customers, suppliers, and other trading partners, as well as to company investors and other stakeholders to get widespread buy-ins. Constant and wide circulation of the initiative and its status should be communicated on a routine basis. This includes information provided in employee newsletters as well as to the press. This helps to position the seriousness of the initiative and convince the company's stakeholders of its worthiness. A good example of the kind of communication needed was a press story done on General Motors (GM) in 2000. It covered GM's order-to-delivery initiative in detail and as such should help GM get strategic buy-ins from their employees, dealers, suppliers, customers, and investors. While this type of communication doesn't guarantee a successful initiative, it does help remove some people from being roadblocks to change.

Assemble an Interdisciplinary Implementation Team

The implementation team assembled to implement an e-supply chain strategy is also important toward getting the organization ready for change. Don't staff it with employees that have nothing to do or are viewed in a bad light. That is a recipe for failure. Much of the success of Cisco Systems is based on the people who implemented their vision and system—the top performers, the people who were too busy for more work, are exactly the people who should be on a project of this nature. Important strategic change requires work be done by movers and shakers who never quit and thought leaders who never lose sight of the importance of the strategic goal.

The best implementation team for an e-supply chain project is one that represents a cross function of the value chain. In this regard, a project team will likely need representatives from operations, marketing, sales, customer service, purchasing, and finance. Also, don't be afraid to put customers and suppliers on an advisory board to the project team. Essentially implementing important e-supply chain processes impact multiple functions and many trading partners; the sooner they get involved, the better.

CONCLUSION

In this chapter we essentially discussed two things. First, we introduced the E-Supply Chain Evolution Model and detailed the types of processes companies might consider implementing to achieve each evolutionary stage. Second, we prescribed a detailed approach to use toward developing an e-supply chain strategy. In the next chapter, we will discuss the types of e-business tools and methods that can be used to enable each stage's supply chain processes. Our basic underlying premise is that regardless of the e-supply chain stage a company is trying to achieve, the e-business tools and methods covered in this book will be useful to help enable them. As such, their implementation would provide some practical next steps for companies to take toward achieving their future e-supply chain visions.

chapter 8

Practical
Next Steps

If you've read Chapters 2 through 7, you are now almost prepared to help develop your company's supply chain strategy road map for change that leverages e-business. The only basic question that remains is, What are some of the things you can do next that are practical? In other terms: What are the steps that can be taken along the way that are digestible (so that your company is not biting off more than it can chew) and that provide enough value so that benefits can be realized all along the way toward achieving the ultimate e–supply chain strategic vision? All of the success stories and benefits begin with execution; that said, this chapter will help you with the execution of your company's supply chain strategy.

From Chapters 2 and 3 we hope you've obtained a good understanding of the basic tools and methods of e-commerce and e-business that can be used to leverage your company's future supply chain operations. While all such strategies are important, more emphasis was dedicated to public and private trading exchanges, since these will play an important role in future supply chain operations. In Chapter 4 we discussed what is currently going on in seven industries: automotive, aerospace, chemicals, defense, fulfillment, consumer products, and high tech industries. This should help you develop the direction you need to go within your own industry, as well as provide you with real-world case studies of practical next steps others are taking. Chapter 5's role was to provide you with a sense of where things will be heading over the next 5 to 10 years and beyond. Chapters 6 and 7 provided thoughts and advice on how to develop an e-business and e-supply chain strategy that leverages the tools and methods of e-commerce, respectively.

While all the prior chapters lay the foundation for moving forward, it would be not be uncommon for most readers at this point to be overwhelmed, wondering exactly what should be done next and what technologies should be deployed. Asking questions such as "What does my first business release and associated technologies look like? What about the second?" This chapter is aimed at helping readers identify answers to these types of questions.

LEVERAGING THE E-BUSINESS TOOLS AND METHODS

Driving this chapter is the basic notion that the tools and methods of e-business are needed to enable and support supply chain business processes. There is a profound distinction between business processes and tools and methods. Business processes are composed of a set of steps to be followed to execute various supply chain operations and activities. Tools and methods, on the other hand, represent the technologies and procedures that merely support supply chain managers and their systems as they execute business process steps. The tools and methods of e-business are mostly technology based and, in and of themselves, do not suffice in enabling business processes. Along with technology, process and organizational changes are needed. Readers should recall the learning of many system implementation failures over the years that were caused by the belief that just installing a computer system would improve operations. In these failed implementations, often successful computer system installations did not lead to business improvements because supply chain managers just kept doing the same things they did before implementation—frequently working around the system!

In this chapter we will look at the four stages of the E–Supply Chain Evolution Model and discuss how the tools and methods of e-business can be used to enable and support the processes inherent in each of the stages. To some extent this may seem somewhat contrary to a commonly held belief that these tools and methods are meant to be used by only stage 3 and 4 companies looking to leverage e-business to improve external supply chains, involving trading partners all along the supply chain. However, one of the major premises of this book, especially within this chapter, is that e-business tools and methods can be used within all four stages to enable improved supply chain operations. These tools are even useful among companies focused on the first two stages of e-supply chain—namely, those improving internal operations and just starting to reach out to customers and suppliers.

> *The impact of these tools and methods will be profound. In the future, multiple companies will be interconnected and use supply chain management tools across the value chain. The importance of standardized processes and systems cannot be overstated.*

ENABLING SUPPLY CHAIN OPTIMIZATION

The tools and methods covered in Chapters 3 and 4 are not the only ones that companies can use to leverage e-business. While the term e-business is new, often associated with the use of the Internet, e-business as defined as the electronic support of business operations is not. From a perspective of supply chain management, the last decade has seen a growth in the use of traditional e-business tools and methods such as transportation management, warehouse management, inventory management, and advanced planning and scheduling (APS) software applications. AMR Research has been tracking the market for these applications for some time. It estimates that software vendors in this market generated $3.7 billion in revenues in 1999 and expects this figure to grow 38% annually until 2004, when revenues will reach a whooping $25.7 billion. Much of the historical growth has been fueled by companies looking to implement these applications to enable stage 1 and, to a lesser extent, stage 2 processes.

Many of these traditional supply chain management software applications have been Web enabled, extending their support of stage 1 supply chain optimization processes. Web-enabled software allows users within and outside a department, as well as from anywhere in the world, multiuser access to the same software application and data, often using just a simple PC browser. This feature helps integrate processes within a department and further allows departments to collaborate and share information. These newer Web-enabled e-business applications, therefore, help synchronize internal supply chain operations, helping break down functional silos.

Functional Process Improvement Tools and Methods

As covered in Chapter 7, the stage 1 supply chain optimization stage of e–supply chain involves improving internal operations from a functional as well as from a cross-functional perspective. Historically, stage 1 companies— including most of the *Fortune* 500—have begun leveraging e-business by implementing point-solution software applications that address a single functional area, such as transportation, distribution, or manufacturing. In a similar fashion, we expect the majority of future activity and resources of stage 1 companies to be applied toward using the traditional and new tools of e-business to improve processes within a single functional department. Logistics professionals seeking to improve their functional areas of responsibility will use some of the new Internet-based tools and methods such as trading exchanges, ASPs, and Internet buy-side software applications as described in the following sections.

Transportation Management

In the area of transportation management, e-business tool usage has primarily been based on the purchase of software applications to support optimized rating, routing, and scheduling, as well as tracking and tracing. Leveraging the Internet, software application vendors are Web-enabling these types of solutions to allow users in a traffic department, as well as other (potentially remote) company users, access to the same real-time transportation information. In this way, for example, everyone can have access to consistent track and trace information.

Traditional transportation management software applications can be replaced over time by the use of logistics exchanges (LXs). These will leverage the Internet to provide substantial opportunity to drastically reduce a shipper's freight costs and improve deliveries of its inbound, outbound, and interfacility shipments. The use of LXs are expected to improve transportation operations in four general areas:

- Market efficiency
- Transaction efficiency

- Asset optimization

- Coordinated execution

In recognition of these opportunities, AMR Research expects the LX market to generate about $2.5 to 3.0 billion of revenue by 2004.

As an illustration of the transportation benefit potential of LXs for users, consider the National Transportation Exchange (NTE), one of the first LXs. It started its business by posting less-than-truckload (LTL) back-haul shipments of transport carriers on its Web site. Shippers looking for a deal were able to come on the site to see whether they could secure one of these low-cost back-hauls. Like NTE, many of the startup LXs have dealt with just the spot-market portion of transportation services. However, over time NTE and other LX auctions, portals, and marketplaces are expected to expand their services beyond just posting spot hauls, to offering a broad range of transportation services. This will help shippers improve their internal transportation management processes. Additional value-added services offered by LXs are expected to include functionality such as:

- request for proposal and quotation tools,

- transportation service content such as routing and rating tables, and international documents and regulations,

- compliance monitoring,

- transportation optimization, and

- match and pay.

As an illustration, let's look at the transportation optimization functionality. In time, a shipper will be able to submit a multitude of transport orders to an LX and have it develop a low-cost, high-quality shipment plan for them, as well as automatically tender the loads. The LX would do this deploying similar transportation optimization software shippers previously used to support rating, routing, and scheduling decisions. Logistics.com, for example, plans to offer such functionality, as well as carrier-bid optimization, within its Digital Transportation Marketplace, an LX.

Warehouse Management

In the area of warehouse management, e-business tool usage has been based on the purchase of application software to support warehouse operations. The functionality includes support of the receiving, put-away, storage, pick, pack, and ship functions and, more recently, cross-dock and yard management operations. To leverage the Internet, warehouse management software vendors are Web-enabling and extending their solutions. This allows warehouse and distribution personnel, as well as other company employees in remote locations, access to the same set of warehouse-related real-time information, allowing, for example, everyone to have access to consistent inventory and order status information.

Over time, traditional e-business warehouse applications will be supplemented by LXs that specialize in securing warehousing services. While these types of LXs are mostly a concept right now, a startup in this area is GOwarehouse.com. On its hosted Web site, the company posts available warehouse space from among its participant public warehouse sellers. Buyers can come on the site to search for and procure space. This type of service can be especially useful for contracting space on a temporary basis to handle overflow situations, such as when needing to store excess, promotional, and seasonal goods. Use of these types of LXs can help companies optimize the use of their own distribution facilities.

Inventory Management

In the area of inventory management, e-business tool usage has been based on the purchase of application software to support inventory planning and control. This software functionality includes support for setting inventory targets and safety stocks and for generating replenishment orders based on min/max order sizes, as well as on optimizing for truckload, quantity discount, and promotional economics. To leverage e-business, software vendors are Web-enabling and extending these applications to enable logistics personnel, as well as other company employees in remote locations, access to the same real-time inventory-related information. Allowing, for example, everyone to have access to a set of consistent on-hand, on-order, and in-transit inventory quantities, on a worldwide and prospective basis.

Some of the new tools of e-business can also be used to support internal inventory management processes. Independent and consortium trading exchanges can be used by companies to auction off their excess inventories. Retailexchange.com, for example, is setting up operations to help retailers get rid of their surplus goods. Covisint, the automotive industry's consortium exchange, runs auctions to help its participants rid themselves of excess inventories, such as tires. In addition to trading exchanges, ask-bid software applications can leverage the Internet to help companies get rid of or bid on the purchase of excess inventories, providing channels for managing down their obsolete and slow-moving inventories, as well as for procuring scarce goods.

ASPs can also be used to provide Web-hosted inventory management services. Long's Drug, for example, contracts with NONSTOP Systems to process its warehouse and store-level sales/inventory data to make replenishment purchasing recommendations that support Long's purchasing department. NONSTOP uses sophisticated optimization algorithms running within their hosted Web site to develop these replenishment plans. Service providers such as Genuity and Worldcom are starting to make their mark in the area of providing connection and bandwidth services for supply chain activities.

Cross-Functional Process Improvement Tools and Methods

All the tools and methods discussed so far that help support transportation, warehouse, and inventory management deal with improving a single functional area or department. Stage 1 supply chain optimization processes also include cross-functional processes within the four walls of an enterprise.

Over the last 5 to 7 years, software applications to support these types of cross-functional processes, such as sales and operations planning (S&OP) and advanced planning and scheduling (APS), have been among the hottest in the software application market. Leading companies, especially in high tech and discrete manufacturing, have been purchasing these types of software applications and implementing them to enable cross-functional processes that improve their internal supply chain operations. In addition to these 'traditional' applications, supply chain professionals seeking to improve cross-functional processes can also use the new e-business tools that include Web-enabled and collaborative planning applications and ASPs.

Sales and Operations Planning

In the area of supporting S&OP processes, companies have historically enabled these by using and integrating two types of software applications: demand planning/forecasting and supply chain planning. Demand planning/forecasting software applications incorporate a set of statistical routines for developing baseline forecasts from historical demand data and multidimensional OLAP data analysis (a.k.a. slicing and dicing) functionality for soliciting market intelligence input from a cross-functional S&OP team. The forecasts developed with these applications are automatically input to an integrated supply chain–planning application that supports multifacility, cross-functional operational/tactical planning. The integrated software applications are used by an S&OP team to conduct "what-if" analyses to assess supply conditions under a variety of demand forecasts, thus supporting the cross-functional development of a balanced supply-demand plan.

Many of these S&OP systems have operated within an intranet or local area network environment, allowing only corporate-based personnel in the same general vicinity to work with them. This approach has limited the domain of many S&OP processes to planning for one business unit or one country. Recent Web enablement of these types of applications, however, now allows them to be run within an Internet-based extranet environment. This allows personnel from around the world to participate in an S&OP process and provides an opportunity for companies to expand the planning scope of their S&OP processes to plan for multiple business divisions and countries, offering the potential to truly operate a global S&OP process.

In addition to Web-enabling their traditional planning applications, software vendors have also developed specific collaborative applications, designed for users to share information and collaborate via the Internet. While initially designed for interenterprise use, some companies are using these applications to support internal S&OP processes. For example, Eastman Chemical Company uses Logility's Voyager software products, designed to support external collaboration, to gather forecast information from its sales representatives around the world.

Advanced Planning and Scheduling Process Tools and Methods

In the area of other internally based APS processes, companies have enabled them using software applications sold by APS vendors, such as i2 Technologies and Manugistics—historically the software vendors that played leading roles in establishing this class of software application. APS vendors often sell integrated suites of products to support cross-functional planning processes that includes the following functionality:

- Demand planning/forecasting
- Supply chain planning
- Manufacturing planning
- Distribution planning and deployment
- Production scheduling

Similar to the use of the software applications discussed earlier in support of S&OP processes, these integrated suites support cross-functional advanced planning and scheduling within an enterprise. The applications are integrated so that plans developed within each software application are automatically propagated to others. This allows a company to plan centrally or plan collaboratively, with each function planning in the context of each other's plans. As in S&OP, since these applications were designed to operate within an intranet environment, the scope of APS processes were limited. However, Web enablement of this class of software now provides the means to expand the scope of APS to planning for global intraenterprise supply chain operations.

APS software applications offered under an ASP model also offer an opportunity to leverage e-business tools to improve supply chain optimization processes. Similar to functionality provided by Web-enabling S&OP applications, offering APS software under this model allows personnel throughout a company access to the same system and data, helping integrate internal supply chain processes from a cross-functional perspective.

ENABLING ADVANCED SUPPLY CHAIN MANAGEMENT (SCM)

As previously discussed, much of the historical growth in the use of SCM software applications has been fueled by the move toward enabling stage 1 and, to a lesser extent, stage 2 processes. This is because up to now the lion's share of companies have been working on improving their stage 1 processes. Use of these software applications in support of stage 2 advanced SCM processes is expected to increase, especially since many vendors have now Web-enabled these applications. Web enablement allows external users such as customers, suppliers, and other trading partners to access a company's systems and data, potentially using just a simple PC browser. This can extend a company's processes to external partners, helping synchronize a supply chain on an interenterprise basis. Thus, these Web-enabled applications and, as discussed later, trading exchanges can be leveraged to support stage 2 e–supply chain processes.

Jointly Managed Inventory Programs Tools and Methods

In the area of supporting other jointly managed processes, companies have historically enabled them using inventory management, distribution planning and deployment, and collaborative planning applications sold by software vendors.

In response to a customer's request to conduct a jointly managed inventory program, suppliers have often implemented stand-alone inventory management systems that develop forecasts and replenishment plans on behalf of their customers. Another approach is to incorporate the customer's operations into the supplier's distribution planning and deployment system. While both these approaches certainly support jointly managed inventory programs, they are cumbersome and have severe limitations. They are a far cry from enabling a joint process! Both partners cannot participate, since they cannot jointly access the same system and data. In addition, these applications cannot seamlessly support the transactional aspects of the programs, such as enabling purchase order management, invoicing, and payment.

E-Business tools, including Web-enabled applications and trading exchanges, help overcome some of the limitations in the traditional approaches used to implement jointly managed inventory programs. Web-enabled applications allow trading partner access to information via the Internet, allowing the joint generation and sharing of forecasts and inventory information. Public and private trading exchanges can also enable more cooperative and collaborative programs. As an on-line hosted site, a trading exchange is used by suppliers and their customers, and it can become a natural place to conduct joint inventory management programs. In addition, since transactions are also likely to be supported on an exchange, it can more easily support the transactional aspects of jointly managed inventory programs.

Other e-business tools have been developed by software application vendors to support jointly managed inventory programs. As previously mentioned, software vendors have developed specific supply chain collaboration applications designed for users to share information and collaborate via the Internet. While they can be used for intraenterprise collaboration, they were initially designed for interenterprise use. Used in this way, they can be run on a hosted Web site or on a server-based computer that sits outside a company's firewall to ensure that sensitive data are not seen by a company's trading partners. Examples of these types of applications include products from Syncra Systems, used by retailer K-Mart to initially enable CPFR® processes with their suppliers, and from Logility, used by brewer Heineken USA to do collaborative inventory replenishment with its U.S. distributors.

Collaborative Planning Program Tools and Methods
Collaborative planning processes, based on electronic communication, have

been supported primarily through the use of value-added network (VAN)–based EDI. EDI is often thought of as the first B2B e-business tool. VAN-based EDI, however, has several severe limitations in supporting collaborative planning processes. EDI requires a lot of specialized support from information technology departments. That has limited the number of trading partners who could make effective use of EDI. EDI also used competing standards, suboptimizing its use. This drove the use of relatively expensive EDI translation software and VAN service charges, again limiting the number of trading partners that could participate to those with skilled technical resources and those with deep pockets. In addition, EDI represents a very structured data approach toward communicating, making it less amenable to the unstructured information needed to support collaborative processes. Lastly, collaborative processes require the bilateral communication of information; however, EDI supports primarily unilateral communication. These limitations in using EDI have led companies to implement supplier synchronization programs with only their top-tier strategic suppliers and customers, and only in a unilateral-based information sharing, not bilaterally based, collaborative fashion.

Enabling collaborative planning processes using the Internet promises to be a lot less painful. Once a company sets up a system to communicate electronically with its trading partners over the Internet, it is a lot easier to convince partners big and small to participate. First and foremost, the Internet is virtually free, eliminating excessive VAN service fees. Second, trading partners do not need expensive software. They can choose to use just a simple PC browser to participate, eliminating the need to buy special software. Lastly, the XML protocol promises to make it easier to communicate unstructured, bilateral information among partners, reducing the need for expensive and technically sophisticated translation software. Thus, we believe the Internet itself will be the most important e-business tool for enabling collaborative planning processes and that there are a variety of ways to leverage it to enable collaborative planning.

To provide products that leverage the Internet for collaborative planning purposes, software vendors have developed three types of applications. First, as previously mentioned, software vendors have Web-enabled their software applications to allow companies to open up their planning systems to customers and suppliers. However, since this would usually involve going behind a company's firewall, this would be limited to a few very strategic trading partners. Second, also previously mentioned, these software vendors have developed specific collaborative planning applications that run on servers in front of a company's firewall. These can be used to collaborate and share information with strategic and nonstrategic trading partners alike, as well as of all sizes. Lastly, a variety of software vendors, such as i2 Technologies and Manugistics, have developed trading exchange platform technology that is starting to include joint planning functionality. These will allow a company and its trading partners to jointly plan on a private or a public trading exchange.

In addition to these collaborative planning applications, another class of evolving software, enterprise application integration (EAI), can be used to enable a collaborative planning process, allowing interenterprise machine-to-machine communication with direct integration to back-end planning systems. While the software is a work in process for supply chain collaboration, broad specifications efforts such as XML plan to enable this machine-to-machine exchange. What is needed are semantic standards described in XML and specific industry standards efforts are in various states of completion. Structured and unstructured documents need to be efficiently exchanged, in the context of particular intercompany planning workflows. Industry standard efforts are important for widespread use, but some software vendors such as Extricity, OnDisplay, and WebMethods already provide platforms for implementing these intercompany workflows.

Improved Order-Promising Tools and Methods

In the area of supporting order-to-promise initiatives, companies have historically enabled these initiatives using distribution planning and deployment, production scheduling, and supply chain planning applications. Distribution planning and deployment applications can enable ATP-based promising of finished goods to a potential customer order. The applications support this with functionality to view and soft-allocate inventories that reside in a company's stocking locations, particularly useful in multiwarehouse, make-to-stock manufacturing and distribution environments. In a similar fashion, production-scheduling applications enable CTP by soft-allocating available production resources, labor, and materials at a particular plant to satisfy a customer order. This is particularly useful in single-plant make-to-order and build-to-order manufacturing environments. In addition, supply chain planning applications can support ATP/CTP in environments where customer orders can be filled using raw materials and components, work in progress, production resources, and finished goods available within a multitude of plants and warehouses.

Supplementing these types of applications, the Internet can be leveraged to support improved order promising in a variety of ways. First, using Web-enabled versions of the types of applications mentioned earlier, they can enable a company's customers, in a self-service mode, to access promising functionality that would normally support internal personnel, such as in sales and customer service. Second, ATP/CTP functionality can be extended to incorporate supplier capabilities. The Internet can be leveraged to allow suppliers to update information on their inventory of materials, work in progress, production resources, and finished goods that can be made available to fulfill a company's customer order. Lastly, software applications running on a public or private trading exchange can be used to offer a customer self-service promising functionality, with a company, and potentially its suppliers, providing availability information.

A supplier can provide availability to support a company's ATP/CTP functionality on a trading exchange or via Web-enabled applications in two ways that leverage the Internet: by populating the company's internal ATP/CTP system directly or via an ask-bid application. In the former, suppliers would transmit information into the company's systems via the Internet on a routine basis. In the latter, a supplier might be part of a set of potential suppliers that would be asked to provide delivery and pricing information via an Internet-based ask-bid system. The company's ATP/CTP system would tie into the system to determine the winning bid based on each supplier's pricing and delivery commitments.

ENABLING LEVERAGING E-COMMERCE

Stage 3 e-supply chain processes that start to leverage e-commerce include supply chain outsourcing, Internet procurement, and the support of Web selling. The tools and methods of e-business to support these processes are relatively new, especially software applications that are just starting to be developed.

Increased Outsourcing Tools and Methods

Outsourcing your problems can create even bigger ones if not done right. While the trend is toward a growing use of supply chain outsourcing, especially of manufacturing, fulfillment, and logistics, if not done well it can cause problems in meeting customer demand. Outsourcing does not abrogate a company's responsibility for meeting customer requirements. Maintaining good customer service requires a company to take responsibility for all its supply chain operations, even those that have been outsourced or contracted out.

Ideally, outsourcing requires that real-time communication links be set up with a provider of outsourcing services. This helps a company offload supply chain activities without significantly adding to order cycle times. Companies that need to place orders through its provider's customer service representatives will needlessly incur delays that result from manual order entry operations. Historically, communication links have been manual, resource-intensive, and not real-time, since they have been enabled via communications modes such as phone, fax, and VAN-based EDI. Over time, this type of communication can be replaced with Internet-based real-time methods that enable the input of orders directly into an outsource provider's systems. The e-business tools that will be leveraged to do this include customer self-service via a Web site, Internet-based EDI, and XML messaging.

Private and public trading exchanges can also be used to support the supply chain activities a company has outsourced. Trading exchanges can become the means by which a company can communicate with its providers. Communication links to logistics exchanges can be used to not only procure services from transportation providers but also to communicate and coordinate operations among them. The exchange essentially becomes the communication hub among shippers, carriers, and distribution intermediaries, such as freight forwarders, brokers, and financial institutions.

Private trading exchanges used to support outsourcing can be operated by a company (the outsourcer) or its logistics provider (the outsourcee) to help manage supply chain operations. General Mills, a large shipper, for example, has chosen to contract with Nistevo Corporation to build a private exchange to manage its existing transportation suppliers, as well as to build a community of participants outside of its supply chain, eventually offering public exchange services. J. B. Hunt Transport Services, Inc., is launching Transplace in conjunction with five other major North American carriers, to offer truckload, refrigerated, and intermodal transportation services over a hybrid public and private logistics exchange.

Internet Procurement Tools and Methods

One of the hottest areas of use for e-business tools and methods is Internet procurement. Most companies started in B2B by implementing buy-side procurement software applications to purchase indirect production items—namely, those goods that are not a component or raw material built into a finished product; these are also termed MRO items. These indirect production procurement implementations led to the fast growth of two influential B2B software vendors, Commerce One and Ariba. They, along with their competitors, are starting to also offer Internet software products and services for purchasing direct production goods; those items that go into a finished product and have a profound, direct impact on supply chain operations.

These types of buy-side applications can also be used within public and private exchanges to enable Internet procurement. We expect that stage 3 companies will enable Internet procurement processes using both, depending on the types of goods being purchased, from the perspective of whether the goods are commodities and strategic in nature.

In support of Internet procurement, companies will generally need to segment their purchased goods into at least three classes of goods and services for the purpose of developing a trading exchange strategy:

- For commodity-like, nonstrategic direct and indirect production goods and services, companies will tend toward the use of private trading exchanges to electronically procure them over the Internet. Spot-buy purchased goods is an example of the type of items that would fall into this category. For these types of goods and services, price and availability dictate purchase decisions, so conducting business over a public exchange will allow buyers to cast the broadest net over a wide range of potential sellers. Also relationships among buyers and sellers of these types of goods are relatively loose, typically lasting less than a year. Thus, a public trading exchange is most appropriate as it allows connections to these suppliers to be easily enabled and severed, as pricing and availability conditions change over time.

- For noncommodity, low- to medium-volume strategic direct production materials and services, companies will tend toward the use of private trading exchanges to purchase them via the Internet. These types of goods and services require tighter ties with suppliers, as price and availability are less important purchase decision criteria. Also tighter, longer-term relationships and contracts, 1 year or longer, need to be established with these types of suppliers, possibly requiring electronic connectivity to facilitate information sharing and collaboration. Thus, the use of private trading exchanges is more appropriate as most users feel the information transmitted through these exchanges will need to be more private and secure. Establishing longer-term relationships with these suppliers mitigates the concern that these private exchange connections are less easily enabled and severed, in contrast to a public exchange.

- For strategic, high-volume direct production materials and services, companies will tend toward the use of private trading exchanges supplemented by VAN- or Internet-based EDI and other means of communication to electronically purchase these goods from suppliers. EDI transactions over a VAN or the Internet may be needed because these goods represent large transactional volumes. In addition, many Fortune 1000 companies already use EDI to connect to suppliers of these types of goods and services. Tight and specialized ties with suppliers of these goods are also required, as price and availability are relatively unimportant purchase decision criteria. Long-term partnerships, lasting for several years or longer, also need to be established to facilitate collaboration, such as about product design and development, in addition to production scheduling and demand planning/forecasting. Private exchanges in conjunction with EDI will enable these longer, strategic, and high-volume direct production goods suppliers to be tightly linked into a company's procurement processes. As mentioned previously, the long-term relationships with these suppliers also mitigate the concerns that connections into these exchanges are not easily enabled and severed, in contrast to those of a public exchanges.

In a similar fashion, a direct production item might be purchased using different types of public and private trading exchanges, depending on availability. Figure 8.1 depicts a supply-demand planning process that incorporates the following escalating use of different types of trading exchanges:

- As the figure depicts, the first place a company would look to procure a direct production item would be in a tier 1 private exchange that is shared among internal organizations.
- If the item could not be procured there, the process dictates that the company next look within a tier 2 private trading exchange that is shared with trusted, strategic suppliers.

Typical Planning Portal to Service Online Trading Exchanges

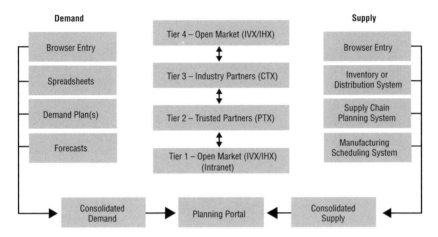

Source: AMR Research, 2000

figure 8.1

- If the item is not available among these suppliers, the company would next look for availability in a tier 3 consortium trading exchange that is shared with suppliers common to other companies in the industry.

- Lastly, having not obtained the item among these exchanges, the company would, as a last resort, look for availability on a public trading exchange.

Support of Web Selling Tools and Methods

Taking and fulfilling an order over the Internet is not as easy as it may at first seem. A company's marketing and IT departments often do not understand that while they can move information in nanoseconds, logisticians' planning horizons typically take days and weeks, sometimes longer. Coordination is critical to not set customer expectations that cannot be met.

Back-office ties to a Web site need to be tight and need to be bilateral. As discussed in Chapter 7, one aspect of satisfying Web-based customer demand is providing supply chain–related information on the Web site, such as product availability, expected delivery dates, and real-time order status information. Another aspect is flawless, speedy fulfillment of orders taken via a Web site. Fulfillment of Web orders must match, if not exceed, ones taken via traditional means such as phone, fax, and mail. Web buyers typically believe that your Industrial Age supply chain processes are as lightning fast and as seamless as your Web-selling processes.

The major tools of e-business that a company can use to establish a Web-selling presence are Internet-based sell-side applications that help a company configure and tailor a site to effectively market, sell, and upsell its products. These are used to configure the graphical user interface (GUI) that allows a customer to navigate the site efficiently to obtain product and service information, place orders, and get product recommendations and use advice. It is these sell-side applications that have to be integrated with a company's back-office enterprise systems to execute the order fulfillment seamlessly—from order to cash payments. EAI software products can be used to do this type of integration.

AMR Research has identified four levels of technology evolution for Web-selling supply chains (see Figures 8.2 to 8.5):

- Level A: Internet Presence Established
- Level B: Commerce Is Initiated
- Level C: Demand-Centered E-Business
- Level D: Demand Web Fulfillment

Level A: Internet Presence Established

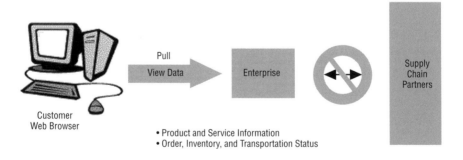

Source: AMR Research, 2000

figure 8.2

Level B: Commerce is Initiated

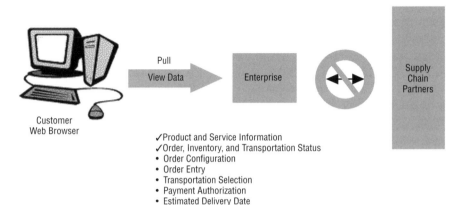

Pull

View Data → Enterprise

Supply Chain Partners

Customer Web Browser

✓ Product and Service Information
✓ Order, Inventory, and Transportation Status
• Order Configuration
• Order Entry
• Transportation Selection
• Payment Authorization
• Estimated Delivery Date

Source: AMR Research, 2000

figure 8.3

Level C: Demand-Centered E-Business

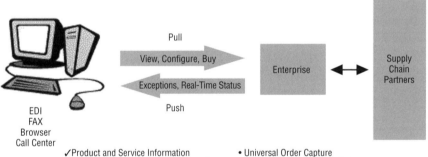

Pull

View, Configure, Buy → Enterprise ↔ Supply Chain Partners

Exceptions, Real-Time Status ←

Push

EDI
FAX
Browser
Call Center

✓ Product and Service Information
✓ Order, Inventory, and Transportation Status
✓ Order Configuration
✓ Order Entry
✓ Transportation Selection
✓ Payment Authorization
✓ Estimated Delivery Date

• Universal Order Capture
• ATP and CTP, Guaranteed Delivery
• Sourcing and Allocation
• Real-Time Order Validation and Confirm
• On-Line Returns Approval
• Event Tracking and Alerts
• Supply Chain Collaboration

Source: AMR Research, 2000

figure 8.4

Level D: Demand Web Fulfillment

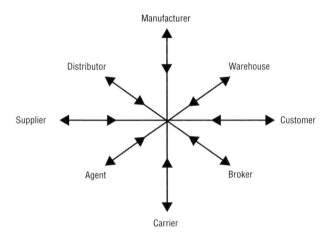

✓Product and Service Information
✓Order, Inventory, and Transportation Status
✓Order Configuration
✓Order Entry
✓Transportation Selection
✓Payment Authorization
✓Estimated Delivery Date
• Event Driven

✓Universal Order Capture
✓ATP and CTP, Guaranteed Delivery
✓Sourcing and Allocation
✓Real-Time Order Validation and Confirm
✓On-Line Returns Approval
✓Event Tracking and Alerts
✓Supply Chain Collaboration
• Rules Based, System Managed

Source: AMR Research, 2000

figure 8.5

The first three levels represent those that support stage 3 leveraging e-commerce e-supply chain processes, while the last starts to approach what is needed within stage 4 e-business optimization processes.

The vast majority of companies today are at level A, "Internet Presence Established," with a growing percentage moving to level B, "Commerce Is Initiated." As trading partner integration grows toward collaborative execution, performance is greatly enhanced. Level C, "Demand-Centered E-Business," represents a very real target for the near term, while level D, "Demand Web Fulfillment," is a conceptualized view of how Web-based systems will work together across companies and enterprises, given current technology direction. A description of these four levels follows:

- Web-selling Level A—Internet Presence Established: Marketing, not selling on the Internet begins with this stage. It is a unilateral flow of information, generally providing product and service information to customer inquiries. Often, this is nothing more than an online brochure. Its value comes from informing the customer. Users can access supply chain-related information such as order, inventory, or transportation status. Third-party logistic (3PL) providers have made it a common service offering. Companies afraid of channel cannibalization caused by selling directly on the Internet are often afraid to move beyond this level.

- Web-selling Level B—Commerce Is Initiated: Selling on the Web begins at this second stage. Customers can place orders directly, using a company's commerce server, configure the order, authorize payment, and be notified of expected delivery dates. Integration to various back-office supply chain management systems and, ideally, integrated end-to-end order fulfillment systems figure prominently in these initiatives, helping seamlessly provide inventory, transportation routing and scheduling, and order management information to the customer.

- Web-selling Level C—Demand-Centered E-Business: This is the stage at which a company starts to enable what it needs to deliver and set new customer expectations. The Web site is integrated into APS applications that are leveraged for ATP/CTP functionality to provide order promising, order sourcing, and order delivery updates. Proper execution becomes critical, and order-related collaboration among supply chain partners is essential. Acting as the demand center, the company coordinates and makes sure the entire supply chain is focused on serving its Web customers. The Web becomes a key strategic channel and is treated as such by all members of the corporation. An information backbone connects the supply chain community. The company starts to get visibility into supply chain inventories, purchase-order status, transportation status, and supply-related alert notification. Information is also pushed to the customer as opposed to the pull-only model in the first two levels.

- Level D—Demand Web Fulfillment: At this level supply chain management moves from art to science. The fourth level is a vision of a totally integrated supply chain, supported by technology providing the scalability, breadth of functions, and communications required for this level. Completely event driven, information and data flow two ways throughout the entire trading community in support of Web-selling activities. Systems also automatically optimize for disruptions in supply and demand, with rules built to manage fulfillment and automation of business decisions between systems and enterprises. (E-Business tools to support movement to this Web-selling vision will be discussed in the e-business optimization section of this chapter.)

It is not necessary for a company to achieve any of these levels of Web-selling support on its own. A company can, for example, outsource its whole Web-selling business to a third party that can actually run the Web site, as well as fulfill orders.

In the area of fulfillment of orders taken over a Web, a company has three options it can choose from. The first is to create its own end-to-end order fulfillment system by linking it Web sites with enterprise systems that are integrated to seamlessly support financial transactions, customer service, and order, inventory, warehousing, and transportation management. The second is to work with suppliers on drop-ship programs in which they execute fulfillment for orders sent to them from a customer's Web site. In this case, suppliers pick and pack orders, and ship them directly to its customers' Web customer. An obstacle to the use of this approach for a broad range of products is that most suppliers are not prepared to handle the unit-level, small, and frequent orders that are generated via Web selling. For example, B2C customers order in units that lead to parcel shipments, while suppliers are used to shipping in pallet and truckload quantities.

The third, and most promising, approach for many companies is to outsource the fulfillment to one of the many fulfillment service providers (FSPs) that are emerging in the market. These providers specialize in Internet fulfillment, with some of them evolving from established distribution companies and 3PLs. For example, GATX, USF Logistics, and Modus Media International are positioning themselves to provide Internet fulfillment services, especially for B2C e-businesses. Other FSPs are evolving from catalog or express delivery organizations that are positioning their core expertise in parcel shipment fulfillment to primarily offer outsource fulfillment services for B2C businesses. Some of these are JCPenney Company, Federal Express, and United Parcel Service. Interestingly, Fingerhut Business Services, with expertise in fulfilling small-value catalog orders, had been selected by Wal-Mart to do the fulfillment of some orders it takes over its B2C Web site.

ENABLING E-BUSINESS OPTIMIZATION

Stage 4 e-supply chain processes that start to enable e-business optimization include the development of a supply chain keiretsu and virtual e-businesses. Many of the tools and methods of e-business used to support the prior three stages need to be in place to reach this stage of e-supply evolution. Generally a company will make a significant investment in e-business tools to enable these types of e-supply chain processes.

Supply Chain Keiretsu Tools and Methods

Enabling supply chain-wide keiretsu requires the innovative use of a variety of e-business tools and methods, many new and untested. The few pioneering companies, such as Cisco and Ingram Micro, that have begun to emulate supply chain keiretsu operations, did so using dated, resource-intensive e-business tools and did a lot of custom system development. They used these methods to connect electronically to their trading partners in real time, a prerequisite for establishing the supply chain ecosystem needed to emulate keiretsu-like operations outside the four walls of their enterprise systems. To support the real-time bilateral sharing of information needed to coordinate activities across a supply chain, they have relied heavily on leveraging VAN-based EDI, earlier versions of EAI, and system development software tools. Blended together, these technologies allowed them to create customized systems that supported the integration of external and internal supply chain processes and information. Cisco, Ingram Micro, and others used the first-mover advantage to their benefit. Even though many tools and processes were custom, they still provided significant competitive advantage.

However, as previously discussed, electronic connectivity via VAN-based EDI is expensive and takes a long time for companies to implement. This realistically limits the number of trading partners to which a company can connect to only a fraction and often only the largest. Enabling real-time electronic connectivity using the Internet promises to be a lot less painful. Thus, we expect the more ubiquitous use of the Internet will allow companies to more easily emulate supply chain keiretsu operations. In addition, we also don't expect the use of VAN-based EDI just to go away in the short run, because companies will be reluctant to throw away what works and took a long time to implement.

In addition to the use of Internet messaging, emerging supply chain event management (SCEM) software applications can also be used to support supply chain keiretsu processes. These includes alert notification software applications that utilize business rules to receive and send Internet messages to various trading partners and systems, allowing them to do exception management for unplanned and nonevents. Software application vendors, Categoric Software and Vigilance, are two of the many specialized startups in this area, providing technology that acts like a "traffic cop" in handling supply chain alert notifications. The technology can allow event management to take place among supply chain trading partners using a multitude of communication protocols and devices, including the Internet, phone, fax, pager, e-mail, and personal digital assistant.

Trading exchange technology also offers great promise in enabling trading partners to connect in support of a supply chain keiretsu. One class of software technology, which AMR Research terms order visibility exchanges (OVEs), is an example of this. OVEs provide four types of order management functionality that together support broad SCEM functionality:

- First, the foundation functionality provided involves data translation services that enable trading partners to send and receive information to an exchange in a variety of communication protocols, including EDI, XML, Internet, pager, fax, and e-mail, as well as via simple PC browser software. The OVE uses this functionality to translate messages from each protocol into any of the other protocols. This allows trading partners with different levels of technical sophistication to communicate with the site

- Second, OVEs offer transaction management functionality, keeping track of the real-time status of orders in a secure environment. It does this by storing or accessing information gleaned from POs, order releases, acknowledgments, advance shipment notices, load tenders, back-order notifications, invoices, and payments.

- Third, these exchanges send alert notifications to trading partners when the status of an order changes or when something goes awry, allowing exception-based order management.

- Fourth, OVEs provide analytical functions that enable users to generate performance reports from order histories.

Examples of a software company that offers this type of technology is Eventra. Pitney Bowes and its suppliers use its OVE technology to support the real-time tracking of purchase orders placed on the suppliers.

In addition to OVEs, public and private trading exchanges offer great promise for enabling the real-time electronic connectivity needed to support supply chain keiretsu operations. There is a so-called SCM exchange concept that supports this. This can be enabled using an exchange in a hub mode with connections to a network/channel master and its multitiers of suppliers and service providers (see Figure 8.6). Used in this way, an SCM exchange forms the basis for connecting all the trading partners to allow them to share the same real time information. This can support the execution needs of fulfillment and replenishment. Order information and demand signals, for example, sent to the hub by the master partner can be simultaneously passed on to all tiered suppliers. Similarly, a supply or unplanned event signal can also be propagated up and down a supply chain in real time, enabling all trading partners to act in unison to these types of signals. More value can be added by the exchange if it supports planning and scheduling. If the exchange has bill-of-material explosion functionality embedded within it, demand needs can be automatically translated and sent to each partner in terms of its own part numbering scheme. While this is only a vision right now, software, such as trading exchange platform technology, is currently under development by software vendors to support these types of supply chain management exchanges.

An example of a scaled-down version of this is being implemented by Sun Microelectronics, a division of Sun Microsystems. As a virtual manufacturer it outsources the manufacture of its electronic boards to contract manufacturers. i2 Technologies is hosting a private trading exchange that is accessible by the division's contract manufacturers, itself, and its customers. The system has APS functionality in it that allows all three tiers of partners access to information on demand and supply needs.

Support of Virtual E-Businesses
The e-business tools needed to enable virtual business models are largely the same as those previously discussed for supply chain outsourcing and include some similar to those discussed for enabling supply chain keiretsu processes. Virtual e-business models require the outsourcing of non-core supply chain functions such as distribution and manufacturing.

Supply Chain Management Exchange

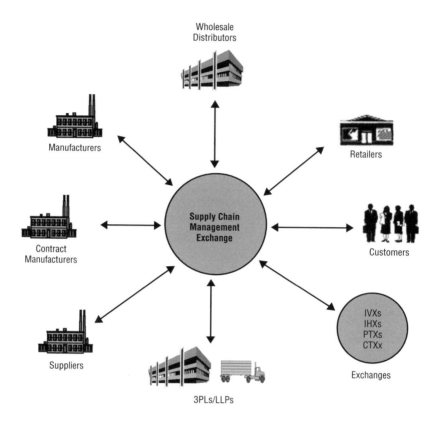

figure 8.6

In the case of a virtual distribution model, a company (holding no finished goods inventories) takes an order and works with manufacturers to direct-ship the order to the customer. It may also work with logistics service providers to perform order delivery services. To enable this virtual distribution model, real-time electronic connectivity needs to be established with the manufacturers and the logistics service providers to minimize any delays in the order fulfillment process.

The same type of enabling technology is needed to support a virtual manufacturing e-business model, efficiently. Under this model, a manufacturer (which does no manufacturing) relies on contract manufacturers to fill customer orders or logistics service providers to perform light-duty final assemble-to-order manufacturing operations as well as deliveries. To enable this virtual manufacturing model, real-time electronic connectivity needs to be established with the contract manufacturers and logistics service providers to minimize any delays in the order fulfillment process.

In addition to the real-time connectivity needed to support a virtual e-business model, in terms of coordinating fulfillment activities, supply chain collaboration applications are also necessary to ensure that outsourced activities are jointly planned and scheduled among trading partners. This helps ensure that each trading partner is adequately prepared to address the same anticipated demand.

Conclusion

In this chapter we have discussed how processes within each of the stages of the e–supply chain evolutionary model can be enabled using a myriad of tools and methods of e-business. Some of these tools, such as SCM software applications and EDI, were traditional ones that have been around for a decade or more, yet they can still be leveraged to support advanced e-business. Many companies, likely exceeding 80% or more of the Fortune 1,000, have yet to use them to their fullest advantage to improve the performance of their supply chains.

Added to these more traditional tools, we discussed the new tools and methods of e-business, such as Internet procurement and trading exchanges. These tools are just starting to be leveraged. Like prior tools, it will take a decade or more of innovation before we realize their fullest potential. (Witness the business use of the telephone, which is still changing, yet is a 100-year-old technology). Yet we know today that they have potential to massively change the way business is conducted.

In the next chapter, we argue that supply chain managers need to embrace the tools of e-business and get started. However, many are currently baffled by the market hype that e-business has conjured up and believe every use of e-business tools will involve huge efforts and resources. This is not the case. In this chapter we've shown that no matter what stage of e-supply chain your company is in, e-business tools and methods can be leveraged to improve your company's supply chain operations.

chapter 9

Beyond the Horizon:
The Call
to Action

A spokesperson for a presidential candidate once summarized the issues of concern to the voters by saying, "It's the economy, stupid!" History proved that this issue was a very dominant factor in determining which candidate won that election. We could use a similar phrase to characterize our summary position regarding the issues we have been considering. In terms of going forward with advanced supply chain, logistics and the integration of e-commerce, it's the execution that counts.

Supply chain managers and logistics professionals have a lot on their plates. In addition to the daily pressures of managing and balancing complex business processes, dealing with resource issues and trying to optimize the use of assets under their direction, there's constant pressure to manage costs, better utilize resources, and optimize supply chain processing. Many managers also have to align strategies and programs to support ever-changing business objectives. Then there's the need to respond to customer demands to keep satisfaction ratings as high as possible. This situation places a lot of demands on the supply chain and logistics professionals, who must make it all come together and turn the effort into increased profits.

Our research has clearly indicated that there's plenty to get done, but there are also better practices that can be adopted or adapted to fit with existing efforts. The analysis and synthesis of ideas and best practices that we've brought to this book reflect an attempt to recognize the amount of work facing the average business manager, while showing new tools and techniques for getting the job done faster and more effectively. One problem remains—getting to execution without a lifetime of study while attaining some measure of positive results.

We've shown the impact that e-commerce and the emerging e-business models are having or will have on companies and industries and their supply chain efforts. We've discussed the new digital economy and the emerging digital marketplace and the implications to advanced supply chain management and logistics efforts. We've considered strategic and global practices and suggested a new, collaborative environment that can lead to significant further improvements and new, profitable revenues. The missing link is getting into the action. The evidence we've considered shows there's far more talk going on about what to do next than there is about getting the company moving.

In this final chapter, we'll take one last look at our hypotheses and the implications they can have on improvement to supply chain and logistics. We'll also discuss the inhibitors to attaining the potential benefits and make some suggestions on how to get a meaningful effort under way.

CURRENT PRESSURES SEEM TO OFFSET A CALL FOR ACTION

When you stop and consider our research and future state hypotheses, it's clear that going to the future and having success require combining best supply chain and logistical practices across an end-to-end network of response to customers and consumers. It demands a total blending of the best applications of both areas of concentration—supply chain and logistics. The more we studied the subjects, the more we saw them merge into one discipline that is critical to meeting the needs we project for future networks of response to ever-demanding customers and consumers. Within that network, the constituents must work collaboratively, share critical resources, and demonstrate their core competencies in the areas designated as their responsibility.

It's also absolutely imperative that the linked constituents make as much use as possible of the emerging e-commerce features being adopted by the leaders to enable their processes to be as quick, accurate, and flexible enough to meet the ever-changing market demands placed on their system. This is not a new concept. E-Business, as we know it today, has been around now for about 2 years. The implications to business and the speed of change that have become the offspring of these new business tools are creating new dimensions for how to measure business effectiveness. With effective application, benefits will be seen from end to end of an entire value chain, of which a particular firm may have more than one membership.

The subjects and material covered in this book are intended to be useful for those managers faced with meeting these necessities. At the same time, it's apparent from our studies that getting the ideas into practice faces a major stumbling block. The complication is the average manager is spending too much time studying the type of material provided and not aggressively stepping up to the applications that take advantage of the opportunities described.

From our interviews, we found the topics of advanced supply chain, network logistics, e-commerce and the need for new e-business models to generate high levels of interest among senior supply chain and logistics managers, but it's not among the top three items on their prioritized improvement list. This conclusion is based on responses to an AMR Research study conducted at the Logistics Forum trade show in May 2000. For most companies interviewed, the application of e-business within the supply chain hasn't reached the level of full management commitment. Supply chain managers and decision makers, for example, have yet to embrace e-business as a means to leverage overall effectiveness and efficiency. Most managers continue to pursue supply chain as an effort to increase internal operational excellence and to minimize freight and storage costs for their firm. The use of external resources such as 3PL providers is still limited to about one-third of potential users.

Where core competencies are demonstrated outside a company, managers still tend to resist outsourcing that part of the total process.

Not fully understanding the overall value proposition, as well as a lack of consensus and cross-organizational commitment, inhibits e-business adoption. The subject continues to be viewed as an opportunity and a threat. Hopefully, this book will shed some light on this dilemma and incite some action, because that's precisely what is needed if firms are going to benefit from one of the most important tools to be introduced to business since the printing press.

ACT NOW OR FALL FURTHER BEHIND

So what are the next steps? Survey data indicate most companies use the Internet mainly for marketing and customer information delivery. Pathfinders are needed within most industries to show there are other much more beneficial applications, many of which we have described. Within supply chain and logistics processes, the Internet can be used to cut transaction costs on purchases, eliminate errors, and speed the time for order entry. It can greatly improve the cycle times from order-to-delivery and order-to-cash, by connecting the planning and scheduling that goes on between partners in a supply chain. It can reduce the need for inventory and safety stocks as inventory status becomes accurate and visible and as it moves online so promises can be made and kept. It can further reduce the cost of storage and transportation as viable aggregations are used to take advantage of online access to available warehouse and truck, rail car, and airplane space. It certainly is the new means of moving collaboration from a nice concept to a practical business application that creates market advantage.

The Internet becomes a new tool to improve the effectiveness of virtually every business function across the value chain networks that the leaders are forming as the next competitive entity in the drive to secure the end consumers. In short, it can be the tool that defines the difference between normal or exceptional performance, and it is destined to be the measure of differentiation between the competitors of tomorrow—the e-commerce-enabled value chains that dominate an industry.

Internet application in transportation and logistics, for example, can bring significant improvement to a firm and its supply chain allies, but only if organizations pool their resources, form the kind of networks that will develop the correct business models, and use the Internet effectively. Large companies or those well positioned with strong brand equities or central industry positions have to take the lead in this area. The need is to begin forming the types of aggregation mentioned in the General Mills–Nistevo arrangement. Firms that are not direct competitors can begin to lay out maps showing the manufacturing and delivery sites. They can then overlay similar locations from eight to twelve other firms having high traffic in the same area. By forming a legal consortia and linking their computer systems with the appropriate software, these firms can begin a trial effort to see how close they can collectively come toward optimizing the use of the least amount of physical equipment to get the job done properly.

The reality is that e-business is a different way of doing business. Companies need to understand how e-business redefines cross-functional, inter-enterprise, and network partnering relationships. They also need to understand that information has to move in tandem with the goods and services, which will be done electronically. They develop these concepts best by forming pilot operations for a time period sufficient to prove or disprove the concept. They should do so rapidly or risk falling behind a more aggressive competing network that could contain firms unknown to the traditionalist a year or so ago. Moving toward execution, even when learning along the way is part of the effort, becomes a viable action. Wireless tracking via Web-enabled cellular telephones and hand-held palm devices is just one example of an advanced technique that requires a test application before rollout.

As the now linked firms move forward together, these value chain members need to develop a compelling value proposition that includes deliverables for the members of the network and a compelling reason for the desired customers to do business with the network. Consistent and value-based practices for enhancing transportation services, collaborative planning, and customer relations have to be included as part of what becomes a digitally connected supply chain. Companies have to accept the fact that they have no choice but to integrate some form of electronic communications into their supply chains and the pilot test as a good opportunity for finding the best systems and applications.

Earlier we've mentioned all the positive reasons to get moving on e-business. Let's give you some of the negatives. If your company doesn't start implementing a strategy for e-business, when the year 2010 rolls around:

- competitors will gain a strategic advantage with lower costs, higher asset utilization, and more customer responsiveness;
- many network masters will be reluctant do business with your company;
- new e-business-savvy customers may not see your company;
- your company won't get to partner with the best suppliers, customers, and network masters; and
- small companies won't be able to afford to work within your company's value chain.

PRACTICAL NEXT STEPS

Steps forward include the following:

- Make a thorough analysis of your industry and your firm's position within the industry. That means drawing a map showing where the industry practices are moving as they apply to changing the way business will be conducted. You must be certain to delineate the front and back ends of that continuum. That means understanding who is in front and who is trailing in the industry. Then you position your firm on that continuum and determine the gap, if any, between your position and the recognized leaders. Be sure to check other industries that are different but have similar characteristics to see if even further progress is possible. With this analysis, your company or business unit needs to be prepared to start a serious dialogue with other members of what will become the supply chain network, so best practices can be shared, optimization approached, and a plan for securing new revenues together can come into view.

- Include e-business as part of your top three supply chain and logistics agenda items. Increase efforts to articulate and outline the dimensions of a value proposition for e-business within your company and the impact it will have on your supply chain network. Seek and gain cross-functional and inter-enterprise alignment on a joint vision and strategy that will mobilize the effort and excite the participants.

- Continue to seek out additional learning opportunities, from both the early adopters and industry leaders and other e-business-oriented companies and subject matter experts in supply chain management. Lessons must be learned in both the B2B and B2C domains. Take advantage of the guidelines and templates presented in this text, and don't be afraid to seek external counsel.

- Broaden your perspectives on e-business beyond customer interaction and supply chain cost savings. Consider the broad implications of supplier and trading partner visibility and the opportunities for collaboration. A broadened perspective can yield greater opportunities for leveraging e-business processes within the supply chain.

- Consider some form of electronic marketplace adoption as part of your supply chain strategy. Evaluate the long-term presence of trading exchanges according to the value-added services they can provide that are over and above procurement transactional cost savings. Evaluate your strategies to impact both the sell-side and buy-side processes.

IT'S ALL ABOUT FULFILLING EXPECTATIONS

As firms work together to build the new value chain networks, they must also keep in mind what is the central purpose. In the past, the emphasis was on cost reduction and increased profits for the firm. That ethic will never disappear, nor do we advocate that it should. The new emphasis has to shift, however, to building revenues through a network effort and defending the network members against onslaughts from competing networks, many containing newcomers with Internet capabilities. In this environment, the customer and end-consumer take on significantly more importance, and the focus shifts to responding to their real needs. Now the network moves its attention to fulfilling its commitments. Demand-driven e-business networks become the vehicles for accomplishing that purpose.

IS YOUR COMPANY PREPARED?

Not every organization is prepared for the changes required. That's why it's important to test the temperature for e-business change in your company. If it's not there, educate your organization on it. Give them a copy of this book. Do whatever it takes to get them to hear the important call to action for e-business. If the company is prepared, but inertia is keeping people from moving ahead, do something small to show them how it could work toward achieving benefits, or take them on a benchmarking field trip to a company that has successfully implemented e-business.

BE FLEXIBLE—THE FUTURE STATE IS DYNAMIC

No matter what you plan to do, expect that it may not work exactly as you planned it and may need to be altered. A big bang approach won't work in e-business because there are few models for success just yet, so implementing big change with unproven models could lead you astray, worse off than you originally started. That's why we advocate the use of the business release approach here. Implement with small changes and learn as you go are the key watchwords.

CONCLUSION

Demand-driven e-business networks, with all constituents synchronized to deliver superior customer and consumer satisfaction, are the entities we see evolving into the future dominant business structures. These networks will be molded around nucleus firms that become network masters. The members will be technologically enabled to conduct business through a physical channel of response or through cyberspace, but they will agree the secret is to focus on what happens before and after the order has been received. These networks will be as good and strong as their weakest link and will, therefore, have built a supply chain and logistics infrastructure that guarantees success fulfilling orders as small as one unit.

We leave you with the paraphrased words of one U.S. president: "If not now, when?" and "If not you, who?" How about now, and how about you? Be one of the heroes in your company and heed our call to action!

REFERENCES

Adams, D. (1998). Delivering sales daily. *Progressive Grocer* (November): 21–22.

Alexander, S. (1999). Mass customization. *Computerworld* **33**(36): 54.

Amerom, M. V. (2000). XML and supply chain management. *Inform* **14**(1): 26–28.

AMR Research, "The Enterprise Applications Report, 1999-2004", *The Market Analysis and Review Series*, 2000

AMR Research, "Supply Chain Strategies Outlook: E-Business is Morphing Supply Chains", *The Report on Supply Chain Management*, AMR Research, January, 2000

Andel, T. (1998). Managing supply chain relationships. *Transportation & Distribution* **39**(10): SCF10–SCF14.

Angus, J. (2000). The perfect price-fixer. *Informationweek* **779**: 135.

Anonymous. (1998a). Scan-based streamlining. *Progressive Grocer*: 18.

Anonymous. (1998b). Study shows efficiencies of scan-based trading. *Frozen Food Age* **47**(3): 30–32.

Anonymous. (1999). Mass customization: The new frontier in business competition. *Journal of Manufacturing Systems* **18**(5): 380.

Anonymous. (2000a). i2 rolls out HightechMatrix.com. *Electronic Buyers' News*: PG52.

Anonymous. (2000b). Dow Chemical to invest $100 million on e-business programs this year. *Chemical Market Reporter* **257**: 6.

Anonymous. (2000c). Pratt & Whitney joins blue292's early adopter program. *PR Newswire*.

Anonymous. (2000d). TRW's on-line spares Web page wins e-business award. *Business Source Premier*.

Ansley, M. (2000). Virtual manufacturing. *CMA Management* **74**(1): 31–35.

Archbold, R. (2000). Next frontier for EMS: Mass customization. *Electronic Buyers' News*: 96.

Bade, D. J., and J. K. Mueller. (1999). New for the millennium: 4PL. *Transportation & Distribution* **40**(2): 78–80.

Bailey, J. P. (1998). Intermediation and electronic markets: Aggregation and pricing in Internet commerce. Ph.D. diss., Massachusetts Institute of Technology, Boston.

Bakos, J. Y. (1991a). Information links and electronic marketplaces: The role of interorganizational information systems in vertical markets. *Journal of Management Information Systems* **8**(2): 31–52.

Bakos, J. Y. (1991b). A strategic analysis of electronic marketplaces. *MIS Quarterly* (September).

Baron, J. P., M. J. Shaw, et al. (2000). Web-based e-catalog systems in B2B procurement. *Association for Computing Machinery, Communications of ACM* **43**(5): 93–100.

Bartholomew, D. (2000). Jockeying for position. *Industry Week* **249**(3): 11–12.

Bauer, Michael J (2000). The E-ffect of the Internet on Supply Chain and Logistics. *World Trade Magazine* (September 2000): 71-80

Bauer, M., and C. Poirier. (2000). *E–supply chain: Using the Internet to revolutionize your business.* San Francisco: Berret-Koehler.

Bermudez, J., B. Kraus, D. O'Brien, B. Parker, and L. Lapide. (2000). *B2B commerce fore-cast: $5.7T by 2004*. Boston: AMR Research.

Biggs, M. (2000). Enabling a successful e-business strategy requires a detailed business process map. *InfoWorld* **22**(10): 64.

Birkner, G. (2000). Eastman chemical draws customers online. *Sales and Marketing Management* **152**(6): 40–42.

Blackmon, D. A. (2000). E-Commerce: The view from above—Price buster: E-Commerce hasn't had an impact on the economy's overall price structure. *Wall Street Journal*: R12.

Booker, E. (1999). XML greases supply chain. *Internetweek*: PG1.

Bowersox, D. J., D. J. Closs, and T. P. Stank. (1999). *21st century logistics*. Oak Brook, IL: Council of Logistics Management.

Brown, S. F. (2000). How e-tailers deliver within hours. *Fortune* (May 29): T210B–N

Brunelli, M. A., and B. Milligan. (2000). Ford and GM drive to build e-procurement systems. *Purchasing* **128**(2): 139–140.

Brynjolfsson, E., and M. Smith. (2000). Frictionless commerce? A comparison of Internet and conventional retailers. *Management Science* **46**(4): 563–585.

Business Wire. (2000, June 20). TRW's on-line spares Web page wins e-business award.

Cahill, J. M. (2000). Virtual supply chains drive e-business. *Transportation & Distribution* **41**(5): S30–S32.

Caldwell, B. (1999). Scan-based trading. *Informationweek* **725**: 20.

Callahan, S. (2000). Big three exchange launches as Covisint. *B to B* **85**(6): 8, 36.

Carbone, J. (1999). Most OEMs build to order. *Purchasing* **126**(6): 37–38.

Cetinkaya, S., and C.-Y. Lee. (2000). Stock replenishment and shipment scheduling for vendor-managed inventory systems. *Management Science* **46**(2): 217–232.

Chabrow, E. (2000). Buying a piece of e-business: Eastman invests in partners. *Informationweek*: 54.

Chandrashekar, A. (1999). Toward the virtual supply chain: the convergence of IT and organization. *International Journal of Logistics Management* **10**(2): 27–39.

Choudhury, V., K. S. Hartzel, et al. (1998). Uses and consequences of electronic markets: An empirical investigation in the aircraft parts industry. *MIS Quarterly* (December): 471–507.

Cimento, A. P., M. Denham, et al. (1999). What's behind the move to virtual manufacturing? *Machine Design* **71**(17): S2–S10.

Cohen, S. G. and D. Mankin. (1999). Collaboration in the virtual organization. *Journal of Organizational Behavior* **6**: 105–120.

Cone, E. (1998). Cautious automation. *Informationweek*: October 19.

Cooke, J. A. (1998). VMI: Very mixed impact? *Logistics Management and Distribution Report* **37**(12): 51–53.

Cooke, J. A. (1999). Web browser brings product demand into focus. *Logistics Management and distribution Report* **38**(5): 67–70.

Cooke, J. A. (2000a). The dawn of supply chain communities. *Logistics Management and Distribution Report* **39**(2): 44–48.

Cooke, J. A. (2000b). New wave? *Logistics Management and distribution Report* **39**(1): 67–70.

Cort, S. G. (1999). Industry corner: industrial distribution: How goods will go to market in the electronic marketplace. *Business Economics* (January): 53–55.

Cottrill, K. (2000). Encounters of the 4th kind. *Traffic World* **261**(1): 27.

Covill, R., and H. Knudson. (2000). *Managing cannibals, conflicts, and competition across e-channels*. Boston: AMR Research.

Covill, Randy and Hilary Knudson, "Sell-Side Content Management--Your Web Production System", *The Report on E-Commerce Application Strategies*, AMR Research, August 2000

Crockett, R. (2000). A digital doughboy. *Business Week* (April 3): EB79–86.

Crooke, J. A. (2000). Scan and supply. *Logistics Management and Distribution Report* **39**(6): 65–67.

Cross, G. J. (2000). How e-business is transforming supply chain management. *Journal of Business Strategy* **21**(2): 36–39.

D'Amico, E., R. Westervelt, et al. (2000). The empire strikes back. *Chemical Week* **162**(19): 31–37.

Dalton, G. (1998a). Ford turns to extranet. *Informationweek* **695**: 30.

Dalton, G. (1998b). XML makes inroads into the enterprise. Informationweek: 30.

Danielson, R. E. (2000). CPFR: Improving your business without being limited by technology. Apparel Industry Magazine 61(2): 56–57.

Delaney, R. B. (2000). *11th annual state of logistics report* (June 5). Washington, D.C.: National Press Club.

DePrince, A. E., Jr., and W. F. Ford. (1999). A primer on Internet economics. *Business Economics* **34**(4): 42–50.

Desaritz, J. (1999). Good chemistry: Dow's e-commerce strategy. *Modern Paint and Coatings* **89**(2): 28–29.

Dresner, M. (2000). Case studies: Andronicos, Dreyer's, and viaLink use Web data to execute scan-based trading. *Food Logistics* **Suppl.** (July/August): 52–53.

Drucker, D. (2000). Ford, dealers to link online efforts closely. *Internetweek* **802**: 7.

Edelheit, J. A., and M. R. Miller. (1997). Electronic commerce comes to the net. BT *Technology Journal* **15**(2): 24–31.

Ellertson, J. (1999). XML as a business solution. *Inform* **13**(2): 16–19.

Ellis, S. (1998). Not just selling chemicals. *Chemical Week* **160**(45): 43–46.

Elsawy, O. A., A. Malhotra, et al. (1999). IT-intensive value innovation in the electronic economy: Insights from Marshall Industries. *MIS Quarterly* **23**(3): 305–355.

Emigh, J. (1999). Vender-managed inventory. *Computerworld* **33**(34): 52.

Eriksen, L. (2000). To B or not to B. *Manufacturing Systems* **18**(6): 96.

Ferrari Robert, "Get Your Supply Chain Ready for Trading Exchanges", *The Report on Supply Chain Management*, AMR Research June 2000

Ferrari, Robert, "Supply Chain Managers Struggle With E-Business", *The Report on Supply Chain Management*, AMR Research August

Fine, C. H. (1998). *Clockspeed: Winning industry control in the age of temporary advantage*. New York: HarperCollins.

Fingar, P. (2000). E-Commerce: Transforming the supply chain. *Logistics Management and Distribution Report*: E7–E10.

Fontanella, John, "Exchanges: Logistics in the Fast Lane", *The Report on Supply Chain Management*, AMR Research, March 2000.

Fontanella, John, "The AMR Research Holiday Survey: Internet Retailers Are Still E-Fulfillment Amateurs", *The Report on Supply Chain Management*, AMR Research, May 2000.

Fontanella, John, "Trading Exchanges Will Accelerate The Adoption of Web-Based Supply Chain Execution Services", *The Report on Supply Chain Management*, AMR Research, July 2000

Forsyth, G. (2000). Who's who in e-commerce. *American Shipper* (September): 34–35.

Foster, T. A. (1999). Who's in charge around here? Logistics Management and Distribution Report **38**(6): 61–67.

Fraza, V. (1998). Streamlining the channel. *Industrial Distribution* **87**(9): 73–74.

Frazelle, E. H. (1998). Plan on these trends. *Transportation & Distribution* (December): SCF4–SCF5.

Frick, K. (2000). E-Commerce: On the battlefield—Food fight: Nestlé has grand plans to create a business-to-business marketplace. *Wall Street Journal*: R51.

Friedman, D. (2000). plan an e-commerce strategy. *Supply House Times* **43**(2): 45–46.

Gavirneni, S., R. Kapuscinski, et al. (1999). Value of information in capacitated supply chains. *Management Science* **45**(1): 16–24.

George, T. (2000). Eastman Chemical to launch ShipChem.com in June. *Informationweek* **774**: 52.

Gilbert, A. (2000). Companies partner on high-tech Web marketplace. *Informationweek* **767**: 24.

Gooley, T. B. (1998). Mass customization: How logistics makes it happen. *Logistics Management and Distribution Report* **37**(4): 49–54.

Gourley, C. (1998). What's driving the automotive supply chain. *Warehousing Management* **5**(10): 44–48.

Graham, G., and G. Hardaker. (2000). Supply-chain management across the Internet. *International Journal of Physical Distribution & Logistics* **30**(3/4): 286–295.

Gregory, A. (1999). The master plan. *Works Management* **52**(2): 18–20.

Guyer, L. (2000). Ford's online effort clicks into gear. *Advertising Age* **71**(17): S8.

Hackbarth, G., and W. J. Kettinger. (2000). Building an e-business strategy. *Information Systems Management* **17**(3): 78–93.

Hadjiconstantinous, E., ed. (1998). *Quick response in the supply chain.* Heidelberg: Springer.

Halliday, J. (2000). AutoNation tests dual strategy in Florida. *Advertising Age* **71**(29): 3.

Hart, P. J., and C. S. Saunders. (1998). Emerging electronic partnerships: Antecedents and dimensions of EDI use from the supplier's perspective. *Journal of Management Information Systems* **14**(4): 87–111.

Helper, S., and J. P. MacDuffie. (2000). E-volving the auto industry: E-Commerce effects on consumer and supplier relationships. Working paper.

Hibbard, J. (1998). Supply-side economics. *Informationweek* **707**: 85–87.

Hibbard, J. (2000). Supply-side economics. *Information Week* (November 2).

Hill, S., Jr. (2000a). More than just talk. *Manufacturing Systems* **18**(4): 69–72.

Hill, S., Jr. (2000b). Say goodbye to supply chains. *Manufacturing Systems* **18**(1): 30–34.

Hirschfeld, S. (2000). Consumer products firms plan Web exchange. *America Online* (March 16).

Hof, R., D. Spoarks, E. Newborne, and W. Zellner. (2000). Can Amazon make it? *Business Week* (July 10): 38–43.

Holmstrom, J. (1998). Implementing vendor-managed inventory the efficient way: A case study of partnership in the supply chain. *Production and Inventory Management Journal* **39**(3): 1–5.

Huppertz, P. (1999). Market changes require new supply chain thinking. *Transportation & Distribution* **40**(3): 70–74.

InternetWeek Newsletter Staff, "Dell's Hard Lesson", *InternetWeek Newsletter*, newsletter@news.internetwk, 9/18/00

Ireland, Ron and Robert Bruce, "CPFR: Only the Beginning of Collaboration" *Supply Chain Management Review*, September/October 2000 Issue

Jarvenpaa, S. L., and B. Ives. (1991). Executive involvement and participation in the management of information technology. *MIS Quarterly* (June): 205–227.

Joachim, D. (1998). Dell links virtual supply chain. *Internetweek* **739**: 1.

Joachim, D. (1999). Ford rebuilds extranet as supplier portal. *Internetweek* **765**: 1.

Johnson, Rod, Menconi, Peggy "E-Business Platforms Are Now Core Competencies", *The Report on Enterprise Application Strategies, AMR Research*, September 2000

Kaplan, S., and M. Sawhney. (2000). E-hubs: The new B2B marketplaces. *Harvard Business Review* **7**8(3): 97–100.

Karpinski, R. (2000). Dow chemical commits to e-market. *Internetweek*: 13.

Kay, E. (2000). From EDI to XML. *Computerworld* **34**(25): 84–85.

Keebler, J. S., K. B. Manradt, D. A. Durtsche, and D. M. Ledyard. (1999). *Keeping score: Measuring the business value of logistics in the supply chain*. Oak Brook, IL: Council of Logistics Management.

Kemp, T. (2000). When it has to be there now: E-retailers tune systems for same-day delivery. *Internetweek* **815**: 1, 56.

Kerwin, K., M. Stepanek, et al. (2000). At Ford, e-commerce is Job 1. *Business Week* **3670**: 74–78.

King, J. (1999). Eastman Chemical pulls customers online. *Computerworld* **33**(41): 44.

Konicki, S. (2000). Nestle taps SAP for e-business. *Informationweek*: 185.

Kunii, I. (2000). From convenience store to online behemoth? *Business Week* (April 10): 64.

LaMonica, M. (2000). Buying an e-business strategy on the cheap. *InfoWorld* **22**(17): 5.

Lapide, Larry, "Are We Moving From Buyers and Sellers to Collaborators?", *The Report on Supply Chain Management*, AMR Research, July 1998

Lapide , Larry. "The Innovators Will Control the E-Supply Chain", *The Report on Supply Chain Management*, AMR Research May 2000

Latham, Scott, "Evaluating the Independent Trading Exchanges", *The Report on E-Commerce Application Strategies*, AMR Research, March 2000

Lee, H. L., V. Padmanabhan, et al. (1997). Information distortion in a supply chain: The bullwhip effect. *Management Science* **43**(4): 546–559.

Lee, H. G., T. Clark, et al. (1999). Research report. Can EDI benefit adopters? *Information System Research* **10**(2): 186–195.

Lee, H. L., K. C. So, et al. (2000). The value of information sharing in a two-level supply chain. *Management Science* **46**(5): 626–643.

Levy, M., P. Powell, et al. (1999). Assessing information systems strategy development frameworks in SMEs. *Information & Management* **36**(5): 247–261.

Lewis, L. (2000). CPFR solutions. *Progressive Grocer* **79**(4): S28–S32.

Malone, T. W., J. Yates, et al. (1987). Electronic markets and electronic hierarchies. *Communications of the ACM* **30**(6): 485–497.

Mann, P. (1999). Linking virtual supply chain. *Manufacturing Systems* **17**(11): 22–24.

Mecham, M. (2000). E-marketplace should help achieve the cost-saving benefits of consolidation that have eluded the industry so far. *Aviation Week & Space Technology* (April 3).

Mecham, M. (2000a). An old-time industry picks up the pace. *Aviation Week & Space Technology* **153**(4): 160–165.

Mecham, M. (2000b). Primes embrace virtual consolidation. *Aviation Week & Space Technology* **152**(14): 26–27.

Min, H., and W. P. Galle. (1999). Electronic commerce usage in business-to-business purchasing. *International Journal of Operations & Production Management* **19**(9): 909–921.

Mitchell, Pierre, "Indirect Procurement: Let the Buyer Beware", *The Report on Enterprise Application Strategies*, AMR Research, September 1999

Mitchell, Pierre, "Content Management Strategies", *The Report on E-Commerce Application Strategies*, AMR Research, May 2000

Mitchell, Pierre, "Trading Exchange Infrastructure: 13-Stop Shopping", *The Report on B2B Marketplace Strategies*, AMR Research, July 2000

Montgomery, Nigel, "European Trading Exchanges – Play or Pass", *The Report on European E-Business Strategies*, AMR Research, October 2000.

Moran, N. (1999). E-Commerce based procurement solutions for the chemical industry. *Chemical Week* **161**(31): S9–S11.

Newton, C. (2000). *Introspective SCM: Focus on CPG Manufacturing.* Boston: AMR Research.

Newton, Chris, "Demystifying E-Fulfillment" *The Report on Supply Chain Management*, AMR Research, April 2000.

O'Marah, Kevin, *Where is the Supply Chain Value in B2B?*, *The Report on Supply Chain Management*, AMR Research, October 2000

Osterle, H., E. Fleisch, et al., eds. (2000). *Business networking: Shaping enterprise relationships on the Internet.* Basel: Springer.

Pachura, R. (1998). When is enough, enough? *IIE Solutions* **30**(10): 33–35.

Palmer, J., and C. Speier. (in press). Quick response: Internal efficiencies and supply chain management in specialty retailing.

Parker, Bob, "Internet Procurement--Low Risk, High Return", *The Report on E-Commerce Application Strategies*, AMR Research, October 1999

The Performance Measurement Group. (1999). *Dimensions executive summary.* N.p.: Author.

Piszczalski, M. (2000). The auto industry goes dot com. *Automotive Manufacturing & Production* **112**(4): 30–32.

Preston, R., and R. Yasin. (2000). Dow's new chemistry. *Internet Week Online* (July 20).

Rayport, J. F., and J. J. Sviokla. (1995). Exploiting the virtual value chain. *Harvard Business Review* (November–December): 75–85.

Reuters. (2000). Sony can't meet Playstation 2 Demand. *Reuters On-line News Service* (September 29).

Richardson, H. L. (2000). Virtually connected. *Transportation & Distribution* **41**(3): 39–44.

Roberts, M. (1999). Vertical vs. horizontal e-commerce solutions: Which way to go? *Chemical Week* **161**(45): S11.

Rosen, C. (2000). Nestle launches speedy online site. *Informationweek*: 75.

Rosenthal, D., S. K. Shah, et al. (1993). The impact of purchasing policy on electronic markets and electronic hierarchies. *Information & Management* **25**: 105–117.

Rossant, J. (2000). Birth of a giant. *Business Week* (July 20): 170–176.

Saccomano, A. (1998). Tea leaves on the Internet. *Traffic World* **255**(4): 36–37.

Savage, E. V. (2000). In its infancy: E-Commerce in Asia. *Chemical Market Reporter* **257**(16): F12.

Schulman, R. (2000). Rethinking the way business is done. *Supermarket Business* **55**(2): 29–30.

Schwartz, E. (1999). Build-to-order drives change. *InfoWorld* **21**(39): 1, 30.

Schwartz, E. (2000a). Enabling the channel for e–business. *Infoworld* **22**(17): 8.

Schwartz, B. (2000b). Online automotive exchange: Big change or pipe dream. *Transportation & Distribution* **41**(5): S4–S8.

Shulman, R. (1998). Scan-based trading: An attainable goal? *Supermarket Business* **53**: 42–43.

Shulman, R. (1999). Something old, something new—Both called DSD. *Supermarket Business* **54**(11): 33–35.

Siekman, J. (1999). Where build to order works best. *Fortune* **139**: 160C–160V.

Sirbu, M., and J. D. Tyger. (1995). NetBill: An Internet commerce system optimized for network delivered services. Unpublished paper, Carnegie Mellon University.

Sivara, D. (1998). Develop a game plan for IT success. *Apparel Industry Magazine* **59**(2): 60.

Smith, K. M., D. A. Grimm, et al. (2000). Setting new supply chain standards: A chemicals industry e-commerce cast studies.

Sriniasan, K., S. Kekre, et al. (1994). Impact of electronic data interchange technology on JIT shipments. *Management Science* **40**(10): 1291–1305.

Stank, T., M. Crum, et al. (1999). Benefits of interfirm coordination in food industry supply chains. *Journal of Business Logistics* **20**(2): 21–41.

Strader, T. J., and F.-R. Lin. (1998). Information infrastructure for electronic virtual organization management. *Decision Support Systems* **23**(1): 75–94.

The Supply Chain Council, The Supply-Chain Operations *Reference Model SCOR Version* 4.0 *Reference Guide*, August 2000

Tattum, L. (1999). Staying at the cutting edge of supply chain practice. *Chemical Week* **161**(11): S11–S12.

Trombly, M. (2000). Real-time reporting. *Computerworld* **34**(19): 64.

Trunick, P. A. (1998). New demands for tomorrow's manager. *Transportation & Distribution* **39**(12): 18–19.

Trunick, P. A. (1999). TMS takes a strategic role. *Transportation & Distribution* **40**(10): SCF6–SCF8.

Tucker, D. and L. Jones. (2000). Leveraging the power of the Internet for optimal supplier sourcing. *International Journal of Physical Distribution & Logistics Management* **30**(3/4): 255–267.

Venkatraman, N. (2000). Five steps to a dot.com strategy: how to find y our footing on the Web. *Sloan Management Review* **41**(3): 15–28.

Venkatraman, N., and J. C. Henderson. (1998). Real strategies for virtual organizing. *Sloan Management Review* (Fall): 33–48.

Verwoerd, W. (1999). Value-added logistics: The answer to mass customization. *Hospital Material Management Quarterly* **21**(2): 31–36.

Violino, B. (1999). Grocery extranet. *Informationweek* **722**: 20.

Waller, M., M. E. Johnson, et al. (1999). Vendor-managed inventory in the retail supply chain. *Journal of Business Logistics* **20**(1): 183–203.

Walton, B., and M. Princi. (2000). From supply chain to collaborative network: Case studies in the food industry.

Warner, F. (1998). Ford uses Internet to slash the costs of ordinary tasks. *Wall Street Journal*: B11C.

Warner, F. (2000). AutoNation goes back to basics with an Internet twist: Car retailer leverages scale, cuts dealership costs, expands online business. *Wall Street Journal*: B4.

Warren, S. (2000). E-Commerce: On the battlefield—Big reaction: Giant chemical companies are rushing to keep the start-ups from muscling in on their business. *Wall Street Journal*: R24

Weil, M. (2000). Segments emerging rapidly. *Manufacturing Systems* (March): 16–21.

Weinstein, S. (1999). SBT for the common man. *Progressive Grocer* **78**(8): 81–84.

Weinstein, S. (2000). The price is righter. *Progressive Grocer* **79**(5): 89–94.

Welch, D. (2000). E-marketplace: Covisint. *Business Week* **3684**: EB62–EB68.

Wellman, D. (1999). The direct approach to the bottom line. *Supermarket Business* **54**(8): 15–20.

White, J. B., and J. Baglole. (2000). Rivalry for online auto sales intensifies with AutoNation-AOL link, Ford test. *Wall Street Journal*: B19.

Whiting, Rick, "Value, and Pain, In Integration: Some Click-and-mortars are merging their traditional and online operations", *Informationweek.com News*, September 4, 2000.

Wilder, C. (1999). E-transformation. *Informationweek*: 44–62.

Wilder, C. (2000). Dow Chemical partners with online exchange. *Informationweek* **768**: 93.

Wilding, R. (2000). *E-implementation in the supply chain: A time-based approach.* Oxford: Cranfield School of Management.Wilson, T. (2000). XML standards: A problem of physics. *Internetweek*: PG35.

Willis, Clint, "B2B...to Be?" Mapping the Future of Business-to-Business Commerce", *Forbes ASAP*, August 21, 2000

Yang, J. (2000). Interoperation support for electronic business. *Association for Computing Machinery, Communications of ACM* **43**(6): 39–47.

Yao, Y., M. Dresner, et al. (2000). Motivations and consequences of the adoption and Use of electronic supply chains: An empirical study in the food industry. Working paper, University of Maryland.